THE RED RIVER SETTLEMENT

A00801411001

F1063.R65 1972

1252889

SOUTH CAMPUS LIBRARY

TARRANT COUNTY JUNIOR COLLEGE

FT. WORTH, TEXAS 76119

Front view of Upper Fort Garry: Red River Settlement

THE
RED RIVER SETTLEMENT

ITS

RISE, PROGRESS, AND PRESENT STATE

WITH SOME ACCOUNT OF

THE NATIVE RACES AND ITS GENERAL HISTORY

TO THE PRESENT DAY

BY

ALEXANDER ROSS

CHARLES E. TUTTLE COMPANY
Rutland, Vermont & Tokyo, Japan

Representatives
Continental Europe: BOXERBOOKS, INC., *Zurich*
British Isles: PRENTICE-HALL INTERNATIONAL, INC., *London*
Australasia: PAUL FLESCH & CO., PTY. LTD., *Melbourne*
Canada: M. G. HURTIG LTD., *Edmonton*

*Published by the Charles E. Tuttle Company, Inc.
of Rutland, Vermont & Tokyo, Japan
with editorial offices at
Suido 1-chome, 2–6, Bunkyo-ku, Tokyo, Japan*

© *1972 by M. G. Hurtig Ltd.*

All rights reserved

Library of Congress Catalog Card No. 72-170105

International Standard Book No. 0-8048-1005-2

*First edition published 1856 by Smith, Elder and Co., London
First Tuttle edition published 1972*

PRINTED IN JAPAN

TO

DUNCAN FINLAYSON, Esq.,

FORMERLY GOVERNOR OF RED RIVER COLONY,

Who, during many years' administration of its affairs, evinced unwearied zeal in the development of its resources, and in the amelioration of the general condition of its inhabitants; who, by the energy of his rule, and by the wisdom of his policy, established order and maintained peace; and who, by officially promoting in the wilderness the benevolent causes, as well of missionary enterprise as of general education, besides fostering with the hand of power the germs of agricultural industry, laid a solid basis, not only for the prosperity of the white man, but also for the Christian civilization of its aboriginal inhabitants,

THESE PAGES ARE,

WITH SENTIMENTS OF THE HIGHEST REGARD,

RESPECTFULLY DEDICATED

BY

THE AUTHOR.

TABLE OF CONTENTS

Introduction to the New Edition . . xv
Preface xxv

CHAPTER I.

The Hudson's Bay Company's Charter—Legal opinions on its validity—Remarks on the same—Lord Selkirk's grant—Observations thereon—Geographical position of Red River Colony—Indian Treaty—The Saulteaux Indians—Country described—Conflagrations in the plains—Effect—Cold—Heat—Wolves—The four opinions—Lord Selkirk's motives considered 1

CHAPTER II.

Emigrants to Red River—Perilous voyage—Reception by the employées of the North-west Company—Critical position—Contract—Trip to Pembina—Comparison—Half-breeds—Winter quarters—Wheat sown—Returns—Blackbirds—Pigeons—Pembina—Plot—Provisions—Plans defeated—Proclamation—Result—Churchill—Gun-locks—Cruelty—New emigrants—Join the North-West—Proposals—Emigrants abandon the North-West—Skirmishing—A man shot—Houses burnt—Emigrants in exile—Recalled—Last brigade arrive—The four conditions—Scotch minister—Conditions—Marriages—Baptisms—Mr. Sutherland . 20

CHAPTER III.

The Scotch emigrants—Gloomy prospects—Privations—Hostile feuds—North-West intrigues—Manœuvring—Hardships of the emigrants — Starving adventures — Bright prospects—Sudden change—Prospects blighted—Hopeless condition—Hudson's Bay Company—Civil war—Bloodshed—Trying scenes—Colony destroyed by the North-West—Flotilla—Emigrants in exile—Parting admonition—Mr. Grant's heroic conduct—Bold front—Pillaging parties—Incidents—The first shot—Fatal result—Short triumph—Scenes changed—Events—Reprisals—North-West downfall—The de Meuron regiment 32

CHAPTER IV.

Emigrants recalled from banishment—The colony re-established—The free grant—Church and school lots—Sites described—Deeds promised—Scotch and their minister—Lord Selkirk's departure—Seed—Returns—Pembina—Winter adventures—Cold—Severe trials—Camp hospitalities—The Scotch—Mr. Sutherland—Pleasing prospects soon blighted—Grasshoppers—French emigrants—Pembina again—Grasshoppers—Total ruin—The Scotch turn hunters—Last thought the best—Prairie de Chien adventure—Wheat—Communication from Red River to St. Peter's—Party arrive—Hope revived . . . 42

CHAPTER V.

Scotch minister—Fruitless attempts—Conjectures—The reproof—Strange things happen—The disappointment—Mr. West—Missionary efforts—The disputed point—Coalition—Happy results—Indian quarrels—Grasshoppers take flight—Swiss emigrants—Watchmakers—Pastry-cooks—Handsome young women—Hunger—Pembina—Beggars no choosers—The Swiss discouraged—Comparison—High notions in high life—Starvation—The silver watch—Gold eyes—The snuff-box—The cat-fish—Hard bargain—Summing up—Perseverance of the settlers—Bourke's sufferings—Remarks 52

CHAPTER VI.

Colony store—Lord Selkirk—Governor McDonell—Officials, their doings—Things that ought not to be—Drunken squabbles—The hour-glass—A new method of keeping accounts—The grains of wheat—The paper-box in the corner—The hubbub—The mêlée—Partiality—Credit system—Colony work—Trickery—Confusion—Mr. Halkett—Grievances redressed—The guinea—The lost keys—The discovery—The papers—The revenge—General remarks—Buffalo Wool Company—High expectations—Gloomy result—Intemperance—Mismanagement—The yard of cloth—Bankers rewarded—Remarks 63

CHAPTER VII.

Supply of domestic cattle—Change of system—The lucky hit—Profitable speculation—Reciprocal advantage—Mr. West's return—Mr. Halkett's reply to the Scotch settlers—The disappointment—Conjectures—Remarks—Pembina quarter abandoned—People return—Governor Bulger—Hay-field farm—Mr. Laidlow—The dead loss—Spirit of the times—Causes of failures—Farming progress—Returns—Canadian voyageurs—The people reassemble—Census—Novelty—Mongrel squatters—Harmony—Scene changed—People divided 73

CHAPTER VIII.

Second importation of cattle—Enlivening scenes—Encouraging progress—The unscrupulous visitors—Feathered heads—Fishing and hunting occupations—The ways and doings of Baptiste L'Esprit—Summer adventures—Winter trip to the plains—The industrious rib—People calling themselves Christians—Assiniboine trip—New scenes—Pipe habits—Tobacco and tea—Flammond and his family—The happy couple—The people's mode of life—Tea-drinking in Red River—Tea-drinking in Koondoz—The Uzbeks—The delicious compound—The mice . . 82

CHAPTER IX.

Hunters and their habits — Rumours — Visit Pembina — Reports confirmed—Steps taken—Hudson's Bay Company—Sympathy—The fatal snow-storm—Train of disasters—Woman and child—Human misery—Lives lost—Cling to old habits — Hunters relieved — Colonists in distress — Gloomy scenes—Sudden rise in the water—Settlers abandon their houses—The river becomes a lake—Property adrift—Floating spectacle—Waterfall—Prices rise—Settlers return—Colloquies—Discouraging scenes—The man and his two oxen—Honest fellows—Precarious times—Cattle diminish—De Meurons—Cause of the high water—The question answered—More floods than one—Features—Indications—Shores of Hudson's Bay—Phenomenon . 98

CHAPTER X.

Swiss and De Meurons emigrate—The Scotch at work again—Discouraging circumstances—Result of perseverance—Ups and downs—Red River climate—Late sowing—New houses—Confidence restored—Orkney men in Red River—Agriculture—The month of May—The seed season—Comparison — Fall ploughing — Fall sowing — Runnet — Defective spot—Ruinous system—Comfort disregarded—Red River malaria—One ploughing enough—Experiments—Fall ploughing recommended—Clover seed—Cold—New feature — Governor Simpson's views — Encouragements versus discouragements — Flour — Butter — Produce condemned — The Company's policy — Hints disregarded — The Governor's table — The difficult question — Who is to blame? 108

CHAPTER XI.

A new experiment—Unsettled state of things—The farmer at a stand—Fixing the price—The governing principle—The market — The Company's wheat — The mixture — The farrago—The flour—The millers—Saddle on the wrong horse—The ice-barn farmers—An example—Visit to an old friend—The establishment in confusion—The barn—The stable with many doors—The corn-yard and the pigs—Fiddling the time away—Anecdote—The father and his sons—The old man in earnest—Scotch settlers and their minister—The comparisons—The Scotch and their petitions—Public meeting—Petition again—Counter petition—The result—Mr. Jones and the Scotch settlers—The Liturgy laid aside—The parson's popularity—Kate and her keg of butter—General remarks—School system revised—Remarks thereon—Doing good to others—The Scotch in Red River—Social relations—Fashion—Dress—The good example . 119

CHAPTER XII.

Governor Simpson—Second experimental farm—Experimental farms in general—The establishment—Ample means—The fur trade farmer—Mongrel servants—Experience disregarded—The sheep speculation—Great projects—Small results—The wolves rejoicing—The humbug—The flax and hemp project—The premiums—The farmers in motion—Strange policy—The Governor's disappointment—The trick—The favourites—The little monopoly—The buildings—Fort Garry—Episcopalians versus Presbyterians—General remarks—The Scotch in Red River . . . 133

CHAPTER XIII.

The windmill—Its history—Red River windmills—The watermill—The dam operations—Keg of rum—The contented master—Men at work—Result—New sheep speculation—Governor Simpson—Contractors—Broils—Going the wrong way to work—Paying for one's folly—The deadly grass—The effect—Marking the road to St. Peter's—The vote of thanks indoors—Murmuring out-doors—Result—Tallow trade—Object—The wolves—Winding up—General remarks—Winter road—The object—Result . . 144

CHAPTER XIV.

The petty trader—Change of men and change of measures—The rich and the poor—The shopping confusion—Steer a middle course—Company's tariff—Great promisers small performers—A petty trader behind his counter—Competition—Hints—The fur trade—Remarks—Indians—The awkward Cree question—Useful hints—Alarm—Patrols—The Saulteaux in Red River—Guns pointed—Mr. Simpson—General remarks—Sioux visits—Wannatah—Half-breeds—Physical demonstrations—Demagogues at work—Manœuvring—First-rank men—Results . . . 155

CHAPTER XV.

Political aspect of things—Colony changes masters—The costly child—Value of the colony—A step-mother's care—The political miracle—The Company's liberality—An overruling power—The mystery—Ground-work of law and order—Prefatory address—Constitution of first council—Law enactments—Their tendency—Presbyterians and their minister—The parson's justification—The Rev. Mr. Cockran—The Presbyterians renew their application—Mr. Governor Christie's policy—The English missionaries—Remarks—Change of opinions—More of form than reality Emigration—The cause—The coincidence—Things as they are—Ariosto and his tempest, a type of parties in Red River 170

CHAPTER XVI.

First petty jury—The flogger flogged—Summer frosts—Crops destroyed—Chain of cross purposes—Preamble—The three imposing months—The stranger—Mosquitoes—Bull-dogs—The black fly—The ramble—Canadians and half-breeds—Their mode of life—The man of consequence—Gossiping parties—Amusements—The effects of habit—Children in their infancy—Votaries of pleasure—Wood-rafters—Squatters—Result—Scene changed—Europeans—Visit the Indians—Fish on dry land—Tea-drinking in the wilderness—Indians and the aurora borealis—Superstition—The Scotch in Red River—Domestic comforts—New habits—The Sabbath-day—The agreeable mistake . . 186

CHAPTER XVII.

Another experimental farm—Remarks—Views of the people at home—Comparisons—The half-pay officer—Great promises—Small performances—The first experiment—The grand operations—Stock—How far for the benefit of Red River—Quality of the hands—The hay party—Captain Cary—Result of the undertaking—Anecdote—The proposition—British Government—Civilization—The Scotch and their minister—The two zealots—Viewing things through a false medium—Mr. Cockran—Observations—Change of system—New laws—Judge Thom in Red River—Opinions of the people—Mr. Simpson, of the Arctic expedition—Subject continued—His death—North American half-breeds—Remarks—Subject concluded . . . 211

CHAPTER XVIII.

Half-breeds in Red River—Parents and children—Company's policy—Relative position of the Company and half-breeds—Steps against interlopers—The French half-breeds change—The cause—The English half-breeds join them—Influence of Papineau's rebellion—Mob-meeting—Half-breeds demand an export trade—Governor Simpson's reply—Foreigners at the buffalo-hunts—Influence of buffalo-hunting on the colonists—The outfit and start—Pembina camp—Number of carts—Dogs—Anecdote—Camp regulations—Honesty of the half-breeds—Officials—Council—Stroll in the camp—Two sides to the picture—First sight of the battle-field—The half-breeds in their glory—Sky darkened—Casualties—Fruits of the chase—Comparison—The risks—The duties—Vallé and the Sioux—Speedy revenge—Pleasures of the chase—Question and answer—Chamois hunter—The mêlée—Perplexing scene—Remarks—The conflict—The waste—Camp raised again—Descent to the Missouri—Tariff—Uncertain travelling—The Sioux chief—Indian telegraphs—The fatal storm—The battle—Loss of life—Sioux warriors—Reflections—Expedition arrives—Effect—Provisions—Result of expedition 234

CHAPTER XIX.

First steps to civilization—Habits change—Influence of the Scotch emigrants—Gospel planted in Rupert's Land—Mr. West—Bishop's visit—Mr. Cockran and the Swampies—Indian settlement—The parson's mistake—Rules for missionary enterprise—Mr. Cockran takes leave of the Swampies—Their character—The Roman Catholic mission of St. Paul—Rev. Mr. Belcourt—Wabassimong mission—Wesleyan mission—Religious opposition—Baie des Canards mission—Partridge Crop mission—Protestants versus Catholics — Sagacious thief—False impressions of Red River abroad—Churches and missionaries—Liberality of the Hudson's Bay Company 275

CHAPTER XX.

New missionary system—Introductory remarks—The text—Neglect of the heathen in Red River—The general principle—Three important conditions—Missionary difficulties—The first stage of progress—Staff of labourers—Governor Kempt's observations—The boon—The converts located—Second stage—Total of expenses—Comparison with the present cost—The missionary qualified—The success of the trader compared—Missionary station in the United States—Rev. Mr. Hunter—The Saskatchewan mission—Rivalry of sects—Coterie of Protestant missionaries in Red River—Crusade against idols—Church privileges—The Bishop of Rupert's Land—Sir George Murray's hints—Concluding remarks 301

CHAPTER XXI.

Sioux and Saulteaux—Treaties—Indian correspondence—Indian feelings—Two Indians shot—Result—Indian hung—Effect—The favourable change—Fulling-mill—The farce—Yankee fur-traders—The two foxes—Friendly intercourse 324

CHAPTER XXII.

Cause of the Presbyterians resumed—Governor Finlayson—The petition—The clergy at work—Criticisms—Correspondence with Fenchurch-street—Affidavits—Doubts removed—The church site question—Company's ultimatum—Appeal to the Free Church of Scotland—Time lost—Friendly aid of Sir George Simpson—The four propositions—The minister in view—Correspondence sent to England—More delay—Bishop of Rupert's Land—The secession—The Presbyterians at home—The churchyard—Frog Plain—The church and the manse—End of the forty years' agitation 341

CHAPTER XXIII.

The decades—Epidemic of 1846—State of public feeling—Deaths—The 6th Royals—The effect—The pensioners—The Company's policy—A military Governor—Government inquiry and result—Character of Major Caldwell—Isbister's controversy—Earl of Elgin's views—Real grievance of the half-breeds—The fur-trade question—Mob meeting—Celebrated trial of Sayer—The Court in jeopardy—Reasons and opinions—Hints for consideration—Judge Thom and the laws—Sacredness of the oath 362

CHAPTER XXIV.

Climate and productions—Woodlands and pasturage—Rearing of cattle—Horses—Brick-makers and other artisans—Prices—Domestic servants—Barter and long credit—The truck system—Imports—Exports—How the money comes—Police—Magistrates—Minnesota and the half-breeds—Fortune's own child—Pembina and the Americans—St. Peter's again—Minnesota government—Vancouver's Island and the constitution of Red River—Danger of neglect—Appendix 387

INTRODUCTION TO THE NEW EDITION

I

ALEXANDER ROSS'S *Red River Settlement* is a classic of the history of the North American West. That reputation is of long standing. But it is important to note that it is not the general subject of the book, the trials and difficulties of the first settlement of the Canadian West, its style or even its substance that are central to its reputation. Two things give the book its essential quality. One is the authenticity: the author writes out of his own experience. The second is an extension of the former. Alexander Ross was married to an Indian woman, and he moved to the Red River Colony to settle and educate his half-breed children. That was the purpose, he thought, of the colony, to make possible a settled and civilized life in the wilderness. To the perceptive reader his book is a study of the attempt to reconcile the nomad and the settler, the savage and the civilized. It was, after all, a theme near to his heart, a theme enacted in the daily life of his home in Red River, the famous Colony Gardens.

II

The theme may well have run deep in Ross's blood, for he was born in Nairnshire, just east of Inverness, which bridled the wild Highlanders, and of Culloden, where the power of the clans was finally broken. When he came to Canada and taught school in Glengarry County, he must have been aware, even as a dominie in a Scots settlement, of how close the wilderness was. Certainly he felt the call of the wild when in 1810 he accepted service with the New York fur merchant, John Jacob Astor, and sailed to the far Pacific coast to help found Astoria on the Columbia River for the Pacific Fur Company. The wild, and its opportunities in new fur country, was to hold him when the North West Company of Canada captured Astoria and the fur trade of the central west coast. In their service he became a fur trader on the Snake River in the Rocky Mountains, and it was there he met and married his Okanagan wife. The wild had claimed him, as it did most fur traders.

Marriage with a native woman was inevitable, however transient it might prove, for most men in the far West. Marriage provided loyal service in the preparation of food and the care of clothing and moccasins. It was good for trade and all dealings with the local Indians. It might well prove an insurance against attack, as it was against the importunities of ambitious fathers or enterprising young squaws. But like all marriage, it was likely to lead to children. For many, perhaps most of the white fathers, the future of the children was simple: they grew as part of their mother's tribe. Where a large trading post gave rise to many half-breed children, they might marry and form a society between that of European and Indian. Such was the origin of the Métis and half-breed of the Red River Colony.

If, however, the white father was a man of conscience and affection, he might not allow his half-breed children to remain the offspring of the wilderness. He would have them educated, in Scotland, as was Cuthbert Grant, in Quebec, as was the father of Louis Riel, or after 1821 in Red River, as were the children of Alexander Ross.

It was bound to be so for his children. Educated himself, he was a man of conscience and affection—of prudence and foresight also, in every way a canny Scot. He was to prove himself much more. Long settled in Red River, comfortable in the bosom of his family and secure in the respect of his fellow colonists, he was not content. He became an author, an author whose books are still sought and read a long century later. For his great wilderness trilogy, *Adventures of the first settlers on the Oregon or Columbia River* (1849), *The fur hunters of the far west* (1855), and *The Red River Settlement* (1856), he elaborated the great theme of the contacts of primitive and civilized man, of the hunter and the trader, the nomad and the settler. Little wonder that he saw in the Red River Colony an experiment in reconciliation of opposites as ancient as Cain and Abel, saw it with insight that moved him at once to satire and compassion.

III

What Lord Selkirk's objects were in founding the Red River Colony is not clear to historians or biographers. Ross was well aware, as he makes evident in his first chapter, that they may well have been several and even diverse. But there, and even more in his preface, he chooses the view that Selkirk had sent his settlers to be the stable core of a colony "forming itself" around them. They would provide the element of settled civilization that would serve to settle and educate the primitive and wandering people of the West, especially the children of those retired from the service of the fur companies— families such as that of Ross himself.

It was in Red River that Ross passed that period of his life from 1825 to his death in 1856, and it was there that he formed his ideas on the history of the old West and wrote the books in which he embodied them. It is this settlement he analyzes and describes in this book, its people, its customs, its tribulations. No one is likely ever to better his description of the colony; what is asked of a reader is to understand Ross, to see as he saw and understand as he understood.

It is not difficult to do so, once one has grasped the elements that made up the colony. The colony itself was a core, a centre of civilized life in a wilderness of hunting tribes. The lives of the Indians had, of course, been greatly modified by the fur trade, but they preserved the custom and belief of their ancient way of life. They therefore moved on the periphery of the circle of which Red River was the centre, little affected by it. Only a few stragglers in the settlement, the Indian parish of St. Peters on the Red and the Salteaux mission of Baie St. Paul on the Assiniboine gave Indian elements to the colony, and even then were peripheral to its life.

Quite different were the roles of the half-caste descendants of the employees of the fur trade. They were integral to the colony and, in Ross's view, the chief reason for its founding and existence. Yet there were two groups of half-castes, so great was the diversity of the fur trade and the settlement.

The larger was that of the Métis. The offspring mainly of French engagées of the North West Company, but with Scots and English surnames among the French, and of Indian mothers, mostly Salteaux and Cree, they spoke French and Indian and were Roman Catholic in faith. They were thus the children of the work force of the fur companies, and pursued the occupations of their parents as hunters, trappers, boatmen. In particular, they became the huntsmen of the Red River buffalo hunt from which came the "country provisions," the pemmican and dried meat of the fur trade, the hunt so elaborately and vividly described in this book. And to a degree, they became under their chief, Cuthbert Grant, warden of the plains of Red River, the defenders of the colony against the Sioux. Or so they were considered, because to hunt on the plains towards the Sioux for the game on which the Sioux lived, they had to be capable of defending themselves on the hunt, and built up much of the discipline and tactical skill of a military force. As such, they were as capable of menacing the settlement as defending it, and the Hudson's Bay Company and the colony had to give much care to placating the Métis.

Distinct from the Métis were the half-breeds. These too were the sons and daughters of employees of the fur trade and their Indian wives. But the fathers were usually attached to a post, and their wives and children lived as part of the order and routine of a post. They were, in short, raised in houses, not in tipis, among the staid ways of civilized homes, not in movement and simplicity of the hunt and the camp. The half-breeds, in consequence, were educated or readily educated folk of grave manners who accepted, most of them, the stability and order of settled life. Some of them did follow the hunt, some did become free traders, most perhaps failed to become good farmers. But in their chief areas of settlement, the parishes of St. Andrews and St. James, they created communities much like those of Kildonan or St. John's, the homes of the Selkirk settlers.

Those settlers of course had founded homes much like those they left, except that they had an abundance of land for their fields and of timber for their houses. They were Scottish crofters on the banks of the Red. Their farming was not of a high order, but it was steady. The crops were sown and fenced, unlike the potato patches of the Métis, sown in spring in the hope of harvest in the fall. Their herds and flocks were watched, if not tended; hay was made for the winters and the cattle stabled. And the livelihood of the settler depended, largely if not wholly, on his crops for sustenance and for sale.

As Ross was keenly aware, agriculture was the heart of the matter for it alone furnished the means of settled existence. It even made possible the winter homes of the buffalo hunters when they had come in from the plains to trade their pemmican and dried meat for, among other things, flour. It was the main effort in the Indian parish to win the Indians from hunting to farming, more important even than winning them from paganism to Christianity, because it was thought one would lead to the other. Hence the continued existence of the colony depended on two things, the improvement of farming methods and the finding of a wider market for farm produce. In this no one tried harder to give a lead than Ross. And it is because Mr. Laidlaw and Captain Cary, the two agricultural experts brought in, failed to make this knowledge practicable in the conditions of Red River that Ross was so critical of them. They had failed to do what it was of the utmost importance to do.

Ross saw even further. It was in fact impossible to widen the market for farm produce, and so improve the quality of farming and the prospects of the settlement, so long as much of what market there was was supplied by the buffalo hunt. The farm and the hunt checked and balanced one another, and the colony stagnated in the equipoise. The nomadic element of the Métis offset the sedentary element of the settler and thwarted the growth of the colony as a centre of civilization. Only the reinforcements of the settlers could check a gathering drag back to nomadic ways. When that reinforcement began, it was to provoke the resistance of the Métis under Louis Riel.

Because of this balance between the hunter and the farmer, the Métis and the settler, the authorities of the colony, the governor and council of Assiniboia were always concerned with law and order, and Ross himself played a large part in the effort to keep the settlement peaceful. The plain truth was that there was no means of raising a public force that could impress the Métis. Ross himself served as sheriff of Assiniboia, captain of the volunteers and of the police, as a member of the council and an officer of the court, but he was well aware that the peace was kept in Assiniboia by influence and persuasion, seldom by authority. He himself witnessed the defiance of government and law by the Métis assembled in arms at the trial of Guillaume Sayer in 1849. It was thought inadvisable to challenge them by calling out the Pensioners, old soldiers sent out to support the authorities.

Yet, until the last years of the colony, the peace was usually kept. Much of this peacefulness was owing to the influence of the clergy. It was properly so, for after agriculture, the Christian religion was meant to be a stabilizing and civilizing influence. The plough was to prepare the way of the cross. Indeed, the two were linked, especially by the Anglican and Protestant missionaries; the Roman Catholics thought of settled life as an aid to, but not a necessary condition of Christianity, and did not despair of the Faith being nomadic as well as sedentary. It followed therefore that Ross saw religion as he saw agriculture, as the joint mainstay of the colony. For this reason he was as critical of the failures and foibles of missionaries as of agricultural experts.

Ross saw the Church too as a preservative as well as a proselytizing force. This was one reason, as well as his own convictions, with perhaps a bit of Scots doggedness, that he worked so hard to obtain a Presbyterian minister for the Scots Kildonan settlers. People would remain firmest in the faith in their own denominations, their own version of the truth, he believed, and so would best preserve the essential core of civilized life.

One may well wince today at the absolute identifications of Christianity and civilization, even of sedentary life and civilization, but that was quite unchallenged in Ross's time. And as the Church and educators went hand in hand then, religion strengthened civilization by its provision for education. Ross, by bringing Rev. John Black to Kildonan, began not only a Presbyterian ministry there, but also a school out of which Manitoba College was to arise, one of the founding colleges of the University of Manitoba and the University of Winnipeg.

The importance of religion, education and a family life resting on them is revealed by his own children. William, his eldest son, became postmaster of Red River, governor of the gaol, collector of customs, and sheriff of Assiniboia. James, his second, became a B. A. and gold medallist of the University of Toronto, a journalist, sheriff of Assiniboia, chief justice of the provisional government of Manitoba, and was called to the bar before his early death. His daughter, Henrietta, became Mrs. John Black and mistress of the manse at Kildonan. There was, in the early death of William and James and the instability of the latter, much that was sad and not unfamiliar in half-breed children, but Ross's family stood like their father for the settled ways of the good life as his generation understood it.

IV

The centre and focus of Alexander Ross's life was Colony Gardens, his home on or near the site of Fort Douglas, overlooking the long reach of Red River to the south at the curve where it turns east to make the loop that forms Point Douglas. It was perhaps the most civilized home in Red River. It is quite gone now. Only the Christian names of his sons survive in Winnipeg streets on the once river lot back from Colony Gardens. But this book is his greater memorial.

W. L. MORTON

Trent College
January, 1969

PREFACE

RED RIVER SETTLEMENT, the subject of this volume, is an isolated spot in the wilds of North America, distant 700 miles from the nearest sea-port, and that port blockaded by solid ice for ten months in the year. Our history dates from the grant of this wilderness to Lord Selkirk, when it was marked by no human footstep but that of the wandering savage or unscrupulous trader: a land inhabited only by the bear, the wolf, and the buffalo, where the bleating of sheep and the lowing of oxen were as unknown as the sound of the church-going bell and the whirr of the grindstone. The settlement of a spot thus characterized, presenting a picture to the imagination of civilized men as gloomy as the Ultima Thule of the ancients, and affording as little promise of reward, cannot be an uninteresting subject to those who love enterprise and honour endurance. To such, the author submits his unpretending narrative, encouraged by the remembrance that his endeavours, on more than one previous occasion, have been amply rewarded by the interest manifested in his disclosures.

From time to time, casual remarks on the colony of

Red River have made the world in some degree acquainted with its history; but this kind of information having generally been put forth in the interest of individuals or parties, nothing has yet appeared which could fairly claim regard as a complete history of the colony. The author's object, therefore, has been to supply this desideratum, more especially to record the hardships and privations undergone by the first settlers, and to show, by the results of their efforts, their constancy in misfortune, and their unremitted industry under the most discouraging circumstances, how much may be effected by men thus situated.

Missionary efforts for converting the heathen also come in for their share of notice in connection with remarks on Indian character, many fresh phases of which are exhibited in these pages. It may here be observed, that Lord Selkirk never intended to rear an extensive colony of civilized men in Red River, but rather to form a society of the natives and the Company's old servants, together with their half-breed descendants. The few emigrants sent out by him were intended merely to diffuse a spirit of industry and agricultural knowledge among these children of nature, and, in fine, to act as the pioneers in the wilderness, who might open otherwise inaccessible paths for the spread of the Gospel.

A colony thus forming itself, by a kind of extemporary process, in the face of many opposing interests, and in the midst of warring elements, may be supposed to exhibit certain aspects, social or material, on which great difference of opinion must of necessity exist.

These points of interest have been a source of continually recurring difficulty to the writer, who has guarded himself, as far as possible, by endeavouring to ground his conclusions, not on opinion, but on facts. After all, he may not have been happy enough to steer himself clear of the prejudices and interested views of all the castes and characters, civilized and savage, noticed in the work; indeed, he never deemed this possible. He rests his claim on broader and surer grounds—on having, from a perfect knowledge of men and things, done justice to all parties, without colouring, or any attempt at artificial construction or polished composition. His statements, it is confidently hoped, will shed a not doubtful light on the past and present condition of the different races, savage and civilized, now inhabiting these lands; and thus will afford materials of the highest importance to the future historian.

The plan of the work will be sufficiently apparent, but it may here be noticed, that when any distinct or specific subject is introduced, it is, whenever convenient, treated throughout, from beginning to end, in one place, though its action may extend over several years; by this means the necessity of wading through different years and chapters for parts of the same subject is generally avoided. Sometimes, indeed, this has not been possible, and especially when one series of events is found connected with another; and hence another general rule—namely, when any year is commenced, that all the following incidents are to be regarded as occurring within the limits of that year, until another is distinctly mentioned, or an exception is pointed out.

The chronological order may thus be a little disturbed, but the order of the subjects treated of is better preserved by this plan. Here, also, it may be noticed, once for all, that the author makes no pretension to the scientific treatment of his subject; his task is the much humbler one of describing the lot of the poor settler, and, in a word, the trials and triumphs of industry.

Finally, cast at an early stage of his career into the depths of the wilderness, far removed from civilized society, and doomed for so many years to an almost exclusive association with the rude and untutored tribes by whom it is inhabited, and choosing at last, for his adopted home, this secluded spot, in which, although it be blessed in some degree with the light of civilization, everyone must yet be prepared in a great measure to resign the intercourse of the literary world, the writer is not so presumptuous as to prefer any claim either to the ornaments of diction, or to the embellishments of imagination. He has, however, had abundant opportunities of observing savage life and manners; and his long experience in a wild country has enabled him to correct the almost invariably erroneous nature of first impressions, by affording him all the elements of sober and dispassionate research in the execution of his plan.

Red River Settlement,
 10th June, 1852.

THE

RED RIVER SETTLEMENT:

ITS RISE, PROGRESS, AND PRESENT STATE.

CHAPTER I.

CONTENTS.—The Hudson's Bay Company's Charter—Legal opinions on its validity—Remarks on the same—Lord Selkirk's grant—Observations thereon—Geographical position of Red River Colony—Indian Treaty—The Saulteaux Indians—Country described—Conflagrations in the plains—Effect—Cold—Heat—Wolves—The four opinions—Lord Selkirk's motives considered.

THE history of a Colonial Settlement is always interesting, whether it be regarded as another link added to the growing chain of civilization; as the means by which new nations and kingdoms may be founded; or only as an additional field of enterprise, calculated to relieve an older country of its redundant population and overflowing resources. Under each of these aspects the settlement on the shores of the Red River possesses its particular claim to regard, but more especially in the respect first mentioned; the primary object of its founder having been the spread of the Gospel, and the evangelization of the heathen. In the course of our narrative, it will appear how far that object has been realized, and by what means. First, we have to exhibit the Colony in its material aspect, and historical associations.

This settlement, it is well known, lies within the territories of the Hudson's Bay Company's charter, granted by King Charles the Second, in the year 1670; in terms of which the Company became absolute lords and proprietors of the soil, and, as a consequence, it is alleged, were entitled to the exclusive right of trade.* On that right, however, or rather on the validity of the charter, we shall here make a brief observation; for not only is it a point of considerable importance to our history, but it is one in which the public have been much interested, and on which the most eminent lawyers both in England and Canada have disagreed.

The validity of the charter is supported by the opinion of Earl Grey, late Secretary for the British Colonies, who in a letter to Sir John Pelly, Baronet, Governor of the Hudson's Bay Company, dated June 6th, 1850, thus alludes to it;—" Steps having been taken

* The charter was granted to the Hudson's Bay Company by King Charles the Second, and includes all the country, the waters of which run into Hudson's Bay.

The Royal License of exclusive trade with the Indians, in such parts of British North America as are not included in the charter, was granted to the Company by her present Majesty, Queen Victoria, for a further term of twenty-one years, upon the surrender of a former grant for the like term, and is dated Buckingham Palace, 30th May 1838.

Another Royal grant was made to the Company of Vancouver's Island, dated the 13th January 1849.

to obtain from the Hudson's Bay Company a statement of its claims, that statement was duly submitted to Her Majesty's law advisers; and Her Majesty's Government received from them a report that the claims of the Company were well founded. It was observed in that report, that with a view to the fuller satisfaction of the House of Commons and the parties interested, it would be advisable to refer the inquiry to a competent tribunal, and that the proper method of raising a discussion on it, would be for some person to address a petition to Her Majesty, which petition might then be referred either to the Judicial Committee, or the Committee of Privy Council for Trade and Foreign Plantations. Such a petition was therefore essential to the complete prosecution of the inquiry. Lord Grey accordingly gave to certain parties in this country, who had taken an interest in the condition of the inhabitants of the Hudson's Bay Company's territories, and had questioned the validity of the Company's charter, an opportunity to prefer the necessary petition if they were so disposed; but for reasons which it is unnecessary to repeat, they respectively declined to do so. Lord Grey having therefore, on behalf of Her Majesty's Government, adopted the most effectual means open to him for answering the requirements of the address, has been obliged, in the absence of any parties prepared to contest the rights claimed by the Company, to assume the opinion of the law officers of the Crown in their favour to be well founded.

(Signed) " B. HAWES."

The decided opinion thus given by the ablest lawyers

in England is supported by some of the most eminent in the United States. "The terms of this charter," says R. S. Coxe, "resemble those granted to some of the Colonies upon this continent by the British Crown, which have ever been construed to confer a proprietary interest in the soil as well as a modified sovereignty over the entire country granted. The territory on the west coast of America was not comprehended within the original charter; but its general provisions have been extended to that region by subsequent Acts:—the statute 43 Geo. III., passed in 1803; the royal grant of 1821, regulating the fur trade; that of 1838; and the treaty between Great Britain and the United States of 1846: this last treaty was framed and its language must be construed with reference to the foundation upon which the rights of the Company then rested. It is well known that the Hudson's Bay Company not only appropriated to its particular and exclusive use, various tracts of land lying within the general description in the grant to it; but also exercised the power of making grants of extensive tracts to sub-purchasers. The authority it exercised was unlimited."

"I entertain no doubt" says the late Honourable Daniel Webster, "that these Companies have a vested proprietary interest in these lands. Their title, to its full extent, is protected by treaty, and although it is called a possessory title, it has been regarded as being, if not an absolute fee in the land, yet a fixed right of possession, use, and occupation, as to prevent the soil from being alienated to others. Some years ago, during the controversy respecting Lord Selkirk's settlement, the nature of these possessory rights was examined, and considered by very eminent counsel in England, with Sir Samuel Romilly at their head. They were all of opinion, that action of trespass, and other usual legal remedies for interrupting the use and enjoyment of land, might be resorted to and maintained by the Companies under their Charters."

" On this part of the case, concurring with Mr. Coxe, I have nothing to add to his remarks."

Similar testimony is borne by John Van Buren, another United States lawyer of great experience, who declared " That the occupation of the Hudson's Bay Company was lawful, and their charter perpetual." Again, Geo. M. Gibb, Esq., strongly urged it on the American Government to purchase the rights of the Hudson's Bay Company, within the territory of the Oregon, as a measure of public policy. " For," says he, " the possessory rights springing out of this perpetual charter, are so wide, so long, so deep, so multiplied, and so indefinite, as to affect seriously our interest there." And further, Edwin M. Stanton, Esq., on the subject of the Company's possessory rights, states, " For not only was the possession of the Hudson's Bay Company recognised by its Government, but also their absolute right to grant and convey vast and unlimited portions of territory to others."

To draw nearer home: " Down to the date of the charter," says Mr. Thom, the able Recorder of Rupert's Land, " the Crown of England confessedly possessed, and habitually exercised, the right of granting foreign trade and colonial dominion to private individuals, or to public corporations, without the consent of the Houses of Parliament; and perhaps no document was ever more frequently confirmed by the paramount authorities of any country than the charter of Prince Rupert and his distinguished associates. By 7 and 8 Wm. III., chap. 22, the proprietary plantations, such as Rupert's Land, were regulated in such terms as expressly involved a parliamentary recognition of all royal grants of colonial dominion. By 6 Anne, chap. 37—a statute which proposed to facilitate the colonial trade—all the estates, rights, and privileges of the Hudson's Bay Company were declared to be saved, notwithstanding the tenor and tendency of the act itself; so that here was a general recognition of the whole charter with a special reference to its commercial provisions. By 14 Geo. III., chap. 83, the northern boundary of Canada was to be the southern boundary of the territory granted to the Hudson's Bay Company, the parliamentary province merely claiming to the northward what the letter of the royal grant, without regard to actual possession, might leave unappropriated. By 1 and 2 Geo. IV., chap. 66, the charter of Rupert's Land was twice expressly recognised: its first section, though its single object was to prevent competition, yet confined the license to the country not covered by the charter; thus positively saving, as in the last-mentioned case, the extent of territory, and negatively assuming the right of trade as an already existing security against the dreaded evil; and the closing section of the Act revived, in the most emphatic language, the chartered jurisdiction which one of the intermediate sections had extinguished.

"But the royal charter has been recognised by public documents more important in their effect, though, perhaps, less obligatory in their character, than Acts of Parliament. In the reign of Queen Anne, the treaty of Utrecht transferred from France to England all right and title to the chartered territories, French Canada, and French Louisiana; thus accepting the charter as the arbiter of their northern boundaries, and rendering to its limits the very homage which English Canada and the Indian territories still render to the same. The Hudson's Bay Company's charter has been sanctioned by every variety of Parliament—by the Parliament of England, by the Parliament of England and Scotland, and by the Parliament of England, Scotland, and Ireland; it has been sanctioned by five of the eight intermediate predecessors of Victoria; it has been sanctioned with respect to its exclusive trade, with respect to its local jurisdiction, and with respect to its geographical extent; it has been sanctioned as against individual subjects, and as against individual aliens; it has been sanctioned as against neighbouring colonies, and as against foreign states; and what is more than all this, it has been proved to be independent of any sanction by triumphing, on merely technical grounds, over a direct attack of the supreme authority of the empire." With these facts before us, we are bound morally and politically to regard the charter of Charles II., with all its doubtful and questionable conditions, as valid, until the British Government pronounce it otherwise.

If such is the law of the case, it is no less true, that respect for this charter is also sound policy. Were it annulled by the British Government, and the country thrown open to competition, there is too much reason to fear that anarchy and bloodshed would take the place of that uniform system and good order which at present is universally enjoyed under the safeguard and protection of the charter. But whatever the result to the aborigines and the colonists, it is certain, however strange it may seem, that the Company alone could be gainers by such a change. In the first place they would be enriched by compensation for their property to the amount, at least, of some two or three millions sterling, and with this capital they would still enjoy the same privileges here as other British subjects. To this must be added the deeply rooted hold they possess in the country, which would virtually be still as much under the Company's control without as with the charter. In a word, the Company would lose nothing by the change but the mere name, while the whole country would be involved in confusion, and suffer we know not what, from the evils attendant on free trade.

Inviting the reader at least to suspend his judgment on these points, we come now to the proper commencement of our history. As early as the year 1811, in the progress of his colonizing system, Thomas Douglas, Earl of Selkirk, purchased from the Hudson's Bay Company a large tract of land comprised within the limits of its charter, for the purpose of planting a colony there. The boundary of this grant "begins at a point on the western shores of Lake Winipeg, 52° 30' north latitude; thence running due west to the Lake Wini-

ITS RISE, PROGRESS, AND PRESENT STATE. 9

pegoos; thence in a southerly direction, so as to strike its western shores in lat. 52° N.; then due west to the place where the parallel of 52° N. latitude intersects the Assiniboine River, then due south from that to the height of land which separates the waters running into the Hudson's Bay, from those of the Missouri and Mississippi; thence in an easterly direction along that height of land, to the source of the Winipeg, or the principal branch of the waters which flow to the mouth of the Winipeg River, and thence in a northerly direction to the middle of Lake Winipeg, then west to the place of beginning."

Red River, one of the feeders of Lake Winipeg, is within this grant, and situated at the south extremity of that lake, in lat. 50° N. and long. 97° W. It is about 300 miles long, but in its windings more than 400, and lies in the direction of south and north; having its source in Ottertail Lake, at the *couteau des prairie*, or height of land. This river, of no great breadth, and having a muddy bottom, is navigable to the Grande Fourche, or Great Forks, about 150 miles from its mouth, with small boats or pirogues (wooden canoes.) Some time after his lordship had made this extensive purchase, it was found that the Americans claimed as far as the forty-ninth degree of north latitude, which of course curtailed his lordship's claim to Pembina, where the international line between both Governments passes. From Lake Winipeg, then, to Pembina was the place selected by his lordship for establishing his colony, although in the Indian treaty, as we shall presently see, " La Grande Fourche" is mentioned. Thus the extent of it, south and north, is in a manner limited to about 100 miles: whereas, on the east and west, it might be extended to almost any distance.

The charter of the Hudson's Bay Company, and the purchase of these lands by Lord Selkirk, clearly establish his right, according to the laws of civilized nations; yet some arrangement with the Indians was necessary, in order to remove all annoyance from the settlers. Lord Selkirk therefore concluded the following treaty, which, although a little out of chronological order, may here be conveniently introduced:—

"This Indenture, made on the 18th day of July, in the fifty-seventh year of the reign of our Sovereign Lord King George the Third, and in the year of our Lord 1817, between the undersigned Chiefs and Warriors of the Chippeway or Saulteaux Nation, and of the Killistino or Cree Nation, on the one part, and the Right Honourable Thomas Earl of Selkirk on the other part. Witnesseth, that for and in consideration of the annual present or quit-rent hereinafter mentioned, the said Chiefs have given, granted, and confirmed, and do by these presents give, grant, and confirm, unto our Sovereign Lord the King, all that tract of land, adjacent to Red River and Assiniboine River, beginning at the mouth of the Red River, and extending along the same as far as the Great Forks at the mouth of Red Lake River, and along Assiniboine River as far as Musk-rat River, otherwise called Riviere des Champignons, and extending to the distance of six miles from Fort Douglas (the first colony fort) on every side, and likewise from Fort Daer (at Pembina), and also from the Great Forks, and in other parts extending in breadth to the distance of two English statute miles back from the banks of the said rivers, on each side, together with all the appurtenances whatsoever of the said tract of land, to have and to hold for ever the said tract of land, and appurtenances, to the use of the said Earl of Selkirk, and of the settlers being established thereon with the consent and permission of our Sovereign Lord the King, or of the said Earl of Selkirk. Provided always, and these presents are under the express condition, that the said Earl, his heirs, and successors, or their agents, shall annually pay to the Chiefs and Warriors of the Chippeway or Saulteaux Nation the present, or quit-rent, consisting of one hundred pounds weight of good merchantable tobacco, to be delivered on or before the tenth day of October at the Forks of Assiniboine River: and to the Chiefs and Warriors of the Knistineaux or Cree Nation a like present, or quit-rent, of one hundred pounds of tobacco, to be delivered to them on or before the said tenth day of October, at Portage de la Prairie, on the banks of Assiniboine River. Provided always that the traders hitherto established upon any part of the above-mentioned tract of land, shall not be molested in the possession of the lands which they have already cultivated and improved, till His Majesty's pleasure shall be known.

" In witness whereof, the Chiefs aforesaid have set their marks at the Forks of Red River, on the day aforesaid.

(Signed) " SELKIRK."

Signed in presence of Thomas Thomas; James Bird; F. Matthey, Captain; P. D. Orsonnens, Captain; Miles Macdonnell; J. Bste. Chr. De Lorimier; Louis Nolin, Interpreter; and the following chiefs, each of whom made his mark, being a rude outline of some animal.

Moche W. Keocab	Ouckidoat
(Le Sonent.)	(Premier, alias Grande Oreilles.)
Mechudewikonaie	
(La Robe Noire.)	Kayajiekebinoa
Pegowis	(L'homme Noir.)

In this treaty we find the Saulteaux mentioned first, as if they had the better claim to priority, and the Crees last, whereas the fact is, the Saulteaux have no claim at all to the lands of Red River, being aliens or intruders. The Crees and Assiniboines are, and have been since the memory of man, the rightful owners or inhabitants of this part of the country. The Saulteaux being a party to the treaty gave great umbrage to the Crees, who, in consequence, have repeatedly threatened to drive them back to their old haunts about Lake Superior: and even threaten till this day the colonists, that they will reclaim their lands again, unless the Saulteaux are struck off the list altogether. These menaces are often held out, to the no small annoyance and dread of the settlers, lest the threat be some day or other put in execution.

The short explanation of this intrusion is as follows: —During the troubles between the rival companies, which we have had occasion to notice so often in a former work, the north-west people had introduced some of the Saulteaux as trappers and hunters into this part of the country, and among those, there were at the time of the treaty one or two considered by the whites as great men, but never recognised as such among their own people; and these are the names that figure so prominently in the treaty as Saulteaux Chiefs. The earliest date that any Saulteaux found his way into this quarter, was about the year 1780; at present they are pretty numerous, and a more bloodthirsty, revengeful race, never raised a tomahawk, or drew a scalping-knife; but more of this hereafter.

The general aspect of the country is determined by the course of the river, which runs through the centre of the colony, from south to north, or rather it is settled on both banks. The west side throughout is one continued level plain, interrupted here and there with only a few shrubs or bushes all the way from Lake Winipeg to Pembina, without wood to yield shelter, or a tributary stream of any magnitude to irrigate the soil, except the Assiniboine, which enters at the forks; nothing to diversify the monotony of a bleak and open sea of plain. On the east the landscape is more varied, with hill and dale, and skirted at no great distance by what is called the pine hills, covered with timber, and running parallel to the river all the way. With the exception of this moderately elevated ridge, however, all the other parts are low, level, marshy, and wooded. The banks of the river are low on both sides, so that when the water rises to any height beyond the level of ordinary years, the waters find an easy access over the banks, flood the fields, and inundate the country.

The extensive plains we have described, possess dull and dreary sameness during winter, which, however, in summer, is changed to one of the finest views and most fascinating prospects in nature. In autumn, when every species of vegetation is dry and withered, alarming and destructive fires break out; the wad of a gun, or a spark from a tobacco-pipe, being sufficient to ignite the long grass and reeds which extend as far as eye can reach. On these occasions, self-preservation calls forth the frightened inhabitants *en masse*, to watch and guard, in anxious forebodings, their little all. These conflagrations, once kindled, march before the winds, it may be for weeks together, encircling at last the whole colony in an ocean of flame. The natives frequently relate that whole families have been overtaken by these irresistible fires while travelling through the plains, and burnt to death. Indeed, we have seen a fatal instance of the kind ourselves, even on the colonized lands, and within three miles of the settlement. In this instance, three whites and two Indians lost their lives, besides seventeen horses, and numbers of horned cattle, while many others had a very narrow escape. The only chance for the traveller, unless some lake or river is at hand, is to burn the grass around him, and occupy the centre of the little clearing thus formed; in which case he will have only the smoke and ashes to contend with. At times, however, the fire advances with such fearful rapidity, as to baffle any attempt of this kind; it has been known to overtake and destroy the fleetest horse.

No sooner has the devouring element of fire been

arrested, but the keen and piercing frosts of winter set in. From the unsheltered state of the country, the settlement is constantly exposed, on the north and west, to bleak and stormy winds, which, during the winter of seven months' duration, are accompanied with deep snows and intense cold. The thermometer in these seasons often ranges from 30° to 40° below zero; the writer has seen it at 45°, and it has been known to fall as low as 49°; yet the soil is rich, crops luxuriant, and the country healthy; catarrhs or obstinate coughs, occasioned by sudden transitions from heat to cold, or the contrary, in the spring and autumn, being the most frequent complaints. In the summer time the range of the thermometer is from 95° to 105° in the shade.

Formerly all this part of the country was overrun by the wild buffalo, even as late as 1810, and of course frequented by wolves, which are always found in the same neighbourhood. At the present time, long after the buffalo has disappeared from the environs of the settlement, the wolves are sufficiently numerous to be very annoying and destructive to cattle; particularly to hogs, calves, and sheep. The former are often torn out of their styes, and neither of the latter can show themselves with safety in the plains. Even grown-up cattle, and particularly horses, are frequently killed about the settlement. To check the evil, the wolves are trapped, run down with horses, hunted with guns, poison is applied, and premiums offered for their destruction; yet after all, they are still numerous during the spring and fall of the year. So long as the hunters frequent the plains, the evil will be incurable.

At every trip, the carts on their return are followed by a train of these unwelcome visitors.

We come now to inquire what his lordship's motives could have been for planting a colony in a place like Red River—so remote, full of obstacles, and forbidding both by sea and land; nor are we sure we shall arrive at the truth; but we shall show the reasons assigned at the time, and the speculative opinions that have been formed by different parties on the subject, and leave the reader to draw his own conclusions, and judge for himself.

1st. According to the North-West creed, his lordship planted the colony to ruin their trade. From the jealous and hostile feuds carried on in the country at the time, by the partisans of the two rival companies, the North-West and Hudson's Bay, it was alleged by the former, and with some degree of reason, that Lord Selkirk, who was a large shareholder in the latter, endeavoured to check the physical superiority of his opponents, and by means of the new colony secure to the Hudson's Bay Company, and to himself, not only the extensive and undivided trade of the country within their own territories, but a safe and convenient stepping-stone for monopolizing all the fur trade of the far west; which would have been a death-blow to their concern. The North-West, therefore, viewing his lordship's object in this light, disputed the validity of the Hudson's Bay Company's charter, and of the grants of land made to him, and consequently unfurled the standard of opposition against it; this hostility and enmity, on their part, was the cause of all the troubles and misfortunes the colonists had to contend with for many years afterwards, as we shall more clearly see hereafter.

2nd. Another strong reason for establishing Red River Colony has been stated; for with reference to these matters, we must regard Lord Selkirk and the Hudson's Bay Company as one, their interests being blended together. It is not, perhaps, generally known, that all dormant or retiring partners, and others leaving the service from time to time, carry off to other countries large sums of money, over which the Company could no longer have any control: with the view, therefore, of preventing this money from going out of the country, the Company, by means of their sub-monopolist, Lord Selkirk, founded the colony in question; that by means of it, all, or the greater part of such retiring partners and others, especially those having Indian families,—and they are many,—might be induced to settle there in preference to going home to their own countries, as being more congenial to their past habits of life. The Company well knew that a colony planted in the bosom of their own trade, must in the nature of things be more or less dependent on them for its supplies, and that by it a double advantage would be gained to the fur trade:—1st. All such sums of money as would otherwise be liable to be carried out of the country by retiring servants, would eventually fall back again into the Company's own hands. 2nd. All the surplus produce, such as flour, beef, pork, and butter, articles the Company require, would by means of the colony be obtained more conveniently, cheaper, and with less risk, than by the annual importation of such articles from England. 3rd. By supplying the Company, the settlers would have a ready market at their door, sufficient to satisfy all their wants. In this last point of view, if in no other, the advantages would undoubtedly be reciprocal between the Company and its colony.

3rd. The next statement, in our opinion, contains his lordship's real object, the pious and philanthropic desire of introducing civilization into this wilderness. Being a pious man himself, he felt for others. His lordship knew from long experience, that poverty and degradation were making long and rapid strides in Rupert's Land; that the wild animals of the chase had almost ceased to exist there, in sufficient numbers, at least, to feed and clothe the aboriginal inhabitants of the soil—not that such numbers had been extirpated by the natives themselves, but by the destroying hand of civilized man. It was now, in this point of view, drawing towards the eleventh hour, when it was high time for them, not only to cultivate the ground, whereby they might live, but prepare to cultivate the mind also, as the best test of their improving condition, spiritually as well as temporarily. To this end, the preparatory step with his lordship was a colony, as a nucleus or rallying point in the wilderness. The object, then, was a laudable and charitable one, strictly in accordance with the character of such a man as Lord Selkirk—a man of a great mind and a good heart— and also in accordance with the spirit of the Company's charter.

4th. For various reasons, therefore, we and many

others here are of opinion, that Lord Selkirk's object was the good of the natives, and theirs alone. What else could it have been? It was not territorial acquisition: that the Company had already. It was not the exclusive right of trade: that they had already. It was not to relieve a redundant population, for that relief was but small; nor could it have been for the bubble reputation. No: he had purer motives. The only prominent objection we have to Red River Colony in a local point of view is its proximity to the boundary line on the south, and his lordship was too clear-sighted not to have foreseen, that eventually it might fall into the hands of the Americans, and should it not, the only outlet for its resources must be south, and not north. Beyond what the Company might require, its market, in the nature of things, must be south also. Hence it is quite evident that his lordship's motives must have been what we have stated; namely, the civilizing and evangelizing of the natives: so that into whatever hands its government fell, he would have attained his end. For its value to Great Britain, if we except the interest of the Hudson's Bay Company, was, and ever must be, small indeed; nor could the Americans expect to benefit much by it, either in a political or commercial point of view. The fears of the North-Westers were fully realized, the anticipations of the Hudson's Bay Company fully borne out by the result, for the colony has become a nursery for its retired servants; but as to Lord Selkirk's view of benefiting the Indians, forty years' experience has proved it, as we shall hereafter be able to show, a complete failure.

CHAPTER II.

CONTENTS.—Emigrants to Red River—Perilous voyage—Reception by the employées of the North-West Company—Critical position—Contract—Trip to Pembina—Comparison—Half-breeds—Winter quarters—Wheat sown—Returns—Blackbirds—Pigeons—Pembina—Plot—Provisions—Plans defeated—Proclamation—Result—Churchill—Gun-locks—Cruelty—New emigrants—Join the North-West—Proposals—Emigrants abandon the North-West—Skirmishing—A man shot—Houses burnt—Emigrants in exile—Recalled—Last brigade arrive—The four conditions—Scotch minister—Conditions—Marriages—Baptisms—Mr. Sutherland.

IN the year 1812, several Scotch families, called the first brigade, emigrated to Hudson's Bay, under the patronage of the Earl of Selkirk, with a view to colonize the tract of country already described, lying contiguous to the American frontiers, but within the territories of the Hudson's Bay Company, called Red River. These emigrants were the first settlers of the only colony that had been attempted upon those inhospitable coasts. Their undertaking was a hard one; but inured to a rough life in the hills of Scotland, the hardy mountaineer is ever ready to embark in any adventure or enterprise, be it ever so perilous, that holds out the slightest prospect of bettering his condition.

The emigrants arrived in safety, after a journey across sea and land which afforded them a slight foretaste of the perilous life in which they had embarked; and but a few hours had passed over their heads in the land of their adoption, when an array of armed men, of grotesque mould, painted, disfigured, and dressed in the savage costume of the country, warned them that they were unwelcome visitors. These crested warriors, for the most part, were employés of the North-West Company, and as their peremptory mandate to depart was soon aggravated by the fear of perishing, through want of food, it was resolved to seek refuge at Pembina, seventy miles distant, whither a straggling party, whom they at first took for Indians, promised to conduct them. The settlement of this contract between parties ignorant of each other's language, furnished a scene as curious as it was interesting; the language employed on the one side being Gælic and broken English, on the other, an Indian jargon and mongrel French, with a mixture of signs and gestures, wry faces, and grim countenances. The bargain proved to be a hard one for the emigrants. The Indians agreed to carry their children and others not able to walk, but all the rest, both men and women, had to trudge on foot; while all their little superfluities were parted with by way of recompense to their guides. One man, for example, had to give his gun, an old family piece, that had been carried by his father at the battle of Culloden, which, under any other circumstances, no money would have purchased. One of the women also parted with her marriage ring, the sight of which on her finger was a temptation to the Indians, who are remarkably fond of trinkets. The journey to Pembina exhibited a strange perversion of things: the savage, in aristocratic independence, was completely equipped and mounted on a fine horse, while the child of civilization, degraded and humbled, was compelled to walk after him on foot. No sooner had the gipsy train got under way, than the lords of freedom scampered on ahead, and were soon out of sight with the children, leaving the bewildered mothers in a state of anxious foreboding, running and crying after them, for their babes. This facetious trick, as their guides doubtless thought it, was often played them; but without any other harm than a fright. In other respects the emigrants suffered greatly, especially from cold, wet, and walking in English shoes: their feet blistered and swelled, so that many of them were hardly able to move by the time they reached their destination.

All things considered, the Indians performed their contract faithfully, and with much indulgence to their followers, who acquired a better knowledge of their character as they proceeded. They were a mixed company of freemen, half-breeds, and some few Indians, and most of them had been attached, at the time, to the hostile party by whom the emigrants had been ordered to leave the colony. They were then acting under the influence of the North-West Company; but in going to Pembina, on the present occasion, they were free and acting for themselves. And here it is worthy of remark, that the insolence and overbearing tone of these men when under the eye of their masters, were not more conspicuous than their kind, affable, and friendly deportment towards the emigrants, when following the impulse of their own free-will. To the Scotch emigrants, who were completely in their power, they were everything they could wish; mild, generous, and trustworthy. From many circumstances, therefore—indeed, from their general conduct on the present and other occasions—the Scotch were convinced, that when not influenced or roused by bad counsel, or urged on to mischief by designing men, the natural disposition of the half-breeds is humble, benevolent, kind, and sociable.

At Pembina the people passed the winter in tents or huts according to Indian fashion, and lived on the products of the chase in common with the natives. This mode of life was not without its charms; it tended to foster kind and generous feelings between the two races, who parted with regret when the Scotch, in May 1813, returned to the colony to commence the labours of agriculture. They now enjoyed peace, but hunger pressed hard on them, and they were put to many shifts to sustain life. Fish, as sometimes happens, was very scarce that season, as were roots and berries: so that their only dependence was on a harsh and tasteless wild parsnep, which grows spontaneously in the plains, and a kind of herbage or plant, equally wild and tasteless, called by our people *fat-hen*, a species of nettle; these, sometimes raw, sometimes boiled, they devoured without salt. While such was their summer fare, the hoe was at work, and a small supply of seed-wheat, procured from Fort Alexander, an Indian trading post on Winipeg River, turned out exceedingly well. One of the settlers, from the sowing or rather planting of four quarts, reaped twelve and a half bushels; but it was with great difficulty they could save it from the fowls of the air. Every spring, we may observe, myriads of blackbirds and wild pigeons pass the colony in their migration to the north, and return again on their way to the south, during the time of harvest, and that in such clouds as to threaten the little patches of grain with total destruction, more particularly in years when there are no berries. On these occasions, bird-nets, guns, and scarecrows, are all in active operation, and also, men, women, and children going constantly about their little parterres, from morning till night, and yet all often proves ineffectual to repel the formidable enemy. Fortunately, however, this evil is diminishing every year.

The fears of the settlers had been dispelled, and their patience and perseverance supported by a cheering ray of hope, that the North-Westers would not disturb them any more. Under this impression, they began to take courage, and prepare for the arrival of their friends, for they expected all the other emigrants, or last brigade, out this fall; but in this hope they were disappointed. It was late in the season before they were made acquainted with the delay, and then, rather than consume the little grain they had secured, they resolved to try Pembina again, and save what seed they could for another year. Here, again, disappointment awaited them. Notwithstanding the extreme kindness shown by the French half-breeds to the Scotch settlers last winter, they now kept aloof, and regarded our people with a jealous eye. Ignorant and awkward as the settlers were in such pursuits, they had nevertheless to think and act for themselves, slaving all winter in deep snows to preserve life. Nay, a plot was discovered to murder two of the party who undertook to hunt, and so this resource was closed against them; provisions, at the same time, which they were compelled to purchase, and drag home with extreme labour, being very scarce, and consequently very dear. Eventually, the settlers returned to the colony once more in a state of great destitution; having had to barter away their clothing for food, many of them frost bitten, half naked, and so discouraged, that they had resolved never to return to Pembina again, under any circumstances.

Such was the situation of the colonists at the commencement of the disastrous year 1814, when a mistaken act of their own greatly aggravated the mischances to which they were liable. At the fall of the year, about the time when the colonists removed to Pembina, Mr. McDonell, formerly Captain of the Queen's Rangers, who had been appointed Governor of the District of Assiniboia, was also nominated by Lord Selkirk to superintend the colony, and to take charge of the settlers. Actuated by a sincere feeling for their interests, and desirous of guarding against want, this gentleman issued a proclamation, in which he forbade the appropriation of any provisions, whether of flesh, fish, grain, or vegetables, to any use but that of the colonists. As much stress has been laid on this document, both in England and Canada, we give it entire:—

" Whereas the Right Honourable Thomas Earl of Selkirk is anxious to provide for the families at present forming settlements on his lands at Red River, with those on the way to it, passing the winter at York and Churchill forts, in Hudson's Bay, as also those who are expected to arrive next autumn, renders it a necessary and indispensable part of my duty to provide for their support. In the yet uncultivated state of the country, the ordinary resources derived from the buffalo and other wild animals hunted within the territory, are not deemed more than adequate for the requisite supply. Whereas, it is hereby ordered, that no person trading furs or provisions within the territory for the Honourable Hudson's Bay Company, or the North-West Company, or any individual, or unconnected traders, or persons whatever, shall take any provisions, either of flesh, fish, grain, or vegetable, procured or raised within the said territory, by water or land carriage, for one twelvemonth from the date hereof; save and except what may be judged necessary for the trading parties at this present time within the territory, to carry them to their respective destinations; and who may, on due application to me, obtain a license for the same.

"The provisions procured and raised as above shall be taken for the use of the colony; and that no loss may accrue to the parties concerned, they will be paid for by British bills at the customary rates. And be it hereby further made known, that whosoever shall be detected in attempting to convey out, or shall aid and assist in carrying out, or attempting to carry out, any provisions prohibited as above, either by water or land, shall be taken into custody, and prosecuted as the laws in such cases direct, and the provisions so taken, as well as any goods and chattels, of what nature soever, which may be taken along with them, and also the craft, carriages, and cattle, instrumental in conveying away the same to any part but to the settlement on Red River, shall be forfeited.

"Given under my hand, at Fort Daer (Pembina) the 8th day of January, 1814.

(Signed) "MILES MC DONELL, *Governor*.

"By order of the Governor.

(Signed) "JOHN SPENCER, *Secretary*."

The publication of this document excited the bitterest feelings on the part of the North-West traders against the Scotch settlers, and to it, as a first cause, may be attributed the ruin of the great North-West Company. It even shook for a time the stability of the Hudson's Bay Company itself.* Each party was on the alert to

* In explanation of this it is proper to remark, that the proclamation was partly issued by way of retaliation for the treatment which the emigrants met with at Churchill. The preceding autumn, some of those bound for Red River had been landed at that place in a state of very bad health. The scarlet fever had been raging with fatal effect on board the ship, several had died at sea, and not a few after landing. What followed, we may relate in the very words of our informant, who was one of the sufferers:—

"On our reaching Fort Churchill," said he, "we were so emaciated and reduced from the fatal effects of the plague, which proved the death of so many of us before our arrival, that we had scarcely strength to stand, and some were dying almost daily. For the sake of those who were recovering, however, some of our people tried to hunt, to get a fresh partridge or something of the kind; but this being observed by Mr. Auld, who was then master at the post, he decoyed our guns from us, under pretence commence the work of pillage. Provisions were taken and retaken, and a sort of civil war commenced, in which many of the colonists sought safety by joining the ranks of their enemies belonging to the North-West Company, whom they deemed the stronger party. The country was patrolled by armed bands; and partly under the influence of terror, partly seduced by the flattering promises they received, the colonists were easily induced to abandon the settlement again by their new friends, in order to seek a home in Canada. In these perplexities they passed the remainder of the year, and though their eyes were gradually opened to the foolish part they had acted, it was absolutely necessary to keep up appearances through the ensuing winter. Having thus, with as much duplicity as their seducers, whiled away that dreary season in safety, they contrived to return to the colony again, without an open rupture, in the beginning of 1815.

The colonists now resumed their agricultural labours, and for some time they cherished the hope of future tranquillity, and a quiet summer. Soon, however, the North-Westers re-appeared amongst them, and aggravated at what they called the treachery of the settlers, they burnt down the colonial establishment; in the encounters which led to this result several

of putting them in better order; and the moment he got them into his possession, so charitable and unfeeling was he, that he ordered all the locks to be taken off, and then, with a sarcastic leer, returned them back to us lockless; adding, 'You shall eat nothing but what can be charged against the colony;' for he could not well charge a pheasant or a rabbit of our own killing."

persons were wounded, Mr. Warren killed, and Governor Mc Donell made prisoner. Anarchy and confusion now reigned triumphant again. Retaliation and mutual recrimination followed, till the whole body of settlers were driven from the colony, and their houses burnt to ashes. The mandate that ordered their immediate departure was brief and imperative: it commanded "All settlers to retire immediately from the River, and no appearance of a colony to remain." This act of banishment was signed by the four chiefs of the half-breeds—"Cuthbert Grant, Bostonais Pangman, William Shaw, and Bonhomme Montour, June 25th, 1815."

Some of them were so far misled by the false representation of a Highlander, of the name of Cameron, who was in charge of the North-West Company's trading post at Red River, as to desert to that station, and afterwards to take passage in the North-West Company's canoes to Canada, under a promise to each family of being put, on arrival there, in possession of 200 acres of land, and of being supplied with twelve months provisions gratuitously. Such of them as could not be allured by those arts and promises, nor intimidated by the reports which were industriously circulated of threatened hostilities from the Indians, quitted the settlement and proceeded in their boats to the north end of Lake Winipeg, where they stationed themselves at Jack River, a trading port belonging to the Hudson's Bay Company, and where they remained for some time.

The Hudson's Bay Company interposed at this crisis, and, under their protection, the settlers were brought back from the place of their exile, a distance of 300 miles. Their case at this time was truly deplorable. To recite all the trying circumstances, hair-breadth escapes, and troubles of this hostile period, might well appal the stoutest heart. To add one evil to another, the last and main party of the emigrants arrived in October, so that their predecessors, instead of preparing a settled habitation for them, only seemed to have performed a longer and more dangerous pilgrimage. The whole party, however, were now brought together, and we may conveniently conclude this chapter by reciting some of the principal conditions by which they had been tempted to seek a home in the wilderness.

First. They were to enjoy the services of a minister of religion, who was to be of their own persuasion.

Second. Each settler was to receive 100 acres of land, at five shillings per acre, payable in produce. It will be seen, however, as we proceed, that in consequence of the first settlers having suffered so many hardships and severe trials, Lord Selkirk remitted the five shillings altogether, and granted them their lands free of all expenses.

Third. They were to have a market in the colony for all their produce.

Fourth. They were to enjoy all the privileges of British subjects.

On each of these several points, we may have occasional remarks to offer as we proceed. With reference to the first stipulation, his Lordship engaged a Mr. Sage, son of the Rev. Alexander Sage, then minister in the parish of Killdonnan, north of Scotland, to accompany the emigrants, an annual salary of 50*l.* having, besides other advantages, been guaranteed to him for a certain number of years. The emigrants, it must be remembered, were all of the Presbyterian communion, and Gaelic their mother tongue, of which Mr. Sage was not fully master, and on this account delayed his departure to the colony for the term of a year, as agreed upon between the adventurers themselves and Lord Selkirk. In the mean time, one of the emigrants, named James Sutherland, a pious and worthy man, who held the rank of elder in the Presbyterian church, was appointed to marry and baptize, from which functions he was never released by the arrival of the ordained minister, in consequence of the difficulties in which the colony was placed.

Mr. Sutherland continued his ministerial labours with unremitted assiduity, till the day he was forced to leave the settlement, as we shall hereafter see, and was a father, as well as a spiritual guide to the colonists. Nor was it the settlers alone that held Mr. Sutherland in high estimation. On his arrival at York Factory, the right hand of fellowship was held out to him by the Governor-in-Chief of the country, as well as by the Governor of the colony. These men, with their followers, gladly heard him expound the Scriptures, and this of itself—considering that he was as unlearned and simple as the apostles of old—showed him to be a man of superior endowments. Of all men, clergymen or others, that ever entered this country, none stood higher in the estimation of the settlers, both for sterling piety and Christian conduct, than Mr. Sutherland. By his arrival with the Scotch emigrants in Hudson's Bay, the gospel was planted in Red River. It was the sunrise of Christianity in this benighted country.

CHAPTER III.

Contents.—The Scotch emigrants—Gloomy prospects—Privations—Hostile feuds—North-West intrigues—Manœuvring—Hardships of the emigrants—Starving adventures—Bright prospects—Sudden change—Prospects blighted—Hopeless condition—Hudson's Bay Company—Civil war—Bloodshed—Trying scenes—Colony destroyed by the North-West—Flotilla—Emigrants in exile—Parting admonition—Mr. Grant's heroic conduct—Bold front—Pillaging parties—Incidents—The first shot—Fatal result—Short triumph—Scenes changed—Events—Reprisals—North-West downfall—The de Meuron regiment.

On the arrival of the last body of Scotch emigrants, gloomy and portentous was the prospect before them. The smoky ruins, the ashes scarcely yet cold, were all that remained to mark the progress of their unfortunate predecessors, and from the appearance of things around them, they had but little reason to expect a better fate. The hostile feuds and lawless proceedings of the rival companies had convulsed the whole Indian country from one side of the continent to the other, but above all in Red River; and the arrival of more emigrants only added fresh fuel to the flame thus kindled. The North-Westers, accustomed to carry all before them, and impatient of restraint, raised a hue and cry against the colony and its promoters. The authority and influence that body had over the Indians, as well as over its own servants, gave them every advantage: for they had so trained and influenced both in the school of mischief, rapine, and bloodshed, that no outrage which the unscrupulous ministers of a lawless despotism could inflict, was too extravagant to dread. Posts were pillaged, robberies committed, and valuable lives sacrificed without remorse.

The partisans of the North-West Company used every art to involve the colonists in ruin, by fomenting dissension amongst them, and terrifying them with stories of Indian cruelty. Having thus heightened the terrors of their forlorn condition, it was easy to deceive them under the mask of friendship, and lure them away from the settlement, with the prospect of bettering their condition. For this purpose they availed themselves of the most extraordinary means, even to the use of the Gaelic language; collecting men from all quarters, and conveying them to the Red River Colony, with the sole object of winning the confidence of the settlers, by the sound of their native tongue. This national charm the Highlanders could not withstand. All else they might have resisted: the influence of the Gaelic alone conquered them! Tossed about on an ocean of troubles as the Scotch then were, any change, however faint the hope it afforded, was hailed with satisfaction. The scarcity of provisions at this time, also weakened the hands and the hearts of the colonists, and turned the balance in favour of their opponents.

In place therefore of sitting down quietly and cultivating the soil on their arrival, they were soon dispersed in search of a precarious subsistence, as the first brigade had been when alone. Some went to Pembina as usual; others to the prairies bordering on the waters of the Missouri: while some again bent their reluctant steps to the distant lakes. In all these quarters they sustained themselves in a wretched manner by means of hunting and fishing among the savages of the country, and often in their wanderings they endured every species of privation which misfortune could inflict or patience endure. In this divided and deplorable condition, they all weathered the storm of adversity during winter, and as soon as the snows were melted, found their whole party reassembled at the colony. Every man, woman, and child now toiled from morning till night, to get a little seed in the ground; though, as events proved, they were only sowing for the fowls of the air to reap.

The North-West party, consisting chiefly of half-breeds, had been augmented to upwards of 300 strong, all mounted on horseback, and armed with various weapons, such as guns, spears, and tomahawks, or bows and arrows. They were painted like demons, their heads plumed; and they rushed to the strife with a yell which gave fatal warning to the industrious but half starved colonists of the danger that threatened them. At the critical period to which we have brought our narrative, these daring marauders had penetrated through the very heart of the Hudson's Bay Company's territories, as far as the shores of the Atlantic, which wash Hudson's Bay, and in their grasping propensities set at defiance every legal restraint and moral obligation. They pillaged their opponents or destroyed their establishments, as suited their views at the time, and not unfrequently kept armed parties marauding from post to post. It was one of these bands, numbering about sixty-five persons, that advanced against the infant colony on the fatal 19th of June, when a rencontre took place in which twenty-one lives were lost; the flower of the Red River colonists strewing the field like the slain on the morning of Chevy Chase. The particulars of this conflict are briefly as follows:—

The approach of the enemy was announced by the women and children of the settlers, who were seen running from place to place in alarm, seeking protection and crying out that the settlers were made prisoners. On this, it appears, Governor Semple,* who was Governor-in-Chief of the Hudson's Bay Company's territories, with several other gentlemen and attendants, walked out to meet the strangers, now discerned to be a party of half-breeds and Indians, all mounted and armed. Their hostile purpose being manifest, the Governor and his party halted, and were seen in a group as if consulting together, while the Indians and half-breeds divided themselves into two bodies, and instantly commenced firing from the shelter afforded by a few willows; first a shot or two, and then a merciless volley. The party of Governor Semple, consisting of twenty-eight persons, was completely surrounded, and of that number no less than twenty-one

* Mr. Semple was eminently qualified for the situation of Governor-in-Chief, being of a mild, steady, just, and honorable character, highly accomplished, and universally beloved.

were killed: namely, Mr. Semple, the Governor; Captain Rogers, mineralogist; Mr. White, the surgeon; Mr. Mc Lean, the principal settler; Lieut. Holt, of the Swedish navy; Mr. Wilkinson, the Governor's secretary, and fifteen men; besides which, Mr. J. P. Bourke, the storekeeper, of whom we shall have to speak hereafter, was wounded, but saved himself by flight. The unhallowed triumph of the murderers was complete. Only one of their number fell in the battle as they called it, and one other, we believe, was wounded, while the colonists who survived the massacre, were ordered once more to leave their homes without farther warning or preparation, on pain of being hunted down and shot like wild beasts, if they should ever appear there again. It is doubtful, indeed, whether one innocent head would have been spared; and that any escaped was due to the generosity and heroism of Mr. Grant, the chief of the hostile party, who rushed before his own people, and at the imminent peril of his life kept them at bay, and saved the remnant of the settlers from extirpation. Their houses, however, were ransacked, their goods pillaged, and the whole colony driven into exile. They again found a refuge at Jack River, now called Norway House, situated at the northern extremity of Lake Winipeg.

As might be expected, the advocates of either party in this catastrophe strenuously denied having fired the first shot, and perhaps it will ever remain in some minds a matter of uncertainty. In the country where the murder took place, there never has been a shadow of doubt, but rather a full and clear knowledge of the fact, that the North-West party did unquestionably fire the first shot, and almost all the shots that were fired; and this opinion is borne out by the testimony of Michael Heyden, the first witness on the part of the Crown, who states distinctly (page 76 of the trials) " That the half-breeds fired the first gun, and by it Mr. Holt was killed, and immediately after another was fired, almost directly after, and Governor Semple fell. This was distinctly seen by some at a distance." Again he says, " There was no firing before that." Chief Justice Powell in his charge to the jury, states (page 263) " That Heyden deposes that a Mr. Holt was killed by the first shot, and by the second Mr. Semple fell" and adds (page 267) " These two shots were the first that were fired." The opinion of the writer is most decided that the guilt of this bloodshed rests on the North-West party, and the following list of casualties may suggest to some how dearly it was visited upon them in the course of a few years. It exhibits the violent or sudden death of no less than twenty-six out of the sixty-five who composed the party.

1. The first person in our melancholy catalogue was a man named Dechamp, who, in crossing the river near to his own house at Pembina, suddenly dropped down dead on the ice; the dog he had along with him, shared the same fate, at the same instant, without any previous illness or warning of his end.

2. Francois Dechamp, son of the above Dechamp, was stabbed to death by his own comrade, his wife shot, and his children burnt to death, all at the same time, near Fort Union, Missouri River.

3. La Grosse Tête, brother to Francois Dechamp, was shot by an Indian between the pickets of a trading post, on the Missouri. These three individuals belonged to the same family.

4. Coutonahais, suddenly dropped down dead while dancing with a party of his comrades, at the Grand Forks, beyond Pembina.

5. Battosh, shot dead by an unknown hand, in Red River colony.

6. Lavigne, drowned in crossing Red River, near Nettly Creek.

7. Fraser, run through the body at Paris by a French officer, and killed.

8. Baptiste Morrallé, in a drunken squabble on the Missouri, thrown into the fire and burnt to death, by his drunken companions.

9. La Certe, died drunk on the high road on the Mississippi river.

10. Joseph Truttier, wounded by a gun and disabled for life in Red River.

11. J. Baptiste Latour, died a miserable death by infection.

12. Duplicis was killed by a wooden fork running through his body in the act of jumping from a hay stack at Carlton, on the Saskatchewane River.

13. J. Baptiste Parisien, shot dead by an unknown hand, while in the act of running buffalo, in the Pembina plains.

14. Toussaint Voudré, lost an arm by accident, and disabled for life in Red River.

15. Francois Gardupie, the brave, shot and scalped

in a sudden rencontre with the Sioux Indians, on the banks of the Missouri, in sight of his comrades.

16. Bourassin, killed on the Saskatchewane; particulars not known.

17. Louison Vallé, put to death by a party of Sioux Indians in the Pembina plains, and in sight of his companions.

18. Ignace McKay, found dead on the public road, White Horse Plains, Red River.

19. Michel Martin, died a miserable death at Montreal, Lower Canada.

20. Thomas McKay, died of intemperance, Columbia River.

21. Ka-tee-tea-goose, an Indian, said to be the person who fired the first shot. This savage, on returning to his family after the massacre, was met by a war party of the Grosse Ventre, or Big Belly tribe, near Brandon House, who after shooting and scalping him, cut his body to pieces, carried off his fingers and toes, and strewed the rest of his remains to the wild beasts, to mark the place where he fell.

22. Cha-ne-cas-tan, another Indian, drowned in a small pool of water scarcely two feet deep, near the Little Missouri River, Brandon House.

23. Oké-ma-tan, an Indian, froze to death in the Pembina plains.

24. Ne-de-goose-ojeb wan, gored to death by a buffalo bull, while in the act of hunting.

25. Pe-me-can-toss, shot and thrown into a hole by his own people.

26. Wa-ge-tan-né, an Indian, his wife and two chil-

dren, killed by lightning on a hunting excursion. Of this unfortunate number, two were Canadians, two English, two Scotch, and fourteen French half breeds; four Saulteaux, and two Cree Indians.

We must in fairness remark that Governor Semple was ill advised in going out with an armed party at all on this occasion, unless he had been able to command a sufficient force to awe his opponents, and protect the settlers. His better plan was negotiation, or stratagem, and he should have gone out alone, or at most taken one or two with him, unarmed. By a little flattery, and good management, the half-breeds and Indians might have been diverted from their mischievous projects, since they are by no means an unreasonable people when an appeal is made to the better feelings of their nature. On the contrary, Mr. Semple and his party being all armed, must have suggested an idea of their hostile intention, and was no doubt the leading cause of the catastrophe that followed.

No sooner was the news of the fatal affray at Red River spread abroad, than the Earl of Selkirk, with an armed force, seized on Fort William, the grand depôt and head quarters of the North-West Company. To account for this summary act of retaliation, we ought to explain that his Lordship was, at this very time, on his way to the colony; his visit being induced by the hostile attitude which the partisans of the North-West Company had assumed. At Montreal, en route, he had engaged about 100 disbanded soldiers of the de Meuron regiment, so called, it is said, after a former Colonel of that name. They were chiefly foreigners, a medley of almost all nations—Germans, French, Italians, Swiss, and others; and, with few exceptions, were a rough and lawless set of blackguards. These men had entered into written agreements with Lord Selkirk, and were to be paid at a certain rate per month, for navigating the boats or canoes to Red River. They were, further, to have lands assigned to them in the settlement, if they chose to remain; and otherwise, to be conveyed, at his Lordship's expense, either to Montreal or Europe. As the event proved, they preferred the former, and were rewarded with small grants of land, situate on a tributary stream, known as Riviere la Seine, entering on the west side of Red River, opposite to Point Douglas, which afterwards, in honour of them, took the name of German Creek. The de Meurons were bad farmers, as all old soldiers generally are, and withal very bad subjects; quarrelsome, slothful, famous bottle companions, and ready for any enterprise, however lawless and tyrannical. Under any circumstances, a levy of this character could be no great acquisition to a new settlement; and at such a juncture as we have described should never have been permitted by the Canadian Government.

These mutual aggressions, however, led to the appointment of a commission of inquiry, consisting of Colonel Coltman and Major Fletcher, who were sent from Canada, armed with full authority to commit the guilty of either side for trial.

CHAPTER IV.

CONTENTS:—Emigrants recalled from banishment—The colony re-established—The free grant—Church and school lots—Sites described—Deeds promised—Scotch and their minister—Lord Selkirk's departure—Seed—Returns—Pembina—Winter adventures—Cold—Severe trials—Camp hospitalities—The Scotch—Mr. Sutherland—Pleasing prospects soon blighted—Grasshoppers—French emigrants—Pembina again—Grasshoppers—Total ruin—The Scotch turn hunters—Last thought the best—Prairie de Chien adventure—Wheat—Communication from Red River to St. Peter's—Party arrive—Hope revived.

ON arriving at Red River, after the exploit we have mentioned, the first step of Lord Selkirk, as a matter of course, was to restore order, as far as possible. The people were all brought back from Norway House, where they had been banished by the half-breeds the preceding summer, and reinstated on their lands. This being accomplished, his Lordship assembled the emigrants at a public meeting, on the west bank of Red River, some two miles below Fort Garry, and in consideration of the hardships, losses, and misfortunes, they had from time to time suffered, he made them several concessions. To some, who had lost their all, he made a grant of land, comprising twenty-four ten chain lots, in free soccage, the holders merely conforming

ITS RISE, PROGRESS, AND PRESENT STATE.   43

to the conditions laid down in the deed of feoffment granted by the Hudson's Bay Company to the Earl. These lots were the only free lands granted to emigrants in the colony. They had lately been surveyed and marked off by Mr. Fidler, on the left bank of the river, and two of them (No. 3 and No. 4) were designated by his Lordship as the sites respectively of a church and a school for the colony. "Here," said his Lordship—pointing to the lot No. 4, on which the Company stood—"here, you shall build your church, and that lot," said he again—pointing to the next, being No. 3—"is for a school." Between the church and school lots there runs a small rivulet, called the Parsonage Creek.*

* The lots alluded to, as the document informs us, and which we shall transcribe for future reference, "are laid out along a line run by Mr. Fidler in the direction North 12° East, or thereby; lot No. 1 commencing at the distance of one mile, or thereby, from Fort Douglas;" which fort was, at the time, situate on the south side or head of the point; " and lot No. 24 ending at Frog Plain. Each lot has a front of 10 chains, or 220 yards, a little more or less, along the said main line, except lot No. 12, which has only five chains. The division lines between the lots are at right angles to the main line, and are marked off towards the river by lines of stakes. Each lot is to extend to the distance of 90 chains, or 1,980 yards back from the river, so as to contain 90 English statute acres, besides which, each lot is to have a separate piece of wood-land, containing 10 statute acres, to be laid off on the east side of the river, at any place which the Earl of Selkirk or his agent shall consider as most suitable for the purpose. These 10 acres are to be preserved by the occupier as wood-land, and not to be used for any other purpose. Till this wood-land be measured and marked off, the occupiers of the aforesaid lots will

My reasons for being so very particular in describing these minor points will be shown hereafter, as the subject to which they relate develops itself.

At this meeting, an urgent application was made for the promised minister, and again solemnly responded to by his Lordship. At the close of its proceedings, he named the parish "Killdonan," a name recognised in the colony at this day, and derived from the parish in Sutherland whence the greater part of the settlers had emigrated. The settlers then busied themselves in erecting a temporary building, to serve the double purpose of prayer-meeting and school-house, until the minister should arrive, and a regular church be built.

The struggles of the opposition began now gradually to cease, and the colonists set to work with heart and

be allowed to take wood for building or fire-wood from any place most at hand on the opposite side of the river. In case of the lands on the opposite side of the river being laid out in lots for settlement, the settlers in possession of the aforesaid 24 lots, shall have the first offer of purchasing the lots opposite to their own, and they shall not be disposed of at a cheaper rate to any stranger.

" In consideration of the hardships which the settlers have suffered, in consequence of the lawless conduct of the North-West Company, Lord Selkirk intends to grant the aforesaid 24 lots gratuitously, to those of the settlers who had made improvements on their lands, before they were driven away from them last year; provided always, that as soon as they have the means, they shall pay the debts which they owe to the Earl of Selkirk, or to the Hudson's Bay Company, for goods or provisions supplied to them, or for other expenses incurred on their account.

        (Signed)   "SELKIRK."
"*Fort Douglas, Red River Settlement,*
  August, 1817."

hand; the more so as the lands were their own, free, and for ever; still, no man yet ventured to call Red River his home. The experienced eye of his Lordship saw things at a glance, and so correct and unerring was his judgment, that nothing he planned at this early date could in after years be altered to advantage. Public roads, by-roads, bridges, mill seats, and other important points were settled; and then he ordered a general survey of the colony to be made, which in due time was completed. Having thus restored order, infused confidence in the people, and given a certain aim to their activity, Lord Selkirk took his final leave of the colony. Accompanied by a guide and two or three attendants, he crossed the wide and hostile plains between Red River and St. Peter's, from whence his journey lay through the United States to Canada.

The industry of the settlers was amply rewarded by the results at harvest time; forty-fold was a common return, and in one case, for a bushel of barley sown, fifty-six were reaped; and for a bushel of seed potatoes, 145 bushels. These facts were related to the writer by John McIntyre, an intelligent settler. Still so little seed was sown this year, owing to the lateness of the season when the people returned from Norway House, and the difficulty of procuring it, that they were again threatened with famine, unless they consumed their all, and ruined their prospects for the next year. To avoid this danger, they resolved, as winter approached, to resort to Pembina again, and draw their supplies from the chase.

This alternative proved a heavier trial than it had been heretofore, as they were less fortunate than on the former occasion. From Pembina they had to extend their journey far into the open plains; dragging themselves and their despairing families, for days and weeks together, through the deep snow, their object being to reach a camp of hunters, freemen, half-breeds, and Indians, where they hoped to live through the winter. On such journeys, the natives of the country are accustomed to travel on snow-shoes, besides which they have horses and dogs to assist them along, and their constitutions are hardened to the climate. Far otherwise was the case of our poor Scotch emigrants. Accustomed in their own country to the shelter of a house, to warm clothing, a mild climate, domestic comforts, and domestic habits, they and their starving families were now exposed, day and night, to the fierce storms of a Hudson's Bay winter, the cold at the time ranging from 35° to 40° below zero! Their sufferings were almost beyond human endurance, and even at this distant day, we shudder at the painful recollection; for many a time, when the last mouthful was consumed, and their children crying for more, they knew not how or where the next morsel was to come from. A rabbit, a crow, a snow-bird, or even a piece of parchment would be found perhaps, and thus from time to time they kept soul and body together, with less hope than the Israelites in the desert. In this condition, they contrived to reach the camp, when the last morsel of their food was gone, and they were almost at their last gasp, on the eve of Christmas Day.

The people of the camp flocked out to meet the wretched travellers, and all were emulous to administer to their wants. They were received as friends, even by the Indians, who furnished them with shoes, and pressed them to eat. After all their trials, and hair-breadth escapes, the wanderers indeed found a home; but they soon discovered that among so many mouths, provisions were not over abundant, the snows were deep, the buffaloes far off, and most of the hunters' horses had died; so that every second or third day, parties on snow-shoes had to start in pursuit of game. The Scotch, tired and worn out, had no hunters among them, neither had they anything to buy provisions with. They were poor as the Indians themselves; for every thing they could spare, every article of clothing, not on their backs, had already been bartered away to sustain life; they had in consequence, while others were hunting, to become the drudges of the camp, slaves of the slave, servants of the savages. Thus, however, they were preserved during the winter.

On the return of spring, and breaking up of the winter camp, the Scotch, as usual, found their way back to the colony, to undergo new trials.

The year 1818, which had now commenced, is an eventful one in the history of the unfortunate settlers. Food was scarce, their hitherto precarious dependence on fish, herbs, and roots, became hopeless, for these all failed; and their misfortunes were crowned by an act of lawless violence on the part of the North-West, who, forcibly carried off Mr. Sutherland to Canada. Still they laboured earnestly to establish themselves, and make this wilderness wear the aspect of a home, for they had resolved on abandoning Pembina for ever. Every step now was a progressive one: agricultural labour advanced, the crop looked healthy and vigorous, and promised a rich harvest. In short, hope once more revived, and everything began to put on a thriving and prosperous appearance: when, lo! in the midst of all these pleasing anticipations, just as the corn was in ear, and the barley almost ripe, a cloud of grasshoppers from the west darkened the air, and fell like a heavy shower of snow on the devoted colony. This stern visitation happened in the last week of July, and late one afternoon. Next morning, when the people arose, it was not to gladness, but to sorrow; all their hopes were in a moment blighted! Crops, gardens, and every green herb in the settlement had perished, with the exception of a few ears of the barley, half ripe, gleaned in the women's aprons. This sudden and unexpected disaster was more than they could bear. The unfortunate emigrants, looking up towards heaven, wept.

While the colonists were thus bemoaning their hard fate and hopeless condition, several French families, headed by two Catholic priests, arrived from Canada, and took up their abode as settlers in the colony. One of those priests has ever since remained in the settlement, and is now bishop, and head of the Catholic Church in Red River. The arrival of these people only increased the evil of the day, by adding so many more mouths to feed; besides the grief it caused the settlers to see them in the full enjoyment of their religion, while they themselves, who had borne the burden and heat of the day, were wholly destitute of spiritual consolation. Their material difficulties, however, called for fresh exertion, and nothing now remained but to place their hopes in Pembina again, notwithstanding the remembrance of their sufferings the year before. It would be tedious to follow them through the catalogue of vicissitudes they had to endure, as this would only be to repeat the story of their moral degradation, under men whose habits and condition in life they had been taught to despise; not to mention the endless misery of providing for themselves and their families among savages.

Early in the spring of 1819, the Scotch settlers returned from Pembina, leaving the Canadian families there, and commenced sowing; all the seed they possessed being the few scattered heads which the devouring grasshoppers had cut down and left, and which had been gleaned in the women's aprons. Much pains was taken, and great efforts made in this almost hopeless attempt, which was again defeated, not by a new flight of the pestilence of last year, but, still worse, by the countless swarms produced in the ground itself, where their larva had been deposited. As early as the latter end of June, the fields were overrun by this sickening and destructive plague; nay, they were produced in masses, two, three, and in some places, near water, four inches deep. The water was poisoned with them. Along the river they were to be found in heaps, like sea-weed, and might be shovelled with a spade. It is impossible to describe, adequately, the desolation thus caused. Every vegetable substance was either eaten up or stripped to the bare stalk; the leaves of the bushes, and bark of the trees, shared the same fate; and the grain vanished as fast as it appeared above ground, leaving no hope either of "seed to the sower, or bread to the eater." Even fires, if kindled out of doors, were immediately extinguished by them, and the decomposition of their bodies when dead, was still more offensive than their presence when alive.

The colony lost all its attractions as the abode of civilized man. The Scotch, with all their patience and perseverance, had now become impatient and discouraged under so many disappointments, and turning their backs on Red River, they sought a life, comparatively free from care, at Pembina again. They now became good hunters; they could kill buffalo; walk on snow-shoes; had trains of dogs trimmed with ribbons, bells and feathers, in the true Indian style; and in other respects, were making rapid strides towards a savage life.

The independence of this mode of life was charming while it lasted, but the colonists knew well how precarious it was; and on reflection, they could not fail to perceive the importance of making another effort to establish themselves, and secure their future comforts on lands which they could call their own, and where themselves and their children might find a home.

Taking this view of things, it was resolved to despatch several men to the "Prairie du Chien," a town on the Mississippi River, several hundred miles distant from the colony, for the purpose of bringing in a supply of seed-wheat, an article not to be found nearer home. The men reached their destination on snow-shoes, at the end of three months; purchased 250 bushels at 10s. per bushel; and, making their way back in flat-bottomed boats, arrived in the colony in June, 1820. The wheat thus introduced was sown, but, being late in the season, it did not ripen well; yet it came to sufficient perfection for seed; so that, from that day to this, in spite of the grasshoppers and other evils, Red River has not been without seed for grain. The cost of this expedition to Lord Selkirk was 1,040*l*. sterling. Exclusive of the main object, that of getting the wheat, it was satisfactory to know, that the state of the navigation between the two countries, during high water, was not only practicable, but offered every facility for future communication; as the same boats that ascended the Mississippi, descended the Red River, with only one single interruption, and all returned to the colony in safety.

CHAPTER V.

CONTENTS.—Scotch minister—Fruitless attempts—Conjectures—
The reproof—Strange things happen—The disappointment—
Mr. West—Missionary efforts—The disputed point—Coalition
—Happy results—Indian quarrels—Grasshoppers take flight—
Swiss emigrants — Watchmakers — Pastry-cooks—Handsome
young women—Hunger—Pembina—Beggars no choosers—The
Swiss discouraged—Comparison—High notions in low life—
Starvation—The silver watch—Gold eyes—The snuff-box—
The cat-fish—Hard bargain—Summing up—Perseverance of
the settlers—Bourke's sufferings—Remarks.

IN the midst of all the disappointments, losses and
misfortunes which the Scotch settlers have had to
contend with since they came to Red River, none has
been so severely felt, nor so deeply regretted, as the
want of their spiritual pastor. That source of consolation temporal or spiritual, which alone sweetens life
here, and cherishes hope in the hereafter, being denied
them, has embittered every other calamity. It is a
subject that has mixed itself up with every action of
their lives in Red River; it has been the daily, hourly
theme of their regret; at every meeting the subject of
deepest interest. To the present hour, application has
been made unceasingly to those in power at the colony

that they would see them put in possession of their rights; but all to no purpose.

Mr. Sage not having come out at the period we have reached in our history, and no communication being made to the colony either by Lord Selkirk or his agent, Mr. Pritchard, application was made time after time to Alexander Mc Donell, who had been recently appointed Governor of the colony, but equally without result. That gentleman, himself a Papist, did not take much interest in Presbyterian politics; but told the Scotch, by way of consolation, that they might live as he himself did, without a church at all. A petition was then sent home to the Rev. John Mc Donald, minister of the parish of Urquhart, Ross-shire, who was well known to them all, stating their destitute condition, and earnestly praying him, in the event of Mr. Sage's not coming, to do something for them in the way of getting a minister: but the application, it is supposed, never reached its destination, for no answer was ever returned to it.

In October of this year (1821) the disappointment of the settlers was aggravated, and their surprise increased, by the arrival of a minister, not of their own persuasion, as had been promised, but a missionary of the Church of England. As nearly all the settlers at this time were members of the Presbyterian Church, Mr. West's appearance was rather the signal of discord than of consolation amongst them, and to this hour it has produced nothing but religious strife and animosity. Attempts at compromise all failed, as Mr. West could not be prevailed upon to discontinue the English ritual, and the Scotch, for their part, could see no spirituality in such forms; besides which, the English language was to them a foreign tongue, and they longed to hear their native Gaelic. Under these circumstances, Mr. West, rather than sit idle, extended his missionary services to the Company's posts, and even visited the Indians; the Scotch meanwhile being assured that he would soon leave the colony, and be replaced by a minister of their own. This promise has not so far been fulfilled. Whether rightly or wrongly, we may here observe, the blame of this whole transaction has been cast on Mr. Pritchard, who, it is said, took advantage of Lord Selkirk's death, an event which happened this year, to disobey his injunctions, and send an agent of his own religion into the colony.

We are here reminded that the Scotch settlers, as we stated in its proper place, had provided a temporary meeting-house to serve them until a minister came out and a church was built—a work finally accomplished by the Scotch settlers, though Mr. West has appeared willing to take the merit of it to himself. Speaking of the subject in his journal, he says (page 27), " I cheerfully gave my hand and my heart to perfect the work. I expected a willing co-operation from the Scotch settlers; but was disappointed in my sanguine hopes of their cheerful and persevering assistance, through their prejudices against the English Liturgy, and the simple rites of our communion." Now, what is the truth? Mr. West might, as he says, have "given cheerfully his heart to perfect the work," for that cost him nothing; but certainly he did not give his hand. The building was erected by the efforts of the Scotch settlers. Their money and their labour began it, and finished it, with some assistance from the colonial authorities.

We dismiss this controversial point to notice a subject of greater importance, which had for its object the peace and tranquillity of the country at large; namely, the coalition between the two great rival companies, which took place in March 1821. This highly desirable event brought about in its consequences the brightest era the colony ever saw, and from which the settlers may date, although the steps were slow, their growing prosperity. It was the death-blow to party strife and rivalry in trade, not in Red River only, but as far and wide as the country extended; and we need hardly say that its advantages extended to the poor Indians, whose degraded passions had been constantly inflamed with liquor and other excesses, that at once shortened their days, and rendered their lives but little better than a feverish and hideous dream. Perfect tranquillity, indeed, is not to be expected in any Indian country, much less in a remote and isolated wilderness like Red River, where the savage races are perpetually at war with each other; but certainly, the first step towards peace must, in any case, be a good example on the part of the whites.

To show by example what savage elements the colonists have to deal with, and what danger they were always in of being implicated in the quarrels of the Indians:—In the midst of the present tranquillity, a trivial circumstance had well nigh set the colony in a flame. A small party of the Sioux Indians had come to the settlement on a friendly visit, and to smoke the pipe of peace with their enemies, the Saulteaux; after which, as is customary on such occasions, both parties mixed together and strolled about to see the settlers. The Sioux were seated quietly enjoying the treat of a few ears of Indian corn, when one of the free-men who had a quarrel with a Saulteaux, and feared to attack the whites, vented his wrath on the innocent Sioux; shot two of them, wounded a third, and scampered off. The Sioux, few as they were, would have given battle; but as the Saulteaux were not to be found, they left the colony. On their way home, however, happening to fall in with a family of Saulteaux on the border of the settlement, they killed and scalped them, for the two friends they had lost. The Sioux Indians are reckoned the most powerful and brave nation west of the Rocky Mountains, and less given to acts of treachery and cruelty than most other tribes, unless forced to it. The brave are always generous, the cowardly alone are cruel. The Saulteaux are noted, beyond most other savages in these parts, for treachery and cruelty, and gave a proof of it on the present occasion.

To return to the affairs of the colonists. The summer of 1821 proved as fruitful as could be expected, and the grasshoppers, which some have dignified with the name of "locusts," now visited the colony for the last time. At first, it was feared the crop, as usual, would be utterly destroyed by them, but vegetation of every kind was abundant, and from some unexplained cause, the whole swarm disappeared early in the season; never, as it proved, to return to the colony again. Still, the quantity of grain could not be over large, and it was deemed prudent for some of the settlers, at least, to resort to Pembina again, that as much as possible might be saved for another year. The resolution had hardly been formed, when it was rendered imperative by the arrival of fresh emigrants, who now came from the Cantons of Switzerland. These families were all of the poorer class, and mostly mechanics; among them were watch and clock makers, pastrycooks and musicians. The delicacy of their constitutions, being inured to a life within doors, rendered them little fit for the hardy employments of the husbandman, and especially in a new settlement, with the disadvantage of a cold climate, such as Hudson's Bay. As to character, they must have proved an acquisition to any community, being a quiet, orderly, and moral people; remarkable withal for the number of handsome young people, both lads and lasses among them. The contrast between these honest adventurers and the de Meurons was complete in all respects, except in their equal unfitness and ignorance of farming operations. Yet this did not prevent their association for some time, as fellow Protestants, and as they arrived, they spread themselves along the German Creek. This neighbourly arrangement did not last long. The character of the de Meurons, and the scarcity of food, darkened the prospect around them; their new homes were destitute of every charm that could win their hearts, and all who were able to undertake the journey to Pembina were but too glad to join the Scotch settlers; trusting that any change must be for the better.

Unhappily, this year, the buffaloes were scarce, and hard to be got, so the poor Swiss, who had neither horses nor dogs, were more dependent upon others than themselves, and not unfrequently upon the Indians, who, to their praise be it said, were always most ready to alleviate misery when in their power. The Swiss received such assistance with but an ill grace. Like the Scotch, they were proud and high-minded, even in distress, and would often run the risk of starving themselves and their families, rather than submit to the degradation of asking relief from a people they so cordially detested as the Indians. Nor was this surprising under the circumstances. After a pursuit of hours, sometimes days it might be, the Indian huntsman has succeeded in killing a buffalo, and having brought the meat home, as a matter of course, he takes his own share first; next he supplies the wants of his relations, and the remainder he dispenses in charity. On such occasions, therefore, the whites were generally served last; the Scotch, the Swiss, the Canadians, or the de Meurons, as it might happen; sometimes much, sometimes little falling to their share, and it might even be none at all. The humiliation of being put off to the last, and then of begging something to eat from an Indian, was what the Swiss could not brook, simply because his benefactor was an Indian.

After a winter thus passed, early in the spring of 1822, the Scotch, Swiss, and de Meurons hastened back to rejoin their friends in the colony, and again suffered all but absolute starvation during seed-time. We need not repeat our oft-told tale of distress, but some particular instances may be interesting. One of the Swiss gave a silver watch, value five guineas, for eight gallons of wheat, not to sow, but to eat. Another, for six small gold-eyes, a fish but little bigger than a sprat, gave five shillings sterling. And one poor man, having nothing else, gave the very snuff out of his box for the head of a cat-fish! The sympathizing fishmonger, on seeing the box emptied, expressed a strong desire to possess it, and when he found that it was highly valued as the gift of a friend, he offered a whole cat-fish for it. The man was in great distress, but still loath to part with his keepsake; he told the fellow the box was a costly one. "It was never purchased," said he, "for less than a guinea."

"That may be very true," said the other; "but I would not see my family starve for the satisfaction of carrying an empty box in my pocket, were it worth twenty guineas."

After much bickering and tardy hesitation, a bargain was struck for the cat-fish, and four gold-eyes along with it! In ordinary times the price of a cat-fish is threepence; sixpence is a very high rate; a shilling exorbitant. The cat-fish is something larger than the Scotch haddock.

We have now travelled through a series of ten years in succession; and a course of greater trials, harder struggles, or more frequent disappointments, than fell to the lot of this little colony, in that eventful period, is perhaps not to be found in the history of any new settlement. From the first arrival of the emigrants, up to this time, every succeeding season had left them, after the most exhaustive efforts, just as it found them, struggling against evils which perpetually returned upon them. The first five years of their pilgrimage and sufferings, were embittered by the enmity of the North-West Company, the effects of which, as we have seen, touched, not their property only, but life itself; the fields, till now untrodden by civilized men, being crimsoned with their blood. The succeeding five years brought afflictions upon them from a cause not of man; as if Providence had appointed this scourge by which they were visited, for the express trial of their faith.

The de Meurons, the Canadians, and the Swiss, we may remark, bore but a small share of these trials, and never made any decided stand or effort to advance the colony; the Scotch, alone, had to bear the whole heat and burden of the day. The brunt of all the difficulties, from beginning to end, fell on them. To them the colony, such as it is, owes its existence; and the meed of praise is justly due to their perseverance.

In the midst of these trying scenes, many cases of individual suffering may be supposed to have occurred, the character of which may be illustrated by the following:—Among the first adventurers, after the Scotch settlers, that were sent out to the colony by Lord Selkirk, were some Irish lads, and a young gentleman from Sligo, engaged as clerk. Mr. John P. Bourke, the person alluded to, proved himself, during the heat of opposition, a trustworthy and faithful servant, industrious, active, and as fearless and determined as most of his countrymen generally are. A man so devoted to the cause of the colony, in those days, had, as might be expected, many implacable enemies among the partisans of the North-West Company; who, as they could neither gain him over to their cause, nor

ITS RISE, PROGRESS, AND PRESENT STATE. 61

intimidate him by their threats, laid many snares and temptations in his way, which Bourke, as wily and cautious as themselves, was at all times proof against.

In 1815, he was among the number of those who took refuge at Norway House, having been previously wounded at the colony, in a skirmish, in which one of his companions was killed at his side. Here, his attachment to the colony was subjected to a trial of another kind. The most liberal offers were made, and promises held out which would have drawn almost any other man from the settlement into the Company's service; but to no purpose. In the midst of adversity, he stood faithful to his master's cause, and the interest of the colony. At length, tired of a life of inactivity, he left his asylum, and after suffering no common hardships, he reached the colony in great distress.

In 1816, poor Bourke was still more unfortunate, being again wounded in the general massacre. On this occasion, also, one of his associates was shot dead at his side, while they were in the effort to save themselves by flight, and Bourke himself was indebted to the fleetness of his horse for safety. He then lay concealed two days and nights, weltering in his blood, without food or water the thermometer at the time standing at 92°. At length he was discovered, relieved, and ultimately saved by an Indian, who not only dressed his wound, but in other respects administered to his necessities.

He was, however, soon discovered, and conveyed a prisoner to Fort Alexander, one of the North-West Company's posts, where he was kept in close confinement. The humane privilege of dressing his wound, and the attendance of a doctor, though there was one on the spot, were alike denied him in this place; from whence he was despatched by the canoes to Fort William, a distance of many hundred miles. During this miserable journey, he was made to lie on a hard wooden box, exposed to a burning sun, and the inclemency of all weathers; after which, on his arrival at Fort William, he was robbed of his trunk, clothing, and watch, and shut up for twenty-two days in a common sewer, water-closet, or necessary, with an allowance of food just sufficient to preserve life. This sickening imprisonment he at last exchanged for a three days' residence in gaol, at Montreal, where, nothing being proved against him, he was liberated.

From Montreal, Bourke made his way back as far as the Sault St. Mary's, and after twenty-three days' walking, reached Fort William in great destitution; but had no sooner arrived at the place of his former sufferings, than he was arrested again, and once more sent to Canada. He was now tried at the Court of King's Bench, and being acquitted, was turned adrift on the hard and unfeeling world without means or friends. Three miserable years passed over his head, before he was able to rejoin his disconsolate family in Red River.

The sufferings poor Bourke endured are felt by him to this day. He is now labouring under the sickness and infirmity they entailed; never since having enjoyed perfect health. Had Lord Selkirk lived, such endurance, such devotedness to his cause, had not passed unrewarded.

CHAPTER VI.

CONTENTS.—Colony store—Lord Selkirk—Governor McDonell—Officials, their doings—Things that ought not to be—Drunken squabbles—The hour-glass—A new method of keeping accounts—The grains of wheat—The paper-box in the corner—The hubbub—The mêlée—Partiality—Credit system—Colony work—Trickery—Confusion—Mr. Halkett—Grievances redressed—The guinea—The lost keys—The discovery—The papers—The revenge—General remarks—Buffalo Wool Company—High expectations—Gloomy result—Intemperance—Mismanagement—The yard of cloth—Bankers rewarded—Remarks.

How the colonists were preserved from actual starvation and supplied with mere necessaries during this protracted period, is a question that must naturally have presented itself to the reader's mind. This much was provided by the care of Lord Selkirk, who sent out a supply of goods and clothing after the departure of the first colonists, as well as a general assortment of the implements of husbandry, arms and ammunition for defence, and a supply of oatmeal to fall back upon in the last extremity. The store in which these articles were kept was erected the first year of the settlement, and regularly supplied from time to time afterwards by shipments from England, and during the dispersion of the settlers towards Pembina, the supplies, when practicable, followed them to that quarter. The direction of this important matter was vested in the Governor of the colony. In fact, his sole duty, for the first few years of his command, was to dole out these stores to the settlers, and all the talent required for such a service was not greater than any petty clerk with a salary of 20*l.* a year might be expected to possess. Yet how was this duty fulfilled by the officials appointed by Lord Selkirk?

Governor Alexander McDonell, whom the people in derision nicknamed the "grasshopper governor," because he proved as great a destroyer within doors as the grasshoppers in the fields, prided himself in affecting the style of an Indian viceroy. The officials he kept about him resembled the court of an eastern nabob, with its warriors, serfs, and varlets, and the names they bore were hardly less pompous; for here were secretaries, assistant-secretaries, accountants, orderlies, grooms, cooks, and butlers. This array of attendants about the little man was supposed to lend a sort of dignity to his position; but his court, like many another where show and folly have usurped the place of wisdom and usefulness, was little more than one prolonged scene of debauchery. From the time the puncheons of rum reached the colony in the fall, till they were all drunk dry, nothing was to be seen or heard about Fort Douglas but balling, dancing, rioting, and drunkenness, in the barbarous spirit of those disorderly times. The method of keeping the reckoning on these occasions deserves to be noticed, were it only for its novelty. In place of having recourse to the tedious process of pen and ink, the heel of a bottle was filled with wheat and set on the cask. This contrivance was, in technical phraseology, called the hour-glass, and for every flagon drawn off a grain of the wheat was taken out of the hour-glass, and put aside till the bouse was over; the grains were then counted, and the amount of expenditure ascertained. From time to time the great man at the head of the table would display his moderation by calling out to his butler, "Bob, how stands the hour-glass?" "High, your honour! high!" was the general reply; as much as to say, they had drunk but little yet. Like the Chinese at Lamtschu, or a party of Indian chiefs smoking the pipe of peace, the challenges to empty glasses went round and round so long as a man could keep his seat; and often the revel ended in a general melée, which led to the suspension of half-a-dozen officials and the postponement of business, till another bouse had made them all friends again. Unhappily, sober or drunk, the business they managed was as fraudulent as it was complicated.

1. Any settler in want of a supply from the store first reported to the Governor, who gave him a note, specifying all the articles. This permit he took to the head clerk, whose duty it was to see the goods delivered and charged; by this functionary he was sent to an assistant, and by the assistant again to his deputy, who was really the storekeeper. Even this irregular and complicated system of routine was not incompatible with eventual correctness; but it often happened that the settler was sent away without the articles he

wanted, the storekeeper giving himself little trouble to search for them. In such cases, the Governor would listen to no appeal; the permit as written by him was sent to the office, and every article in it, whether delivered or not, was charged to the settler's account.

2. It often happened, when the settler had passed through the greater part of this ordeal, and got to the storekeeper with his note, that he would be desired to leave the memorandum and call again, not once, but several times in succession. Thus day after day would be lost, and not unfrequently the note itself; in which case the articles were refused. They were all the same, however, charged to the settler's account. Complaints multiplied, and the system was changed; but, as generally happens in such cases, from bad to worse. Some were charged one price, and some another, for the same article. One would get everything he asked, another could obtain nothing, according as he stood high or low in favour with the men in power.

3. To save time and expedite business after the arrival of supplies, the store was opened on certain days only, and all the settlers invited to attend. As each was anxious to be first, the door was crowded by hundreds of people at a time. The strongest pushed their way to the front, and when one posse was admitted, the door was barricaded to keep the others out, who made a rush at every opening of the door; while favourites were quietly admitted at the windows. Many passed days and nights without tasting food, and weeks expired before they could procure other articles from the store. Nor was better order kept in the office.

ITS RISE, PROGRESS, AND PRESENT STATE. 67

Notes, contracts, and papers of every kind, in place of being kept in regular files, or booked, were thrown promiscuously into an open box, which lay at the end of the counter, till called for, to be entered by the chief clerk. Very few, indeed, were entered; and when called for by parties interested, none could ever be found but such as were favourable to the officials themselves.

4. It is hardly necessary to observe, that all the goods, clothing, implements—in short, everything whatever advanced to the settlers—was supplied on credit, to be paid for eventually from the produce of the land. This is the debt Lord Selkirk alludes to in his note of August, 1817, as already noticed. Equally certain it is that, under such a system, the prices charged were exorbitant. Is it any wonder if the settlers, after so long a period of difficulties and disappointments, should be deeply involved in debt? Many of them, however, during this unfortunate period, had been at various times employed in what was then called "colony work," such as house-building, road-making, or tripping; and at such jobs had earned considerable sums of money, which were to have been placed to their credits as so much reduction of their debts; but such was the iniquity of those entrusted with power in the colony, that the money in some instances was never credited, and the colonist sought redress in vain. False entries, erroneous statements, and over-charges, were afterwards proved in nearly every instance; but most of the officials had then left the country, and their correction was next to impossible: neither contracts nor

vouchers could be found. To crown all, the settlers at the end of each year had been compelled to sign their accounts as correct; for until they did so their credit was stopped by the offended Governor, and necessity soon forced them to submit. On debts thus contracted a further charge of five per cent. was levied as interest.

Such was the condition of affairs when Mr. Halkett, one of Lord Selkirk's executors, and a staunch friend to the colony, arrived from England; to whom, therefore, the Scotch settlers formally applied for redress. The Viceroy and his satellites were now called to account; all the debts were reduced one-fifth, and the five per cent. added yearly was struck off as a fraudulent and illegal transaction. Lord Chief Justice Ellenborough has laid down the rule of law with regard to interest clearly and concisely thus: " Interest ought to be allowed only in cases where there is contract for the payment of moneys on a certain day, or where there has been an express promise to pay interest; or where, from the course of dealing between the parties, it may be inferred that this was their intention; or where it can be proved that the money has been used, and interest been actually made. A note of hand or promissory note does, therefore, legally carry interest. Tradesmen's bills, where there are no special agreements, do not." It was then strictly ordered that all goods from England, on reaching York Factory, should bear $33\frac{1}{3}$ per cent. on prime cost, and on arriving in the colony 25 more; on the York cost; making $66\frac{2}{3}$ on the London invoice, and no more; and that this rate was to be the standard of price for the colony in future.

There was still another system of fraud practised. On passing through a dark and rather secluded passage within the colony fort, Mr. Halkett observed several private doors locked, and as he could get no satisfactory account of what these depositories contained, he ordered them to be opened. He was told that the keys were either lost or mislaid, yet they were immediately produced when he ordered the doors to be burst open, and the tabooed depositories were discovered to be filled with stores of all kinds! The iniquity of the system that had been carried on was now placed beyond question, and with this discovery the last year of Governor McDonell's stewardship was brought to a close. That worthy, however, took ample revenge on the Scotch settlers, by destroying or carrying off all the papers, whether public or private, that had been entrusted to him. Among the documents thus lost to the colonists for ever were all the papers containing promises made to them, at different times, by Lord Selkirk, in consideration of their hardships, and other public documents of value.

The fortunes of the colony were sensibly affected in this year by a new project set on foot by the magnates of the fur trade, who had from time to time visited the settlement and watched its progress with some degree of interest. The plan contemplated by these ambitious and restless men was a joint stock concern, under the highsounding title of the " Buffalo Wool Company." The scheme consisted of one hundred shares, of 20*l.* each, with provisions for remodelling and extending it at any future period; its chief manager being Mr. Pritchard, a gentleman of considerable experience, whom we have already noticed. His calculations appear to have been all based on the supposition that wool and hides, the staple articles required, could be had for the mere trouble of picking them up. The express objects of the company were as follow:—

1. To provide a substitute for wool; as it was supposed, from the numbers and destructive habits of the wolves, that sheep could neither be raised nor preserved in Red River, at least to any extent.

2. The substitute contemplated was the wool of the wild buffalo, which was to be collected in the plains, and manufactured both for the use of the colonists and for export.

3. To establish a tannery for manufacturing the buffalo hides for domestic purposes.

It was the chairman's belief, to quote his own words, that " To accomplish these important ends, neither much capital nor much skill was required; " but others thought very differently of the project, and were assured that much would depend on economy and proper management. Nevertheless, the capital, amounting to 2,000*l*., was no sooner placed in the bank than operations were commenced with as much confidence as if the mines of Potosi had been at their door. All the plain-hunters were set in motion; the men were encouraged to exert every nerve to procure hides, and the women to gather wool. A new impulse was thus given to industry, but it was attended with two evils—evils which might have easily been foreseen. First, the wool and the hides were not to be got, as stated, for the picking up; and, secondly, all who had previously applied themselves to the cultivation of the soil, threw aside the hoe and spade to join the plain-rangers. The hope of realizing gold from articles hitherto perfectly useless, diverted the elements of civilization into the channel of barbarism, and substituted an uncertain resource for the solid reliance of agriculture. The hides, likewise, rose in price proportionate to the demand, and soon cost 6s. each to the company; wool, 1s. 6d. per pound. Still warning was not taken. Orders were sent to England for machinery, implements, dyes, and skilled workmen; a superintendent, a clerk, a storekeeper, and many others, were engaged at high salaries; and as nothing could be done in those palmy days without the bottle and the glass, spirits were imported by the hogshead.

An establishment was formed befitting the dignity of the Buffalo Wool Company. All Red River at work. High wages gave a high tone to the undertaking. A second immigration of operatives consisted of curriers, skinners, sorters, wool-dressers, teasers, and bark-manufacturers, of all grades, ages, and sexes. Boys and girls advanced from 2s. 6d. to 7s. each per day; men had at first 7s. 6d., but they kept ascending the scale till they reached 15s. per day. Such were the prospects, the encouragement, the miscalculation, the extravagance! Light come, light go! Money was spent as if the goose that laid the golden eggs was to live for ever. Meanwhile, provisions became dear, and at length scarce; for while labour obtained these high rates at the manufactory, no one would willingly take the hoe or the spade at 2s. per day.

Such was the state of things in full operation when curiosity led a few disinterested persons, the writer among others, to take a peep at this fool's paradise. Alas! what scenes of disorder! what waste, what excess and folly! Half the people were off duty, officials as well as others, wallowing in intemperance. One man lying drunk here, another there; the bottle and glass set up at every booth, and all comers invited to drink free of cost. The hides were allowed to rot, the wool spoiled; the tannery proved a complete failure. In short, besides expending their 2,000*l.* capital, the company found themselves indebted in the amount of 4,500*l.* to the Hudson's Bay Company, who had been their bankers. This heavy loss hung over their heads for several years, till the honourable Company drew the pen through it, and relieved the bankrupt Buffalo Company from the terrors of a lawsuit. A few samples of cloth had indeed been made and sent home; but that which cost 2*l.* 10*s.* per yard in Red River, would only fetch 4*s.* 6*d.* in England!

CHAPTER VII.

CONTENTS.—Supply of domestic cattle—Change of system—The lucky hit—Profitable speculation—Reciprocal advantage—Mr. West's return—Mr. Halkett's reply to the Scotch settlers—The disappointment — Conjectures — Remarks — Pembina quarter abandoned—People return—Governor Bulger—Hay field farm —Mr. Laidlow—The dead loss—Spirit of the times—Causes of failures—Farming progress—Returns—Canadian voyageurs—The people reassemble—Census—Novelty—Mongrel squatters —Harmony—Scene changed—People divided.

NOTWITHSTANDING the mismanagement and failure of the Buffalo Wool Company, that enterprise was eventually of great advantage to the colony, as it caused the circulation of money, and put many of the settlers in possession of a little capital at the right moment. A drove of some 300 head of domestic cattle had been sent to the colony on speculation, and arriving unexpectedly at this juncture, were eagerly purchased at prices which amply repaid the enterprising Americans by whom they were introduced. Good milch cows sold as high as 30*l.* sterling each; and oxen trained to work fetched 18*l.* a head. These, it may be interesting to remark, were the first cattle ever brought to the colony, with the exception of an English bull and two cows got from the North-West Company. The whole herd was a large-boned and fine breed of cattle; but were not many years in Red River before they deteriorated in size, owing to two causes,— the want of care, and the cold climate.

In 1823, Mr. West left the colony for England, and we then cherished the fond hope that our own minister would have been sent out, as we had been given to understand; but in place of that, we were mortified to see another missionary of Mr. West's creed arrive to take his place, namely the Rev. D. T. Jones. And we might here very naturally ask the question, what must have been the representations made by Mr. West to the members of the Church Missionary Society at home, which could have induced that body to send out, at so great an expense, another of its missionaries to Red River, a place in which he himself had not a dozen hearers of his own communion. It could not have been for the colony that this missionary was sent, nor could it have been for the Indians, for neither Mr. Jones nor any of his successors ever once visited them.

Indeed, with the exception of Mr. West himself, who saw a few on his rambles about the Company's posts, not a missionary of his creed ever came here that travelled a foot out of the settlement to see Indians. On the whole, little as Mr. West did, he was the only Protestant missionary who ever showed the least degree of perseverance beyond the colony; and had he dealt more sparingly in scalps and romance, meddled less with other denominations of Christians, and studied the Indian character a little better, we should not have altogether disliked him nor found fault with his intellectual powers as a missionary. We shall take up this part of our subject by and by; meantime we turn to the settlers.

We have recorded in its proper place the arrival of

several Canadian families in the colony, who were induced by the then distracted state of the country to take up their abode at Pembina. Here they were joined by half-breeds, hunters, and others, with the addition of whose numbers they formed a snug little settlement; so that a Catholic church was built and houses erected. Pembina, however, was on the frontier, and as it was then doubtful where the international line would pass, those at the head of affairs thought it advisable to withdraw the people from that quarter, and place them in a more central locality, where they would be better situated both for instruction and protection. Other arguments were not wanting in favour of the selection of Red River for this purpose. The lands at Pembina were too low and wet for a permanent establishment, and at the period we have reached, there were grounds for believing that a rupture with the Sioux might occur. On the other hand, everything in the mother colony had assumed a more favourable and more tranquil aspect. The implacable enemy of peace and order in the colony, we mean the North-West Company, was no more. The grasshoppers had disappeared from their fields; and cattle having been introduced, the hopes of the husbandman were revived, and it was expected that the colony would, in the nature of things, take root. Here, accordingly, the little settlement at Pembina, after five years' occupation, found it convenient to transfer themselves. The first to suggest the change was Mr. Halkett, whose proposals were warmly seconded by the new and patriotic Governor, Captain Bulger, who succeeded Alexander McDonell, in June 1822.

Governor Bulger was a staunch friend of peace and

order, and certainly had the interest of the colony at heart. He was a just and upright man, strict and impartial. From the misrule of the times, he met with strong opposition; but being a man of judgment and decision, the colony for the first time began to exhibit the character of system and regularity under his rule. During his time the general survey of the colony was completed. He was succeeded at the end of a year only by Mr. Robert Pelly, a cousin of Sir John Henry Pelly, Baronet, who was at that period Governor of the Hudson's Bay Company in London.*

* Mr. Robert Pelly, who had a slight dash of pomp and vanity in his composition, was at the same time a quiet and easy sort of person, and by no means well qualified to reconcile the conflicting interests in the colony, or to govern the heterogeneous mass of which its population was at this time composed, as the following example of his judicial wisdom will sufficiently testify:—In the spring of 1824, the Saulteaux formed a party of some 300 or 400 men, with the view of making an inroad upon the neighbouring country of their hereditary enemies, the Sioux; but they had not proceeded far when it was found necessary to hold a council of war, at which it was decided to abandon the enterprise. The party, therefore, prudently determined on returning home, with the exception of about 20 *braves*, who were determined to do something to retrieve the character of the Saulteaux as warriors. This small band, after prowling about the borders of the enemy's country, found neither man, woman, nor child upon whom they could wreak their vengeance. In this emergency, one of their band, determined not to return without a scalp, murdered a poor old woman of his own tribe, whom he found unprotected within the limits of the colony, and, taking her scalp, passed it off as a trophy of his prowess in the Sioux country. This savage deed was soon noised abroad, and the public voice was loud for bringing the murderer to punishment. At length, therefore, he was brought before the Governor, who was attended on the occasion by

One part of Lord Selkirk's original plan was to establish an experimental farm and dairy, which, it was hoped, would supply the people with seed, and in times of scarcity with bread. The "Hay Field Farm," as it was called, was entrusted to the management of a Scotch farmer, named Laidlow, a person of considerable agricultural experience, who had come to the colony for the purpose; but in this, as in every other attempt to benefit the colony in those early days, mismanagement, disappointment, and ruin, were the only result. A farm on a large scale was got in train, with men and maid-servants not a few, most of whom were sober, industrious persons of good character, and had a fair knowledge of farming operations. Barns, yards, parks, and houses of every description, were provided; and yet all the time there was not an ox to plough, nor a cow to milk in the settlement. To crown the folly and extravagance of the undertaking, a mansion befitting a peer was built at an expense of 600*l*., which, at the moment of completion, was accidentally burnt to ashes in a drunken frolic. After several years' labour, waste, and extravagance, every

some of his officials, so as to form a little court. Having listened with attention to the charge, this sapient gentleman, judging it less troublesome to overlook the crime than to punish the murderer, transferred the case to a higher and a more impartial tribunal than his own in these words:—" Tell him," said he to the interpreter, " that he has manifested a disposition subversive of all order, and that if he should not be punished in this world, he is sure to be punished in the next." The murderer was accordingly discharged, and felt pleased to incur the risk of future punishment in order to avoid the present; while, at the same time, he expressed the most profound contempt for the Governor's sense of justice and for his decision.

vestige of property on the farm had disappeared, the experiment having cost Lord Selkirk 2,000*l*.

In contrast with the failure of the model farm we may here notice the success which followed the introduction of cattle last summer, as mentioned at the beginning of this chapter. The plough was now tried with considerable success; sixty-eight returns from wheat, after the hoe, and forty-four from the plough, were the average reward of the husbandman. The first really fair crop of grain was thus reaped in Red River by the Scotch settlers, after a protracted struggle of twelve years.

The fusion of the Pembina settlers with the colonists of Red River, was productive of a singular result. That event threw a number of French Canadians and others out of voyaging employment, who now came with their Indian families to the colony, in preference to going to their own countries. All the scattered and wandering parties connected with the emigrants were by this circumstance at length assembled together; here, therefore, were the Scotch, the de Meurons, the simple Switzers, and the Canadians, besides a number of retired servants, making in all about 1,500 souls. There was still an outside class called freemen, of different countries, who clung more or less to their former habits, and for a long time seemed unable to decide between the charms of a savage and a civilized life. During the arduous struggle of the preceding years, these people had stood aloof, and allowed the helpless emigrants to fight their own battles; but as soon as they had, by dint of perseverance, effected a permanent settlement, they began one by one to yield themselves to its attractions. Thus the already miscellaneous population of the colony was, we can hardly say reinforced, by a band of wanderers, who had long since lost all relish for habits of industry, and the pursuits of civilized life, whose countenances were a sufficient proof of their degradation, and who, but for a slight difference of tint in the colour of the skin, were marked by no characteristics to prove that they had once been white men.

On approaching the settlement, these new comers squat themselves down, not to cultivate the soil, or betake themselves to habits of industry among their countrymen; but with a shy countenance of mistrust, peculiar to Indians, they camp in the woods for the purpose of hunting, or, for the sake of fishing, locate themselves on the banks of the river, like the aborigines of the country. They have as little regard for the principles of religion as for the usages of civilized society; and men with hoary heads may be seen occupying the hours of the Sabbath in the brushwood, making arrows for their children, it may be, or contriving some new adornment for their own persons. They are generally great talkers, have long yarns to tell, and are not over scrupulous in their narrations, which are made up of an almost unintelligible jargon of the English, French and Indian languages. While the old men thus saunter about in idleness, the young are not slow to follow the example thus set before them. The boys with bow and arrow, the girls with basket and berries, are alike permitted to grow up in ignorance and thoughtless levity—a perfect model of savage life and manners, taught them by their wandering and degenerate parents. Such habits, believe it who will, shed a baneful influence over European children, who mix among them. So degenerate is our nature, and so powerful the force of example, that the amalgamation deteriorates us, without improving them. Curiosity soon leads a civilized boy to handle the bow, shoot an arrow, and stick a feather in his cap; but it is a far more difficult task, almost a hopeless one, to accustom the children of the wilderness to the use of the hoe, the spade, or the plough; even after they have been made to taste of the fruits arising from industry. Civilized habits are altogether out of the question with people habituated to Indian habits. In these respects, there is hardly a line of demarcation to be traced between the pure savage and the freeman whose mode of life we have depicted. In justice we ought to add that our remarks chiefly apply to the Canadian class, or those who are illiterate; for it is matter of general remark, among people in this country, that the educated, either of high or of low life, more frequently improve themselves in the trade, than lose what they had once acquired—unless, as sometimes happens, they abandon society, and associate with the Indians.

We have now seen all the different classes of which this infant colony was composed brought together. The better to advance each other's interest, as well as for mutual support, all sects and creeds associated together indiscriminately, and were united like members of the same family, in peace, charity, and good fellowship. This state of things lasted till the Churchmen began to feel uneasy, and the Catholics grew jealous; so that projects were set on foot to separate the tares from the wheat. Whatever reason might be urged for this division in a religious point of view, it was, politically considered, an ill-judged step; yet the measure was carried, and the separation took place, inflicting a wound which has never been healed to this day. The Scotch, as a matter of course, remained as they were, on their own lands in the centre of the colony; the French of all grades were located in one parish, up the main river; and the half-breeds, under Mr. Grant their chief, were settled some twenty miles up the Assiniboine, at a place called "White Horse Plains;" the Forks being the common centre of the three grand divisions. Each of these sections had its religious instructor: the French and half-breeds, their priests; but the Rev. Mr. Jones was the only officiating clergyman among the Europeans; although he 'belonged to the English, and they to the Scotch church. It was rather anomalous to see, in this section of the colony, an English clergyman without a congregation of his own creed, and a Scotch congregation without a minister; yet such was the state of things in the settlement at this time.

From these original causes, party spirit and political strife has been gaining ground ever since. The Canadians became jealous of the Scotch, the half-breeds of both; and their separate interests as agriculturists, voyageurs, or hunters, had little tendency to unite them. At length, indeed, the Canadians and half-breeds came to a good understanding with each other; leaving then but two parties, the Scotch and the French. Between these, although there is, and always has been, a fair show of mutual good feeling, anything like cordiality in a common sentiment seemed impossible; and they remain, till this day, politically divided.

CHAPTER VIII.

CONTENTS.—Second importation of cattle—Enlivening scenes—Encouraging progress—The unscrupulous visitors—Feathered heads—Fishing and hunting occupations—The ways and doings of Baptiste L'Esprit—Summer adventures—Winter trip to the plains—The industrious rib—People calling themselves Christians—Assiniboine trip—New scenes—Pipe habits—Tobacco and tea—Flammond and his family—The happy couple—The people's mode of life—Tea-drinking in Red River—Tea-drinking in Koondoz—The Uzbeks—The delicious compound—The mice.

IN 1825, another arrival of cattle from the United States gladdened the settlers' hearts, and gave fresh impetus to their exertions; but, unfortunately for the Yankee drovers, there had been no Buffalo Wool Company to lessen by its extravagant operations the value of money. The present supply sold for less than a third of the former prices. Good milch cows were now purchased for 6*l*. each, and the largest trained oxen were got for 20*l*. the pair; some of the latter, indeed, as low as 14*l*. The speculation cleared itself, but the profits made could hardly be regarded as a fair return for the hazard of the undertaking.

These were the last cattle sent from the United

States, and already the first drove had multiplied so fast as to afford hope that the colony would soon be independent in that respect. No country can produce finer heifers, of one or two years old, than Red River; but after that age they grow but little, and the cows in particular are seldom large, which is attributed to their breeding too young. They have their first calf almost invariably before they are two years old, and frequently the second before they are three. But if they diminished in size, they increased fast in numbers. How cheering it was to behold the numerous small bands of domestic cattle that enlivened the plains so lately swarming with the wild buffalo, only those can say who, like the writer, have watched the savage aspect of things daily, hourly, yielding to the more genial fruits of civilization!

In addition to these cheering prospects, this year was one of great enterprise among the colonists. No less than forty-two new houses had been built within a few months. Strings of fencing were made, enclosures formed, and a stirring industry manifested on every side. It was curious to see such scenes diversified by the intrusion of armed bands of savages, their heads barbarously feathered, parading fantastically among the industrious and plodding settlers, and looking down with an eye of contempt and scorn on the slow drudgery of the white man, whose comforts they, nevertheless, envied.

Hitherto our theme has been the trials, hardships, and misfortunes of the Scotch settlers; but having now seen their prospects change for the better, we may here bestow a few words upon the frequenters of the plains, commonly called the half-breeds of Red River, a class we shall have frequent occasion to notice. We ought to remark, by the way, how far this appellation is from expressing the truth, as not a tenth part of their number really belong to Red River, although they have from choice made it the land of their adoption. Hither, in fact, have flocked the half-breeds from all quarters east of the rocky mountain ridge, making the colony their great rendezvous and nursing place; while their restless habits lead them from place to place, from camp to camp, from the colony to the plains, and from the plains to the colony, like wandering Arabs, or the more restless Mamelukes, wherever hunting or fishing hold out to them a precarious subsistence. To do them justice, however, we ought to remark that, like other communities, they are distinguishable into several classes. Some are respectable in their habits; others as improvident as the savages themselves: but the chief dependence of all is upon buffalo hunting or fishing. The boundless prairies, therefore, have attractions for them, which the settled habits and domestic comforts of the industrious farmer can never hope to rival in their estimation.

These huntsmen resort annually to the plains, where the buffalo abounds, and generally go the journey in carts. The number composing these caravans has been of late years about 350; but they are on the increase. An account of their expeditions, and other interesting particulars, we reserve for distinct treatment. It is only the more wealthy or venturesome class of which we here speak as huntsmen—the best of those called by the general name of half-breeds. A second and inferior class of the same people resort to the lakes, and live by fishing, as precariously as their betters, but at the same time less expensively. In the lakes Winipeg and Manetobah, at the door of the colony, any quantities of the rich and finely-flavoured Titameg, or white fish, may be caught; yet, as in farming and in hunting, much depends on the season. The Titameg, for instance, are only to be got in great plenty during the autumn, and at certain places; and with every advantage of place and time, a gale of wind may visit the fisherman with total ruin. As many as fifty-four nets were lost in a single night on one occasion, the whole dependence of twenty-one families through the dreary winter, who were consequently reduced to a state of starvation. Their ruin was complete, for the very nets thus lost had to be paid for with the produce of their fishing efforts at the time.

Exclusive of the huntsmen and fishers, who, with all their improvidence, are somewhat regular in their pursuits, there is yet a third class of these half-breeds deserving of notice, whose numbers are by no means inconsiderable. The lowest or hopeless class, as we are disposed to term them, consist of people extremely poor, chiefly half-breeds, of all ages and sexes, orphans and others, who from time to time have found their way here from the four quarters of Rupert's Land, without friends, means, or habits of industry. They are ever a burden either upon the settlement or their associates. They dog the plain-hunters, follow the fishmongers, and exhibit all the characteristics of pauperism in a land without poor-laws to support a pauper class. They follow no regular calling or profession, not so much as that of the gipsies or tinkers; but live by chance as they best can. To illustrate the character of these people, we select a living example in the person of Baptiste l'Esprit, whose adventures through the year will serve as a portraiture of the whole class.

On the approach of spring, Baptiste, poor fellow, tired of the settlement, and fond of change, wishes to see the plains, still more anxious to see the buffalo; but is in want of everything—has nothing of his own. Wishes to make you believe he is the most honest in the world. Wishes you to trust him, to try him once more; is anxious to borrow, to get his supplies on trust. Promises everything. Tries one; tries him this way, that way, and the other way, tries him every way, but is refused; yet the smile of confidence is never off his countenance while in the supplicating mood. Nor is it an easy task to resist importunities so urgent, and particularly when enforced by an object of poverty; yet Baptiste is refused. But he is accustomed to refusals; such things never discourage him. Baptiste tries another, and another, but with no better success. Unfortunately for Baptiste, his character is known. Nevertheless, Baptiste, still confident in his own cause, tries another; accustomed to persevere, tries again, and again; and at last, by dint of importunities and fair promises, gets a horse to hire from one, a cart from another; but Baptiste having nothing of his own, the risk is great, so the price must be in proportion to the risk. A man of means gets a horse and cart for 2*l.* a trip, but Baptiste promises 4*l.* The temptation is great; Baptiste gets the horse and cart. His present wants supplied, is all he cares for. But Baptiste is in want of ammunition, is in want of everything else, as well as a horse and cart. Baptiste is at it again. Tries one, tries two, tries a dozen, at last succeeds: the rogue and the fool meet. But Baptiste wants many things yet—has neither axe nor knife; and this fact the reader must always bear in mind—that Baptiste has nothing himself. Baptiste wants clothing, something from the merchant as well as the settler. Himself and family are naked. Baptiste sets out again; calls here, calls there, at this shop, at that shop, travels up, travels down, nothing discouraged; gets in the merchant's book. After a month's preparation, and before Baptiste is half ready, the time for starting arrives. The others are off; Baptiste must start too, ready or not ready.

At this stage of things all Baptiste's preparations hang on a hair: he must go or all is lost; but to go without something to eat is impossible. Charity steps forward, for the hand of charity is liberal in Red River. A day after the rest, off goes Baptiste, helter skelter, with his horse and part of his family; but if no horse, as frequently happens, they tramp it on foot, for to the buffalo they must get, cost what it will. Neck or nothing. Fifteen days' anxious travel, and 180 miles behind him, Baptiste gets to the buffalo. Glorious sight! But here all is bustle; no one idle but himself, What is he to do? No runner, no hunter himself. Baptiste goes to one, goes to another; waits many days.

The dogs eat, but Baptiste starves in the middle of plenty; asks, begs, lounges about, but shows no disposition to assist any one. Baptiste is above working—cannot work. Sympathy steps forward: Baptiste must not starve. Gets a piece from one, some from another. Baptiste eats, but cannot make provisions; has no servants; himself indolent, his family still more so. They can do nothing. The meat spoils; but although Baptiste cannot work, he can eat; eats heartily, lives well on the charity of others, and that is all he cares about. Days pass, weeks pass, the summer passes: Baptiste eats, sleeps, smokes, and all is right—but no load; nothing to pay the hire of his horse and cart: the busy scenes of the camp pass unheeded by him. No effort made. Late and early every one is at work. Baptiste alone is idle; but consoles himself by saying, " It is time enough yet." Before he looks about him, the hunters are loaded. Baptiste alone thinks it is time enough yet, till time is no longer. A move is made for home. Baptiste is aroused from his apathy; his cart is still empty; begins now to bestir himself; goes round, asks one, asks two, asks this one, asks that one, asks everyone for something to put in his cart; promises this, that, and the other thing; but the people were shy, but Baptiste was not to be discouraged, did not slacken in his importunities; they upbraided him for his indolence, rejected his promises. The prairie is a place of activity, industry, and perseverance. The half-breeds are generous; but Baptiste is no favourite; nevertheless, he could sing a good song, tell a good story; some pity his family; charity stretches forth her hand, and now the cart is loaded in a trice; Baptiste, the while, as proud as if he had done all himself, quite satisfied, happy as happy could be. After a six weeks' jaunt, the last to start, the last to camp, yet Baptiste, fat as a seal, and sleek as an Esquimaux, arrives to resume the delicious enjoyment of indolence again.

During Baptiste's adventure to the plains, his wife remains at home. It sometimes happens, however, that both go; happens also that the wife goes, and Baptiste remains at home; but this year she remained at home. Let us now see how this industrious rib passed her summer. Pretty much as her *cher mari*—to very little purpose; basking herself on the sunny banks of Red River, smoking her pipe, promenading among her neighbours, and watching a hook and line for her comfort. This industrious helpmate makes shift, with the aid of the hoe, to put down a few grains of Indian corn, and sometimes a few seed potatoes also, which, in spite of all, will grow to maturity, and then the birds destroy the one, the cattle devour the other, for want of care; but misfortunes will happen. As soon as Baptiste arrives with the produce of his buffalo adventure, he sits down, smokes his pipe, then unloads his pony, and tells the story of his journey. Is highly pleased with the trip; praises his own industry and success. "Look," says he to his wife, " look at this piece, look at that piece," turning them over and over at the same time. His wife is charmed; counts his profits. " There is enough to pay all," so the point is now settled, and they enjoy themselves; a day, a week passes; but not a word about paying off debts! till the load gets nearly expended:

then they begin to reflect. Madam is consulted, and the distribution of the plain speculation commences; but commences a day after the fare. This piece is laid aside for a new gown to madam, that piece for a shawl; so much for tea, so much for tobacco, the two great luxuries of Red River; a bit to this gossip, a bit to that gossip. Madam has her cronies. " This man," says she, " helped me with my crop," a bit to him, a bit to some one else. Then there must be a merry let-out. Friends are invited, a feast given, the last morceau disappears. The load is gone. But here Baptiste, for the first time, thinks of the borrowed horse, the borrowed cart, the many generous friends who supplied him at starting. " We must," says Baptiste, " pay something; a little to this one, a little to that one, we owe here, we owe there." The wife is again consulted. A consultation is held. The happy couple reason the matter over and over. The piece put aside for the new gown is cut in two; half goes for the horse, half for present use. " We can do no more now," said the wife. To this Baptiste adds, " Amen. But we will pay all the next trip." The reader is desired to remember the words, " next trip." The new shawl, the tea, tobacco, and other etceteras, are attended to, and the gossips and cronies are not forgotten. After another consultation, Baptiste, with the half piece, value 10*s*., the eighth of what he had promised, goes to settle with the owner of the horse, finds him, hangs down his head, is silent for some time, at last looks up with a sorrowful countenance, tells a pitiful story, and a very different story from the one he told his wife. " I have been unfortunate," said he; " I had bad luck, my horse was sick, I broke my cart in the plains. Most of my provisions I lost in crossing a river. After a hard summer's labour, I had scarcely a mouthful for my own family. Brought nothing home; my cart was empty. Ask my comrades: they will confirm the truth of my statement. Here," said Baptiste, holding up the half piece in his hand, " this is all I can give you now;" but Baptiste l'Esprit never cheated anybody—" if you lend me the horse for next trip, I will pay you all honestly. The prospects before me are good; fear not, I will pay you more than you expect." Sympathy for poor Baptiste's misfortunes, and a desire to be paid next trip, had their due weight. The too credulous lender believed Baptiste, believed all, and was deceived. Lent him the horse again. The rogue and the fool shook hands, and the last trip was like the first, with this only difference, that the debt was doubled, and the disappointment more complete. Falsehood often resembles truth in appearance, so has fiction the appearance of reality; but we are not dealing either in romance or fiction—what we have stated is a true picture of real life as it is in Red River: the way the borrower serves the lender, the way the settlers are duped and tricked by such people as Baptiste l'Esprit. The working of a bad system ruins a people.

But we are not done with Baptiste yet: this is the case in successful years; but every year is not a successful one, for it not unfrequently happens that Baptiste arrives without either horse or provisions, the friendly Indians having relieved him of both. In this case, too, the lender pays the piper. Baptiste, however, accustomed to drag the chain of misfortune, drinks the bitter cup of disappointment with all the *sang froid* of a philosopher. When nothing remains but hope, Baptiste picks up his smoking-bag, lights his pipe, and on foot commences his journey homeward. The enemy is seen on every hill; Baptiste is on the alert. Hides in the day, walks during the night, yet is happy in distress. Dares not shoot to satisfy the pangs of hunger, for the savages must not be apprised. His life is at stake. Goes days without water, nights without sleep, and weeks without shoes. Dreams of plenty, but awakens to remove the delusion; knows no better condition; is happy in adversity. Baptiste reaches home, and takes as much pleasure in recounting his perilous adventures as any other man would in detailing the result of a prosperous trip.

At home, Baptiste joins his industrious spouse in the business of fishing, in which occupation the time is spent as cheerfully in the magic circle of a few piscatory friends as if nothing had happened. Losses and crosses are familiar to him. Never troubles his head about the welfare of society: a firm believer in predestination, he never repines at his lot; never looks beyond self. At length the advanced state of the season reminds him that hoary winter is before him. Baptiste now begins, for the first time, to think how or where he is to pass the winter. He resolves, and resolves again, and as often hesitates, till the proper season for either fishing or hunting slips by. At length decides on betaking himself to labour among the inhabitants; regrets his choice, thinks otherwise. Madam remarks, "Fishing is easier than labour." Baptiste thinks so too, and the happy couple resolve accordingly. Manetobah Lake, as a fishing place, is fixed upon; but here it occurs to them, that the season is too late for Manetobah. Thinks Lake Winipeg is better, because it is nearer. Winipeg is in turn resolved upon. They hesitate again; come to a dead stand. At last, both agree that buffalo meat is preferable to fish. Turn road: buffalo is resolved upon. And here Baptiste flatters himself with the idea, that he will have better luck in winter than he had in summer. This resolution gratifies their senses, gratifies their appetites. The moral obligation is fulfilled; thus they reason, and all is right. So off sets Baptiste and family, late in the fall, to the plains, to pass the winter among the Indians, among the buffalo; but after some twenty days' sore travel, finds to his misfortune, what he might have found long before, that the season is too far spent; the buffalo too far off. They stop short, have not a mouthful to eat, fierce winter overtakes them, famine is around them. They resolve, and re-resolve, and at last resolve to turn back, eat their dogs, eat their shoes. Life is sweet; Baptiste makes for the settlement, arrives more dead than alive, tells his tale of woe. Sympathy is awake, his family are sent for, two already dead, the rest arrive, objects of charity. The benevolent feed them, nurse them, take care of them. But this is not all; spring arrives, and as every returning year brings new events to pass, Baptiste thinks those events will be favourable to him. The experience of the past has no influence on him. Baptiste as anxious as ever about the plains. But this light we may see through the darkness of futurity. The future will be what the past has been, a chequered scene, a mixture of good and bad in this life. But Baptiste never troubles himself about events nor results, so to the plains he goes, and pursues the same path of reckless folly, nor need we wonder that the same results follow.

Among the class illustrated by this character, are to be seen many of the old voyageurs, and other waifs and strays of society, as well as the half-breeds, of which it is chiefly composed. They pretend to the character of civilized men, call themselves Christians, and occasionally frequent the church. In all else they are no better than vagrant savages. Wherever night overtakes them, they are at home. They camp in the open plains, in the woods, among the rocks, and along rivers and lakes. All places are alike to them in the pilgrimage of life. They are notorious tobacco-smokers, and when their means will allow them the luxury, still more notorious tea-drinkers.

The writer was once travelling with a friend on the banks of the Assiniboine, having secured the services of Baptiste l'Esprit as guide, who on approaching a bluff of wood one morning, introduced us into a small log hut built on the verge of the wood, and occupied by a family of four persons, his friends. Mr. and Mrs. Flammond, the parent couple, with a little girl about four years of age, were squatted gipsy-like in one corner of the dwelling, which had neither table, chair, nor stool, to render it tolerable. In another corner was sleeping a grown-up young woman, having before her bed two large pieces of bark to serve as curtains; while other parts of the floor were occupied by four men sleeping two and two, wayfarers, like ourselves, who had found shelter there the night before, and had not yet risen.

The rain, which had driven us hither for shelter, beat through the log walls, driven by the wind, which presently carried away part of the roof, and in a short time we stood ankle deep in water. The sleepers were now roused, and in the midst of the bustle that ensued, plash, plash, across the floor went the little four years' child, to light her mother's pipe at a chimney in the corner. Having returned with the pipe, she began to suck the breast of her mother; but if this surprised us in a child of that age, how greatly was our astonishment increased when she began to cry for the pipe, which was actually filled and lighted again for her use!

After smoking heartily, the child presented the pipe to her father, by whom it was passed to the mother, and from the mother back to the little girl, who still filled up the intervals by sucking. The child was quite an adept in the art, and we ought not to omit that the lady with the bark curtains was supplied with a pipe before she performed her toilet.

Having received a hint, while the kettle was boiling, that the family were "just out of tea," we presented them with some, which, being prepared, was handed round in birchen cups, in genuine Indian fashion; cup after cup, and kettle after kettle was supplied, till the half pound was gone, and a wistful look for more: but not a mouthful of anything to eat was forthcoming; the only food which the family had tasted in three days, being two gold-eyes. In short, we supplied them with food as well as drink; and were amply repaid for all we gave, by the romantic and chequered history they related to us in their own quaint phraseology, spiced with abundant drollery and good humour. The Flammonds were a happy family. Apropos of tea-drinking, the old lady remarked, "We passed a fine winter among the Assiniboines. We were twenty-three families, made buffalo robes, dressed leather, and prepared provisions, the whole winter: all of which we sold for tea as soon as earned. The seven opposition traders told us in the spring, that we had drank twenty-five chests!" These people emulate each other in making the blackest and bitterest tea.

Lieutenant Burnes, in his travels into Bokhara, gives a curious account of tea-drinking in Koondoz:— "Nothing," says that intelligent observer, "is done in this country without tea, which is handed round at all times and hours, and gives a social character to conversation, which is very agreeable. The Uzbeks drink their tea with salt instead of sugar, and sometimes with fat; the leaves of the pot are then divided among the party, and chewed like tobacco." Bad as Red River habits may be, the people here neither use salt nor fat, nor do they chew the article. Probably it would be an improvement were they to mix the tea and tobacco together; and we have no doubt, but time and habit would soon make it a favourite and delicious compound. Tea is so loved that it will even purchase their chastity, which is nevertheless proof against many other temptations. Its magic power is like that of money in other countries.

During the autumn of this year, the colony became infested with a new enemy, hitherto unnoticed. The mice, like the grasshoppers, devoured everything; the grain after being stacked, was almost totally destroyed by them. The straw, the very stubble itself, was cut to atoms; the fields, the woods, and the plains, seemed literally alive with the new and troublesome visitors, whose appearance threatened the settlement with another great calamity.

CHAPTER IX.

CONTENTS.—Hunters and their habits—Rumours—Visit Pembina —Reports confirmed—Steps taken—Hudson's Bay Company— Sympathy—The fatal snow-storm—Train of disasters—Woman and child—Human misery—Lives lost—Cling to old habits— Hunters relieved — Colonists in distress — Gloomy scenes— Sudden rise in the water—Settlers abandon their houses—The river becomes a lake—Property adrift—Floating spectacle— Waterfall—Prices rise — Settlers return — Colloquies — Discouraging scenes—The man and his two oxen—Honest fellows —Precarious times—Cattle diminish—De Meurons—Cause of the high water — The question answered — More floods than one—Features—Indications—Shores of Hudson's Bay-- Phenomenon.

WE are now brought, in the regular course of our history, to the disastrous year 1826, one of the most fatal, both as to life and property, that ever befell Red River. The incidents we have to relate will further illustrate the habits of the class to which Baptiste, in the preceding chapter, belongs; and of the half-breeds generally who depend on buffalo-hunting in the plains, for their subsistence. We must premise that the hunters make two trips to the plains annually; the proceeds of the first are always sold off to supply their wants in clothing and other necessaries for the year, but the second furnishes their winter stock of food; and when it fails, crowds of these people resort to the plains, generally to pass a wretched winter among the Indians; such as we have noticed, in reference to the abode of the Scotch settlers at the same place.

As early as the month of January this year, flying reports had reached the colony, that the hunters who had gone to the plains were starving; but such reports being common in these parts, and as often false as true, they passed for some time unheeded. About the middle of February, however, business led the writer to Pembina, where he found ample verification of the reports, and had the satisfaction of assisting in the benevolent efforts of Mr. Mc Dermot, who was actively engaged in administering to the wants of the sufferers. Having communicated with Mr. Donald Mc Kenzie who was, at the same time, Governor of the colony and the Company's Chargé d'affaires at Fort Garry, that gentleman took immediate steps for their relief, by sending off party after party, with provisions and clothing. At this trying moment, in fact, all depended on the officers of the Hudson's Bay Company; and even with all the assistance they could command, the difficulties were almost insuperable. The distance the sufferers were, even beyond Pembina, was from 150 to 200 miles, and the only practicable mode of conveyance, owing to the deep snows, was by means of dogs, so that the labour was great, the task a tedious and difficult one; but everything was done that either man or beast could do, and such despatch and diligence used, that it was the means of saving hundreds of the people's lives. Private individuals likewise contributed. Sympathy for the plain hunters was universal. Everyone lent a willing hand.

The disaster began in December. About the 20th of that month, there was a fearful snow-storm, such as had not been witnessed for years. This storm, which lasted several days, drove the buffalo beyond the hunters' reach, and killed most of their horses; but what greatly increased the evil, was the suddenness of the visitation. As the animals disappeared almost instantaneously, no one was prepared for the inevitable famine that followed; the hunters, at the same time, were so scattered, that they could render each other no assistance, nor could they so much as discover each other's whereabouts. Some were never found. Families here, and families there, despairing of life, huddled themselves together for warmth, and, in too many cases, their shelter proved their grave. At first, the heat of their bodies melted the snow; they became wet, and being without food or fuel, the cold soon penetrated, and in several instances, froze the whole into a body of solid ice. Some, again, were found in a state of wild delirium, frantic, mad; while others were picked up, one here, and one there, frozen to death, in their fruitless attempts to reach Pembina—some half way, some more, some less; one woman was found with an infant on her back, within a quarter of a mile of Pembina. This poor creature must have travelled, at the least, 125 miles, in three days and nights, till she sunk at last in the too unequal struggle for life.

Those that were found alive had devoured their horses, their dogs, raw hides, leather, and their very shoes. So great were their sufferings, that some died on their road to the colony, after being relieved at Pembina; the writer passed two who were scarcely yet cold, and saw forty-two others, in seven or eight parties, crawling along with great difficulty, to the most reduced of whom he was, by good fortune, able to give a mouthful of bread. At last, with much labour and anxiety, the survivors were conveyed to the settlement, to be there supplied with the comforts they so much needed, and which, but a few weeks before, they affected to despise! But the sufferings of some, who can tell? One man, with his wife and three children, were dug out of the snow, where they had been buried for five days and five nights—without food, fire, or the light of the sun. The woman and two of the children recovered. In all this disastrous affair, and under circumstances peculiarly distressing, the distance, the depth of the snows, and severity of the weather, the saving of so many people was almost a miracle. Thirty-three lives were lost.

Hardly had the colonists recovered themselves, after these exertions, when they were visited by another great calamity. The winter had been unusually severe, having begun earlier and continued later than usual. The snows averaged three feet deep, and in the woods, from four to five feet. The cold was intense, being often 45° below zero; the ice measured five feet seven inches in thickness. Notwithstanding all this, the colonists felt no dread till the spring was far advanced, when the flow of water, from the melting of the accumulated snow, became really alarming. On the 2nd of May, the day before the ice started, the water rose nine feet perpendicular in the twenty-four hours! Such a rise had never before been noticed in Red River. Even the Indians were startled, and as they stared with a bewildering gaze, put their hands to their mouths, exclaiming, "Yea ho! yea ho!" an expression of surprise, "What does this mean? What does this mean?" On the 4th, the water overflowed the banks of the river, and now spread so fast, that almost before the people were aware of the danger, it had reached their dwellings. Terror was depicted on every countenance, and so level was the country, so rapid the rise of the waters, that on the 5th, all the settlers abandoned their houses, and sought refuge on higher ground.

At this crisis, every description of property became of secondary consideration, and was involved in one common wreck, or abandoned in despair. The people had to fly from their homes for the dear life, some of them saving only the clothes they had on their backs. The shrieks of children, the lowing of cattle, and the howling of dogs, added terror to the scene. The Company's servants exerted themselves to the utmost, and did good service with their boats. The generous and humane Governor of the colony, Mr. D. Mc Kenzie, sent his own boat to the assistance of the settlers, though himself and family depended on it for their safety, as they were in an upper story, with ten feet of water rushing through the house. By exertions of this kind, and much self-sacrifice, the families were all conveyed to places of safety, after which, the first consideration was to secure the cattle, by driving them many miles off, to the pine hills and rocky heights. The grain, furniture, and utensils, came next in order of importance; but by this time, the country presented the appearance of a vast lake, and the people in the boats had no resource but to break through the roofs of their dwellings, and thus save what they could. The ice now drifted in a straight course from point to point, carrying destruction before it; and the trees were bent like willows, by the force of the current.

While the frightened inhabitants were collected in groups on any dry spot that remained visible above the waste of waters, their houses, barns, carriages, furniture, fencing, and every description of property, might be seen floating along over the wide extended plain, to be engulfed in Lake Winipeg. Hardly a house or building of any kind was left standing in the colony. Many of the buildings drifted along whole and entire; and in some were seen dogs, howling dismally, and cats, that jumped frantically from side to side of their precarious abodes. The most singular spectacle was a house in flames, drifting along in the night, its one half immersed in water, and the remainder furiously burning. This accident was caused by the hasty retreat of the occupiers. The water continued rising till the 21st, and extended far over the plains; where cattle used to graze, boats were now plying under full sail.

As no one deemed it possible to remain in the colony, the choice of another locality had become a matter of eager debate, when, unexpectedly, on the 22nd of the month, the waters appeared at a stand, and after a day or two, began gradually to fall Wheat, which had fallen to 2s. per bushel at the commencement of the disaster, now rose to 15s., nearly double its former price; and beef, in like manner, from $\frac{1}{2}d.$ per pound to 3d. The height to which the water had risen above the level of ordinary years was fifteen feet. It subsided, of course, very gradually. It was on the 15th of June that the settlers, for the first time, drew near the sites of their former habitations.

During this heavy trial, only one man lost his life by drowning; but many were the hair-breadth escapes that might be mentioned. At one spot, for example, the writer and some others fell in with a man who had two of his oxen tied together, with his wife and four children fixed on their backs. The docile and terrified animals waded or floated as they best could, like a moveable stage, while the poor man himself, with a long line in his hands, kept before them, sometimes wading, sometimes swimming, guiding them to the highest ground. With no slight trouble, we got them conveyed to a place of safety; and, but for our timely assistance, they must all have perished; for the water was gaining on them fast, while they had far to go, and were already exhausted.

The sudden rise of the water, when it once got over the banks of the river, may admit of more vivid illustration from the writer's personal experience. My boat then was drawn up at the house door, to be in readiness, when we were surprised by the rush of the water. I immediately ran out to lock a store door, a few yards off; but before I could get back, the water was knee deep, and the furniture afloat; nor could the door of the house be locked, for the strength of the current. Embarking hastily, we pushed off, and made for a neighbour's barn, but had not rowed 300 yards from the door, when the water began to move and carry off the loose property; a cariole went first, carts and slades followed, so that in the space of an hour the water had made a clean sweep of all moveables, nothing remaining but the houses, which soon followed in the general destruction. In the barn we were joined by fifty others, and, after passing a miserable night there, were compelled to abandon it by the still rising waters. We now erected a stage, four or five feet high, in the open plains, and having there piled up such of our little property as could not be stowed away in our boat and canoes, we made it our refuge for two days longer; but the wind blowing a gale, and the water gaining on us fast, at the end of that period we boated off in haste to another spot, where we were still less fortunate, for now the water disturbed us in the night, and we had no alternative but to shape our course for the banks of the Assiniboine. Here, on a patch of high ground, we found a dense crowd of people, and among others, the rascally de Meurons, who, it was well known, hardly possessed an animal of their own, and yet were selling cheap beef all the time. Disgusted with their near neighbourhood, we removed from this otherwise most favourable spot, and next took up our quarters on the delightful banks of Sturgeon Creek, where we remained in peace and quietness till the water began to fall.

While here, provisions became very scarce; pemican 8*d*. per pound; salt, 2*l*. 5*s*. the bushel. The troubled state of the people increased the evil. The cattle had been driven to some distance, too far to be available to us, but not beyond the reach of the de Meurons, who fed us with our own beef, at 3*d*. per pound. When we came to count our cattle, we had but a Flemish account of calves and year-olds. It was no time to quarrel, and hardly safe for a man to claim his own property, as the de Meurons, and others who profited by their example, helped themselves without scruple to whatever chance threw in their way. These were the boys that had been brought to the country to restore the settlements to order, and keep peace!

The cause of this disaster has been the subject of many conjectures, which, however, will not bear investigation. We prefer to state the only conclusion that appears to us perfectly natural, and consistent with well-known facts. The previous year had been unusually wet; the country was thoroughly saturated; the lakes, swamps, and rivers, at the fall of the year, were full of water; and a large quantity of snow had fallen in the preceding winter. Then came a late spring, with a sudden burst of warm weather, and a south wind blowing for several days in succession; the snow melted at once, and Red Lake, Otter-tail Lake, as well as Lake Travers, all overflowed their banks. To these causes must be added the large quantities of ice carried down by the Red River, which came suddenly in contact with the solid ice of Lake Winipeg; and thus stopping the current, seems to have caused the great overflow of back water on the level surface of the plains; this opinion is strengthened by the fact, that as soon as the ice of the lake gave way, the water began to fall, and it fell as rapidly as it rose.

What has happened once, may happen again. Excessive rains and snows seldom occur, indeed, in one and the same year; but when they do happen, or even when they occur in two consecutive years, they will undoubtedly produce the same disastrous results. The late Mr. Nolin, who was one of the first adventurers to these parts, assured the writer, that when he first entered Red River, in the year 1776, the flood was still higher than on the present occasion; he having sailed that year, as he declared, from Red Lake River, round by the way of Pembina, and down towards the colony; the whole country, therefore, being under water, and the river appearing to him rather like a lake. The Indians likewise mention a flood about the year 1790, and the natives now on the ground affirm that in 1809 the water rose unusually high.

CHAPTER X.

CONTENTS.—Swiss and de Meurons emigrate — The Scotch at work again—Discouraging circumstances—Result of perseverance—Ups and downs—Red River climate—Late sowing—New houses—Confidence restored—Orkneymen in Red River—Agriculture—The month of May—The seed season—Comparison—Fall ploughing—Fall sowing—Runnet—Defective spot—Ruinous system—Comfort disregarded—Red River malaria—One ploughing enough—Experiments—Fall ploughing recommended—Clover seed—Cold—New feature—Governor Simpson's views—Encouragements versus discouragements—Flour—Butter—Produce condemned—The Company's policy—Hints disregarded—The Governor's table—The difficult question—Who is to blame?

As the waters subsided, the future movements of the colonists became the subject of anxious discussion, and they soon found themselves divided into two parties; the one consisting of those who were still resolved, in defiance of all obstacles, to remain at Red River; the other comprising the Swiss emigrants, the de Meurons, and other restless spirits, who, it will be recollected, were never reconciled to the country, and were now resolved to try their fortune elsewhere. This party, now on the wing to be off, were joined by every idler and other person averse to Red River; and so little was their further residence in the colony desired, that food and other necessaries were furnished to them gratis by the Company, with the view of hastening their departure. The emigrating party, consisting of 243 individuals, took their departure for the United States on the 24th of June, and we saw them no more. We subsequently learned, however, that the Swiss had settled on the Mississippi, and were doing well.

The Scotch settlers, meanwhile, not so easily chilled by disappointments, promptly decided on the course they were to take: without a moment's hesitation, or loss of time, they resumed work on their cheerless farms, which were then bare and naked as on the first day they came to the country. This was the fourth time the Scotch settlers had commenced the world anew in Red River, all the fruits of their former labours having disappeared, like the morning dew. The advanced state of the season held out but little hope of their labours being crowned with success; yet barley, potatoes, and even a little wheat sowed as late as the 22nd of June, came to maturity. In such a latitude as Hudson's Bay, this would appear almost incredible; but such was the effect of the short warm summer of those regions.

The patience and perseverance of the Scotch were amply rewarded from this time, for we are now brought to the year 1827, which commences a new era in the settlement. Several causes contributed to this result. The dross had been purged away from our community, so that we were now one people in thought, word, and deed. Before the year 1830 had passed, the colony was completely re-established, and more promising and thriving than ever. In this brief interval of two or three busy years, no less than 204 new houses had been built, besides many enclosures made, and barns erected, on sites far more eligible, and secure from any future rise of the water, than those which the flood had destroyed. To these advantages must be added the favourable crops that ensued, for every wet year in Red River is a crop year, and many years after the high water, the soil was saturated to its full. Late springs have always proved the surest indications of a good crop, as there is then no danger to be apprehended from the frost.

The blank occasioned in the colony by the party emigrating to the States, was, by this time, filling up fast, and that by a people differing very much in character and habits from those who had left it. It is a general observation here, that Orkneymen, the class to which we allude, are less given to change than people of most other countries. In whatever sphere of life they are placed, either high or low, in prosperity or adversity, their well-known habits of industry and frugality follow them; and the same uniformity of character by which they are distinguished at home. It was the good fortune of these men to come at a most favourable juncture, when the permanent prosperity of the colony was secured, and order established; and as they had come out, not as settlers, but servants of the Hudson's Bay Company, the greater part of them had saved more or less money, with which, when their time expired, they at once became comfortably settled on their own lands, in preference to returning home. They are, generally speaking, a degree behind the Scotch settlers, in point of agricultural skill, though not in point of economy. On the whole they are a quiet, honest, and plodding people, satisfied with little; and one circumstance places them at a striking disadvantage compared with the Scotch emigrants. Most of them, having contracted matrimony while in the service, brought into the settlement Indian families, who were in a great degree ignorant of the habits of the white people. We here mention the fact; but its effect upon their interests, as farmers, will show itself more fully when we come to speak of the Red River market and the value of produce.

The mode of farming and state of agriculture in the colony may here be conveniently noticed. The season for the out-door labour of the farmer is rendered short by the long and severe winters; and this being the case, everything is commonly done in a hurry, whence it follows, that it is seldom well done.

The first of May is the earliest reliable period for setting the plough at work, and at latest, by the 20th of that month, all seed, with the exception of barley, ought to be in the ground, in order to ensure a crop. Our springs are, therefore, a month behind most European countries, and later than Canada, where nearly an equal degree of cold prevails, by some fifteen days. May, with us, takes the place of April in other countries, in the renewal of vegetation; but it is only in June, we might say July, that the soil is sufficiently heated to bring forth its produce, and afford the husbandman a fair prospect of a crop.

All kinds of grain thrive well in the colony, and grow to perfection; but wheat is the general crop raised, and it is invariably sown in the spring. Fall sowing was, indeed, once or twice tried; but having failed, the practice was altogether abandoned. Such trials, however, owing to a lack of judgment, indifferent seed, and other unfavourable circumstances, might have failed in any other country; and we would strongly recommend these considerations to the attention of our Red River farmers.

Fall ploughing and fall sowing are distinct and equally important subjects, and here, perhaps, the writer may, without egotism, quote his own experience. On finding my crops falling off greatly, I tried the fall ploughing and summer fallow, to some considerable extent, and it generally answered so well, that I became anxious to see it introduced throughout the colony. First, then, I had a small park, which sowed ten bushels of grain, and finding, from year to year, that it was diminishing, till, at last, it only produced fifty-two bushels in return, after the ordinary routine of spring ploughing, I got it manured and ploughed in the fall, and ploughed it again before sowing in the spring. The season being favourable, I had 255 bushels on it. One of my neighbours tried a similar experiment, and had, after six bushels sowing, 140 in return. A second field, sowing eight bushels, which had been left fallow for two years running, during which time it had been ploughed three different times, and then sown in drills, yielded for a first crop 280 bushels. In addition to these encouraging facts, other instances were not wanting, in course of time, to demonstrate that fall ploughing, and fallow, yielded by far the better crops; besides the advantages of time, which is always saved by labour done in the fall. This being the case, the moment the harvest is over, the plough should be at work. If the spring be wet, and weeds appear abundant, plough your fallow ground before sowing it; but if dry, and the spring be an early one, plough the seed down, or sow it without ploughing, as it then retains the moisture still better, unless too much tramped by cattle. Under the present system, so short is the time allowed for preparing the ground, and sowing, in the spring, that there has never yet been as much grain raised in one year, as would be sufficient to serve the whole population for six months, supposing the farmers not to have sold a single bushel; and yet the hue and cry has been, " There is no market!" The people, we must remark, have depended on the precarious returns of the plains, for the remainder of their supplies.

The only objection urged against fall ploughing here has been, that in some instances, during dry years, it has failed, owing to the snow not lying on the ploughed ground, and imparting that moisture to it which is always derived from the snow lying upon stubble fields. This indeed may be the case in large open fields, swept by winds, but in small parks, where the enclosures are not too far apart, snow will certainly remain; and the writer may state that he has often found the accumulation of snow-drifts along the fences, prevent early ploughing in the spring. In regard to fall sowing, enough has already been said to urge repeated experiments before it is finally condemned.

Grass, perhaps, may be admitted as an exception to these remarks, since the several attempts so far made with red clover have totally failed. Still, it ought not to be forgotten, that in most cases it did appear above ground the first year, but disappeared ever after, solely, it is supposed, from the severity of our winters. Hence, the question remains, whether red clover can be expected to thrive, and resist a cold of 48° below zero. White clover is said to thrive well; but is little used. Timothy is the only artificial grass yet sown here with any degree of success, and it thrives exceedingly well. In truth, the present state of Red River, with its abundance of waste lands and their luxuriance in natural grasses, leaves but little inducement for raising artificial grass of any kind. The natural grass is so easily got, and so nutritive, that it is considered a mere waste of time, and loss of labour, to cultivate any of the foreign species.

Notwithstanding the impetus given to colonial labour after the flood of 1827, agriculture remained in such a backward state, up to the year 1831, or thereabouts, that the Company could never rely upon the settlers for a sufficient supply of flour, or any other article of consumption. About this period, a fresh stir was made; the colonists began to look about them, and take some steps to improve their domestic arrangements. The farmers' wives commenced to spin, and there was made in the colony this very year 185 yards of coarse tow cloth or bagging. The difficulty was to obtain assistance, unless the farmer had an able family of his own; men labourers getting from 2s. 6d. to 3s., and women from 1s. to 1s. 6d. per day, and even at this rate indolent and awkward at their work. It is not surprising, therefore, that prices remained high, and that the Company had to import annually, from England, such articles of consumption as it needed; a rather singular circumstance in a country purely agricultural, and rendered still more singular by the fact, that there was no other outlet or market in the country but that afforded by the Company's servants.

At the period we have reached, great improvements were made and a large extension given to agricultural operations at the instance of Governor Simpson, the chief manager of the Company's affairs throughout Rupert's Land, who promised to take all the Company's supplies from the colony. The promise was effectual in rousing the colonists to fresh activity, so that in a short time all the wants of the Company were adequately supplied. This was no sooner done, however, than the prices fell; flour from 16s. to 11s. 6d. per cwt.; butter from 1s. to 7d.; and cheese from 6d. to 4d. per pound; while dry goods, iron, salt, and every other article the sellers required, remained at the usual prices. The people grumbled for some time; but the storm blew over, and business went on according to the new tariff, which was concluded to afford a fair remuneration. The market, in fact, was getting overstocked; when, unfortunately, a hue and cry was raised throughout the country against the quality of the produce: the flour was said to be heated, sour, and altogether of so very bad quality as to be only fit to poison pigs; in short, wherever it went, it was refused. The butter was pronounced mouldy, rancid, and scarcely fit to grease cart-wheels; cheese could not be eaten. Even the beef and pork were found fault with, at 3*d*. per pound. The consequence was, English produce was again called for, and again imported. The settlers, in fine, were left, after all their improvements, in a worse predicament than if they had never extended their farms; since they were now deprived of that market which their additional labour and additional expense had led them to expect.

The apology for this state of things must be sought for in the circumstances of the colony at that time. Perfection was not to be expected; but even the necessary conveniences for pursuing agricultural operations with success did not exist. In the whole colony, there was not to be found either a smut-mill or fanning machine, to clean the grain, and but few barns to thrash it in, and still fewer kilns to dry it; much, therefore, of the grain had, of necessity, to be thrashed on an ice-floor, in the open air, during all weathers, and then ground in a frozen state, and immediately packed in casks made of green wood, furnished by the Company itself. Of all this, the officials were cognisant; in fact, it was done under their own orders. Little wonder if the flour turned out to be of very bad quality; heated, sour, and even rotten.

With butter, it was even worse. The settlers were in the habit of bringing it into the Company's store, in small quantities; some more, some less. Not in firkins, tinettes, or kegs; but in open dishes, covered with a towel, a napkin, or a cabbage-leaf; in hot, windy, or rainy weather, just as it happened; and at different times of the year: that is, some in the spring—when its colour is that of a pale white; others, again, according to the state of the grass, of a high colour; in fact, at all seasons. Some well, some as ill salted. Some of it made by skilful persons; others, again, by the unskilful natives of the country. Now, all these colours and qualities, of different periods, were generally thrown together in large open casks, where it lay till the packing season arrived. The whole accumulation was then mixed together, and packed by the Company into kegs made of green wood, and incapable of holding brine or pickle; in which state it was sent, in open boats, to the remotest parts of the country; to the Atlantic and Frozen Oceans—hundreds, nay, thousands of miles; exposed, for months together, to a burning summer's sun.

Such were the disadvantages under which the settlers had to labour, and to which they were subjected by the caprice of the Company's servants, who would regard no warning of the consequences, and listen to no remonstrance. Had the buyer and seller conspired together purposely to ruin the character of Red River produce, they could not have hit upon a surer plan for effecting their object. It will, of course, be understood, that remarks of this nature apply, not to the Hudson's Bay Company in England, but to its representatives on the spot; and even then it would be unjust to fix any particular amount of blame upon individuals. In the working of most machinery, there is wheel within wheel. The governor trusts his deputy, the deputy his second, and the second is often imposed upon by his favourites.

CHAPTER XI.

CONTENTS.—A new experiment—Unsettled state of things—The farmer at a stand—Fixing the price—The governing principle—The market—The Company's wheat—The mixture—The farrago—The flour—The millers—Saddle on the wrong horse—The ice-barn farmers—An example—Visit to an old friend—The establishment in confusion—The barn—The stable with many doors—The corn-yard and the pigs—Fiddling the time away—Anecdote—The father and his sons—The old man in earnest—Scotch settlers and their minister—The comparisons—The Scotch and their petitions—Public meeting—Petition again—Counter petition—The result—Mr. Jones and the Scotch settlers—The Liturgy laid aside—The parson's popularity—Kate and her keg of butter—General remarks—School system revised—Remarks thereon—Doing good to others—The Scotch in Red River—Social relations—Fashion—Dress—The good example.

A NOTABLE expedient was now ventured upon with the view of correcting the evils we have described. Instead of purchasing any more of the flour, against which such a hue and cry had been raised, the Governor, always interesting himself in the prosperity of the colony, resolved upon buying up the wheat and getting it dried and milled according to the Company's own liking. The price he fixed was 3s. 6d. per bushel, equivalent to 11s. 6d. per cwt., which had been considered by both parties a remunerative price for the flour, and certainly more, all thing considered, than the Company would have paid for flour imported from England. This principle regulated the Company in all similar cases; and though arbitrary, it would be difficult to find a reasonable objection against its fairness. The settlers, on their part, yielded with a bad grace to the necessity in which they were placed; and when we add that the sale of wheat in the colony is by measure, and that it was at this time taken as it comes, good, bad, or indifferent, at the same price, it is easy to imagine what a door was left open for cavilling and trickery.

The harvest of this year was under an average crop, and got in somewhat late in the season; yet the grain was in general good, and the Company bought in from eight to ten thousand bushels, to be kept in their own granaries over winter. Unfortunately, their buildings were too small for so large a quantity. No space being left to shift it from place to place, it had to be heaped up, often four or five feet deep, and so remained till it got almost baked together; add to which it was neither over dry, nor free from smut, which rendered it still more difficult to keep. Then, again, large quantities of dried buffalo meat had been stored up in the same buildings, the daintiest fragments of which were carried off by the mice and mixed up with the wheat, making a compound of wheat, smut, icicles, dried meat, mice, and mice nests, all more or less heated together, and forming a mass of impurity; the smell of which, without the hazardous experiment of tasting, was absolutely disgusting. In this state, despite all advice to the contrary, and the certainty of bringing disgrace upon the colony, the wheat was ground and the flour shipped off to the different trading posts. The writer having a mill, was among those patronised on this occasion, and can bear witness that the smell was intolerable. When the complaints of the victimised consumers had to be answered, the whole blame was laid upon the millers.*

We have mentioned the dampness of the wheat, and the particles of ice mixed up with it in the Company's granaries, arising from the slovenly and dirty habit of thrashing the grain on an ice-floor, in the open air,

* That some blame, however, was justly attached to the millers, may be inferred from the following analysis of the flour ground at the undermentioned mills, kept separate and tested by Mr. Governor Finlayson:—

	Pounds of Flour.			Pounds of Bran.
No. 1.	In 112 from	John Vincent's mill was found	12
,, 2.	,, 112 ,,	William Bird's mill	,,	12
,, 3.	,, 112 ,,	George Flitt's mill	,,	12
,, 4.	,, 112 ,,	Narcisse Marion's mill	,,	14
,, 5.	,, 112 ,,	Michel Klyne's mill	,,	14
,, 6.	,, 112 ,,	James Inkster's mill	,,	14
,, 7.	,, 112 ,,	Thomas Logan's mill	,,	14
,, 8.	,, 112 ,,	Andrew McDermot's mill	,,	18
,, 9.	,, 112 ,,	Thomas Bird's mill	,,	20
,, 10.	,, 112 ,,	Hugh Polson's mill	,,	20
,, 11.	,, 112 ,,	Robert Sandeson's mill	,,	26
,, 12.	,, 112 ,,	Cuthbert Grant's mill	,,	28

No. 1 and 2. Half-breeds, of English extraction. 3. An Orkneyman. 4. A Canadian. 5. A German. 6. An Orkneyman. 7. A Half-breed, of Scotch extraction. 8. An Irishman, whose mill was the same used by the writer of this book, named above, he having sold it to Mr. Bird. 9. A Half-breed, of English extraction. 10. A Scotchman. 11. A Half-breed, of Orkney extraction. 12. A Half-breed, of Canadian extraction.

chiefly by an indolent and wretched class of squatters, who raise just sufficient to poison the good grain, and destroy the market of the Red River colonists. To some extent, this practice could not be avoided by the most painstaking farmers, but the evil was greatly increased by the policy of the Company, who, to please all parties, took their supplies indiscriminately from all who presented themselves in the markets.

The class to which we particularly allude, have already been described as the "paupers of Red River;" they are voyageurs, hunters, trip-men, lake frequenters, fiddlers, idlers, and last of all, they are farmers. We call them paupers, and as a body they are such in reality, for no class of people can be more improvident and dependent on the exertions of others; yet it is not always poverty that lies at the root of their miserable way of life, but sheer force of habit and indolence, to be found among men of means as well the poorest of those who resemble them. By way of exemplifying the case, the writer may here briefly describe his visit to an old acquaintance, who had settled himself on an extensive farm, among the half-breeds of the place.

This man had not his superior for wealth and influence in the whole parish to which he belonged, for having been long in the Company's service, he had left the fur trade with a fortune of some 4,000$l.$ sterling. As he showed me over his establishment, the first place we went to see was a miserable sort of hovel, without lock or latch, with the snow drifting through the roof, which the old gentlemen called his barn. It was just large enough for two men to work in, but they preferred the ice-floor on the outside, as being safer, and hardly more exposed, since a cat jumped out between the logs as soon as we got in; and for that matter, a dog might have followed her, the holes being ample enough. Lying in our way, as we entered, was a pile of old harness and broken boxes, which in a manner shut up the entrance. At one end of the building were a few boards, on which lay eight bags of pemican, and some bales of dried meat, near to which lay in a heap some barley in the chaff. Across the rest of the floor, were several sleepers raised a foot and a half above the ground, as if on purpose to break the shins of any adventurer who entrusted himself within its precincts. It will be understood that these timbers had originally been laid down for the purpose of carrying a floor, but the work had never yet, and probably never would advance so far. In the other end were a few loads of unthrashed oats, peas, and barley, lying heads and tails together, and scarcely distinguishable the one from the other, being covered with the drifted snow. Across the plating of this strange building were two rough beams, on which were laid two raw hides, on cross sticks, holding up some half cleaned wheat, in one frozen mass, thickly covered with snow. I observed to my friend that the wheat would be spoiled.

"Oh, no," said he: "it is for the Company."

"It is very good of the Company," I replied, "to take such wheat as that."

"Yes," said he, "the Company take from us anything we have got for sale."

At the opposite side, lying on cross sticks also, were

jumbled together heaps of buffalo hides, mouldy, moth-eaten and rotten, bull's heads, old parchment, dog's sleds, snow-shoes, and a thousand other things, all more or less hidden in the snow-drift, and through which we could scarcely make our way. We had almost omitted the descent by means of a break-neck ladder of three wide steps, and glad we were to reascend them, and get out of the so-called barn with whole bones. On reaching the door, the old gentleman, turning round, remarked with a smile, "They have stolen one of my bags of pemmican: I had nine."

Leaving the barn, we went to one of the stables close by; but I saw enough of it from the outside to satisfy me, without going in. The door had first been on the east side of the building; but when that had got choked up with dung, one had been cut out on the west end, then on the north, and as a last make-shift, when I was there, one was cut out on the south side, fronting the dwelling-house door, and not many yards from it; at the same time dung was piled so high all round, that nothing of the building, except the roof, was to be seen. To reach the door, the animals had to slide down, and to get out on their knees. On my observing this difficulty of ingress and egress, the old gentleman remarked, "Losses do now and then occur; we have, however, lost but one this season." When I asked him where he would cut out the next door, seeing no place accessible but the roof; "Oh! we will throw the building away," said he, "and make another!" There were two other stables adjacent, which had been abandoned in a similar manner. The dung of many years was festering on the spot, forming one of the numerous similar sources of Red River malaria.

From the stable we proceeded to the corn-yard, fenced round with a sort of temporary railing, enclosing five half-made ricks of wheat, a little higher than a man's head, which my friend dignified with the name of stacks. They were made in that form which left them as broad, if not broader, at the top than the bottom, and covered with sticks more likely to rot than keep them dry. As we approached the place, the cattle that had been regaling themselves among the stacks, at one end, took fright, and in their onward course roused a nestling of pigs which were burrowing under the ricks, at the other; instantly, all was in motion, and the scene became one of sufficient interest for a Hogarth's pencil. The cattle and pigs held on their course, scampering round and round, tossing, trampling, and destroying, till all was reduced to one common level; the ice floor covered with a foot or more of frozen grain, and that grain, mixed up with at least two feet of snow, dung, chaff, and straw, formed a melange scarcely to be described. With all this, the gravity of my friend never allowed him to change countenance; on the contrary, so familiar did he appear to be with such things, that he enjoyed a hearty laugh on seeing the cattle throw the squeaking pigs in the air, sagely remarking, indeed, "What we lose in wheat we will gain in pork." With such farmers, patronized so impartially by the Company, can it be matter of surprise that a universal cry was raised against the produce of Red River?

After clearing the yard of its unwelcome visitors, we

returned to the house, where we found two of my friend's sons (he had four or five, married and living about the place) rattling away at the fiddle. Instead of rebuking them for neglect, or complaining of the damage done in his corn-yard, he enjoyed the glee, remarking with an air of self satisfaction, that all the half-breeds had a great genius for music; and concluded by praising his own sons, for their skill on the violin. Having been an eye-witness of the general neglect of everything about his place, it was impossible to refrain from asking, why his sons, all young able men, did not keep things in better order?"

"Why," said he, "they take no interest in such matters, and besides, they are now off on their own account, and live by the plains. I have," continued he, " spent 2,000*l*. on them, chiefly in horses; and yet they are as poor as when they got the first shilling. Like their countrymen, they are above the drudgery of farming. They take no delight in cultivating the soil. Their thoughts, their ideas, their energies, are all limited to buffalo-hunting, fiddling, and horse-racing. They are now old enough to judge for themselves, and I allow them to take their own way. When I sow and reap the grain to their hand, they will not thrash it; when I thrash it, they will not take it to the mill; but when ground into flour and baked into bread, they will eat it. Generally speaking, all we do is to raise a little grain for the Company, for we use but little ourselves, preferring meat to bread." Here then is a picture, and would we could render it more like the strange reality, of a class whose very existence we can only deplore;

an honest straightforward man, settled in as fine a farming district on as rich a soil, and as easily cultivated, as heart could wish. I asked him if the Company took all his grain. " Yes," was his answer, " and they would take more if we had it to offer." The regular farmers always complained of this state of things in the colony, that the sound and healthy grain they raised should be invariably mixed up and confounded with the adulterated and poisonous trash produced by such people as the ice-barn farmers.

While the minds of the Scotch settlers were soured by the disappointments we have narrated, they were still without the advantage and consolation which might have been afforded them by a minister of their own persuasion. In our last remarks on this subject we noticed Mr. West's return home, and the arrival of the Reverend D. T. Jones as his successor and chaplain to the Company. As soon as the present troubled state of things in the colony, with reference to our agricultural pursuits, our farms, our produce and our precarious market began to subside, and the prospects of the people had become more settled and favourable, no time was lost in renewing the application for their long-expected pastor, and with a degree of more than usual confidence, arising from the fact that the colony had now fallen into the hands of the Company, who, as we were led to believe, were bound to see all Lord Selkirk's plans and promises carried into effect. This, at least, was what we heard rumoured abroad; for no direct intimation that such was the fact had reached us.

Our hopes, as usual, proved delusive, and the disappointment was aggravated by a circumstance which well nigh excited the worst passions, and did, in fact, create much bitterness of feeling. It was at this period that certain statements made by the Rev. Mr. Jones, and inserted in the "Missionary Register" of December 1827, first came to light in the colony. Speaking of the Scotch settlers at page 630, the reverend gentleman thus expresses himself: " I lament to say that there is an unchristian-like selfishness and narrowness of mind in our Scottish population; while they are the most comfortable in their circumstances of any class in our little community." And then, to heighten as it were the contrast, if not to disseminate the seeds of party feeling, he adds: "The Orkney Islanders are a far more promising and pleasing body of men: there is among them an identity of feeling and disposition; and the energy of their character is, in general, directed in a proper channel." Nay, to finish the picture thus begun, he further remarks: "The half-breeds, in particular, walk in simplicity and godly sincerity!" I have taken the liberty of annexing the note of admiration to the last sentence. Nor do I doubt but Mr. Jones found it a much easier task to dictate to Orkney Islanders, as he calls them, and half-breeds too, than to make stubborn Scotchmen change their creed.

There is, however, every allowance to be made for the Orkney men, and we may here explain the fact, why they never sincerely joined the Scotch in their applications to get a minister of their own persuasion. We have stated that the Orkney men came into the colony from the service, with Indian families, and there being no other Protestant church in Red River at the time but the Church of England, their families had, as a matter of course, to join the church that was, or join none; and being the first they had ever known, they perhaps did right in following it, and remaining within its pale in preference to any other. The Scotch settlers, on the contrary, had brought their religion into the country along with them—a religion as dear to them as their lives, and which they never could conscientiously change without abandoning their first faith. Hence the reason why they never could, nor would, become reconciled to the Church of England, notwithstanding they went to that church in the absence of their own.

If the Presbyterians were not sincerely attached to the Church of England before, they were less contented than ever after their knowledge of the censure thus passed upon them. In the midst of the stir it created they addressed an application to the Governor of the colony on the subject, which was graciously received; the people being told that an answer might be expected by the earliest opportunity. Thus encouraged, they were buoyed up with the most sanguine expectations, till the lapse of time proved to them how delusive and treacherous are the hopes which depend upon the good or ill-will of others. We did indeed receive an answer, but, as the nature of it will show, by an indirect way, and by mere chance. One of the members of the Church Missionary Society, writing to a gentleman in the settlement, let the cat out of the bag; for his letter, which accidentally fell into our hands, contained these expressions:—" Red River," said he, "is an English colony, and there are two English missionaries there already; and if the petitioners were not a set of canting hypocrites, they might very well be satisfied with the pious clergyman they have got." Such was the answer we finally received. Every man for himself in this charitable world. In the expressions of the pious gentleman who wrote the letter, we see the spirit of the dominant party, force riding rough-shod over justice.

The people were highly incensed at the manner in which they had been treated, and a second application through the same channel having failed, Governor McKenzie assembled the people at Fort Garry. Here great complaints were made, not only for want of a minister, but for the want of school teachers; nothing but the routine of church matters being attended to, and the children's time wasted at the sort of schools then in the settlement. At this public meeting, therefore, a petition was numerously signed for a minister of the Church of Scotland, and also for a schoolmaster, and placed in the hands of Mr. Governor McKenzie, by whom it was transmitted home: the fate of that petition was never known. In explanation of this we may observe that Mr. Jones and his satellites got up a counter petition, which was also sent to head-quarters, and probably achieved this brilliant triumph for them.

Before dismissing this subject, Christian charity obliges us to remark that the faults we have noticed were but slight in the character of a man like the Reverend Mr. Jones, who possessed many amiable qualities. After this little breeze with the Scotch settlers, he became extremely kind and indulgent to them, and among other things laid aside such parts of the Liturgy and formula of the Episcopalian Church as he knew were offensive to his Presbyterian hearers. He also held prayer-meetings among them after the manner of their own church, without using the prayer-book at all, which raised him higher than ever in their estimation, especially as they understood that he could only do so at the hazard of forfeiting his gown. His own words were:—" I know I am doing good; and as long as I can do good to souls, the technical forms of this or that church will not prevent me." Mr. Jones was a fine and eloquent preacher; tender-hearted, kind, and liberal to a fault. And so popular was he on account of the last-mentioned trait in his character, that he was all but idolized in Red River. Some time after he had gone home for the last time, one of the Scotch women happened to be passing the writer's house, just as the packet arrived from England.

" What news from home?" said honest Kate to me.

"Oh, nothing particular, madam," said I, "only I hear it reported that your old friend Mr. Jones is coming out again."

" Ah! God bless you for that news!" she exclaimed; and, whatever her thoughts were, she went on her way delighted.

Although the Scotch settlers did not succeed in getting out their minister, nor the Presbyterian party their schoolmaster; yet, so bold and unflinching was the language in which these two capital grievances were set forth, that the great folks both in church and state began to take the alarm, and great efforts were made in behalf of schools throughout the settlement. The drawling system gave way to plans for the introduction of a more healthy and vigorous course of instruction. Even boarding-schools, and an academy for the higher branches of education, Latin, Greek, and the mathematics, were warmed into existence; all quite new things in Red River. It is not uncommon for people with but little experience to leap from one extreme to another, and so it happened in this case. The Presbyterian party derived but little benefit, either directly or indirectly, from these measures, notwithstanding they were the result of their own efforts. It is almost needless to say they were too poor to avail themselves of the advantages held out by the boarding-schools, and of too low birth and fortune for the high school, as that seminary was exclusively provided for the children of Governors, Deputy-Governors, and chief Factors, the great nabobs of the fur trade.

CHAPTER XII.

CONTENTS.—Governor Simpson—Second experimental farm—Experimental farms in general—The establishment—Ample means—The fur-trade farmer—Mongrel servants—Experience disregarded—The sheep speculation—Great projects—Small results—The wolves rejoicing—The humbug—The flax and hemp project—The premiums—The farmers in motion—Strange policy—The Governor's disappointment—The trick—The favourites—The little monopoly—The buildings—Fort Garry—Episcopalians versus Presbyterians—General remarks—The Scotch in Red River.

THE failure of the wheat experiment was not sufficient to deter Governor Simpson from trying other means to render the produce of Red River acceptable, and, indeed, to raise its character. His desire now, was to establish another experimental farm, at the Company's sole expense, with the view of initiating the settlers, and particularly the natives of the country, into an improved system of husbandry and dairy management, the cultivation of hemp, flax, and whatever else might interest the farmer, and ensure a steady market for the fruits of his industry.

The chosen site of the " new experimental farm," for so this grand undertaking was designated, was a rich and fertile spot on the Assiniboine river. Here houses of every description were erected. First, a princely dwelling, then barns, corn-yards, and stables; and, at last, parks and enclosures were formed. With regard to stock, cows of the best breed were purchased. A stallion was imported from England, to improve the breed of horses, at a cost of some 300*l.* sterling; and breeding mares got from the United States, also at a great expense. Servants, both men and women, were provided, to fill every station. Implements of husbandry were collected in profusion. The most costly ploughs, harrows, drills, and whatever else could be thought of, down to the milk-pail, and the axe-handle, as well as seeds of all kinds, were imported; so that no expense was spared to ensure success. An experiment thus provided for ought to have succeeded; but we regret to say that the subsequent arrangements were not so happily adjusted. The practical farmer was still wanting, and that want deranged the whole machinery.

The choice of a manager to carry out this princely design fell on a gentleman of the fur trade; a man of the most zealous, active, and persevering character in all that he was acquainted with; but in no wise qualified to conduct farming operations, even on the smallest scale, far less on a large one, where science as well as industry were required. The appointment of Mr. Chief Factor Mc Millan was the more to be regretted, as, among the Scotch emigrants, there were not a few who had a good practical knowledge of such things; but this was not the sole mistake. The servants appointed to the farm were, for the most part, half-breeds of the country, and knew little more of agriculture than the wild Indian of the plains. Their extent of the skill consisted in having seen wheat, barley, and potatoes raised, and that in the simplest and rudest manner. The dairy, and the process of making butter and cheese, were absolutely new to them. System was never dreamt of; and the want of system ruined all.

As to the flax and hemp, both grew luxuriantly; but after growing, were neglected, and allowed to rot: not a pound of either ever realized a shilling to the settlement. In fine, the most common grain raised at the experimental farm was inferior, both as to quality and quantity, to that raised by the humblest Scotch settler in the colony. The thousands that were lavished away on this scheme, from beginning to end, were rendered nugatory by the foolish desire of placing a favourite in a comfortable situation. After six years' trial, when the whole was sold off, the dead loss to the Company amounted to 3,500*l.* sterling. Indeed, it was the general opinion at the time, that had the truth been told, the actual loss would have more than doubled this sum.

The Governor was never reconciled to the failure of this favourite scheme; for he had hoped it would be the beginning of a happy era in the settlement. It was his excellency's hobby, and on learning the result, he exclaimed, " Red River is like a Lybian tiger: the more we try to tame it, the more savage it becomes. So it is with Red River; for every step I try to bring it forward, disappointments drag it two backward!" Still the colony derived some collateral advantages from the attempt; for example, the breed of horses was decidedly improved. Such a failure did, perhaps, more harm in a country like Red River, than it would have done in any other; it gave such a contemptible idea of the skill of the white man. It became a by-word in the colony, among the half-breed population, "that the ice-barn farmers were bad, but the experimental farmers were worse; and, after all their grand performances, the whites have but little to boast of."

While the Company were at work in their experimental farm, the colonists, no less eager on their part to follow the example, set their heads and hearts together, and became enamoured of a sheep speculation. This project was announced as a joint-stock association, to be called the "Assiniboine Wool Company," a project still more extravagant, not to say foolish, than the Buffalo Wool Company, described in a previous chapter. The thing in itself, indeed, was not unreasonable; but the manner in which it was to have been carried into effect, was wild in the extreme. The proposed capital of this novel concern was 6,000*l*. sterling, divided into 1,200 shares of 5*l*. each—a sum three times greater than all the money in circulation in the settlement, which, at this time, did not exceed 1,900*l*. The operations of the Company were perfectly simple. The sum thus raised was to be laid out in the purchase of sheep, either in England or the United States; the flocks being kept and increased in Red River till they amounted to thousands, and tens of thousands; or, in other words, till the plains groaned under their numbers. The wool thus raised was to form an article of export, and higher expectations were not excited, even by the gold mines of California.

The introduction of sheep, as a branch of rural economy, had it been on anything like a moderate scale, would have been a laudable undertaking, the policy of which no one was prepared to deny; for so far we had to buy everything, and sell nothing; but that men should risk their all, the last shilling they possessed, in a doubtful and uncertain speculation, be it what it might, was certainly, to give it the mildest term, not only a foolish, but a mad scheme; while, at the time, a servant could scarcely be found in the colony to keep a cow, far less sheep, which must have become the prey of wolves, had the money been found for introducing them into the country. This, however, was the very thing that could not be done. Everything went on agreeably till the shareholders were called upon for their money, when the more sagacious among them began to calculate the chances in their favour. This the scheme would not bear, and the wolves were disappointed. After occupying the public mind, and amusing the public ear for more than a twelvemonth, the project was abandoned, in favour of another, which, as we shall presently see, ended in a similar result.

The new project, like the experimental farm, was a child of the Governor's own brain; for he was determined, cost what it would, to drag Red River into notice, one way or other; and it is sincerely to be regretted, that his policy and views were not in many respects backed and supported with more zeal and perseverance on the part of others. But, unfortunately, there was in all our undertakings and councils, a poisonous mixture of petty jealousy, the jarring elements of peevish little minds—men fond of talking, but seldom of active business habits; and these not pulling together, never failed to frustrate the best intentions of the Governor. His present proposal arose from his wish to divert the efforts of the people from the over-production of grain, for which there was no adequate market, into a more advantageous channel. His choice fell upon flax and hemp, for promoting the cultivation of which, on a large scale, with a view to exportation, certain premiums were announced to be continued for three years in succession.

The people of Red River grasp at everything new, as a hawk pounces on a bird, and then abandon it as easily, without waiting with patience for the anticipated result; but their interest was redoubled on the present occasion, by the prospect of a double reward. The premium, to speak truth, on the present occasion, was the great point with them, and flax and hemp but secondary considerations; not the end regarded, but the means to a more selfish one. Every man, accordingly, prepared himself for the new experiment, or rather for the premiums. The Scotch settlers, the ice-barn farmers, the plain hunters, the lake frequenters, the squatters, all were moved by one impulse.

The simple facts we have to relate will prove that this charge of cupidity is not over stated. The low loamy valleys along the banks of the Red River are peculiarly adapted for the growth of flax; and for the three years the premiums were awarded, favourable crops were produced, and the flax, after the different processes of growing, steeping, rotting, bleaching, and drying, was pronounced excellent, even of first quality; and these were the only operations required: to those, therefore, who excelled, the premiums were given. After the production of these specimens, incredible as it may appear, the flax was left from year to year to rot, like dung, upon the ground. The premiums being paid, no further notice was taken of the produce; and when ceased to be given, the flax was no longer grown.

There was another and most iniquitous feature in the working of this scheme, which deserves mention. The quantity of flax seed in the colony, at the time the premiums were offered, was very small; and before the scarcity was generally known, every ounce of it was bought up, and came into the possession of a favourite few, by the connivance of those in power. Those who got the seed, got the premiums too, as a matter of course. This was the case for the first year. Nor would the producers sell or part with an ounce of the seed to anyone else, even the second year; no money that could be offered would purchase a grain of it; and so the favourite few got the premiums the second year also; and so they did the third, even to the end of the chapter.

With the hemp it fared precisely the same as with the flax. The favoured few who contrived to monopolize the one, monopolized the other, and would have made a handsome property of it, had it lasted long enough. The soil of Red River produces as good hemp as can be grown in any country, rich and luxuriant. In alluvial ground it succeeds best, and our short hot summers seem to favour the growth of that coarse but tender plant exceedingly well. Most of it grew to the height of six feet nine or ten inches; but the moment the premiums expired, the hemp, like the flax, expired also. The whole crop was allowed to rot. Thus was added another item to the catalogue of our failures, without the least benefit to the settlement generally. Besides the spectacle of flax and hemp rotting in the fields, a costly flax-mill, finished and in working order, might be seen standing idle, because no one persevered in the work to which he had set his hand.

Tired by the endless repetition of delusive and vexatious experiments, which have resulted, one and all, in fruitless disappointment, we turn to the more solid subject of stone and lime. In Red River, as in Canada, and most other new countries, the people, for a long time, contented themselves with what are called wooden houses, of such humble appearance as might be expected where means are low, workmen scarce, and wages at a high rate. The cost of such houses depends on a variety of circumstances; but the average may be taken at 60*l.* sterling. These frame buildings, simple, yet commodious and comfortable, differ in size as in cost, but are seldom more than thirty feet in length, or less than twenty; the other dimensions being of corresponding proportion. A superior class of dwellings have shingled roofs, stone foundations, windows, doors and partitions paneled and painted, and the walls rough-cast with lime. One of this description, forty or fifty feet long, and well finished, will cost 300*l.* Such was the cost of one built for the writer; but it was the best in the settlement of its size. Of late, a decided improvement in the character of our wooden buildings has become manifest. Several are of two stories high, some with galleries, and two ornamented with verandas. Taste, as well as convenience, begins to receive its due share of consideration; the luxury of glass windows, and a lock on the outer door, things hitherto scarcely known in Red River, have become fashionable, indeed, almost general. Such houses, white as snow, look well, and have a very gay appearance.

The more solid structures of stone and lime are also, in some few instances, beginning to be introduced by the Company; and this, at no distant time, will be resorted to generally, as wood is becoming scarce, even for fuel. In the upper part of the settlement, where wood may still be got, stone is not to be found; but in other places, towards the lower end, limestone quarries are abundant. Lime was made here as early as the time of Governor Bulger; but the article was only used for practical purposes, such as building and the whitewashing of houses, very lately. The first instance was at the building of a small powder-magazine, erected by the Company at Upper Fort Garry, in 1830. This magazine claims the proud distinction of being the first stone and lime building in the colony.

In the year following, the Company commenced building on an elevated spot, at the head of the sloop navigation, twenty miles below the forks—being half way between the latter place and Lake Winipeg—an establishment of stone and lime, on a large scale, intended as a stronghold and safe retreat from any foreign enemy, or the destructive visitation of high water—should such a catastrophe ever occur again. This establishment, called "Lower Fort Garry," covers about as much ground as St. Paul's Cathedral, in London. The fort is square, and built on a rock or limestone quarry, surrounded by a stone wall, and protected by four round towers or bastions. It was at first designed as the seat of Government, and the Company's head depôt; but that intention has been relinquished in favour of "Upper Fort Garry," situated about 400 yards above the confluence of the Assiniboine and Red River, in latitude 49° 53' north, and longitude 97° west; a situation more central than the former, and certainly better adapted both for the defence and the transaction of business pertaining to the colony.

This fort has therefore been rebuilt on a more elevated site than it formerly occupied, and on an improved plan. Its form is nearly square, being about 280 feet from east to west, and 240 from north to south. It is surrounded by a stone wall of 15 feet high, and of considerable thickness; having two large gates on the north and south sides, and four round towers or blockhouses at each corner, with port and loop holes for cannon and musketry. In the inside of the wall is a gallery which runs round the fort, and which affords a pleasant walk, and an extensive view of the surrounding country. The principal dwelling-house—a large and commodious building—occupies the centre of the square, behind which, and near the northern gate, stand the flagstaff and belfry. There are also houses within the walls, for the accommodation of the officers and men attached to the fort; together with stores and granaries, and—would it were not necessary to add—a jail and court-house for the colony. It is a neat and compact establishment, and reflects great credit on Mr. Governor Christie, under whose eye the work was accomplished.

These splendid establishments, for such they really are in a place like Red River, impart an air of growing importance to the place. Upper Fort Garry, the seat of the colony Governor, is a lively and attractive station, full of business and bustle. Here all the affairs of the colony are chiefly transacted, and here ladies wear their silken gowns, and gentlemen their beaver hats. Its gay and imposing appearance makes it the delight of every visitor; the rendezvous of all comers and goers. Lower Fort Garry is more secluded, although picturesque, and full of rural beauty. Here the Governor of Rupert's Land resides, when he passes any time in the colony. To those of studious and retired habits, it is preferred to the upper fort.

While speaking of architectural subjects, we shall be excused departing a little from chronological order to mention, that at the date we are writing, the colony boasts of two Protestant churches, and a Roman Catholic cathedral, built of stone. Two or three handsome stone houses have also been erected by the Scotch settlers, which may be regarded as unmistakeable indications of prosperity—a prosperity dearly purchased by years of trouble and patient endurance. We might say more, but it is useless to be continually repeating the story of wrongs, which now perhaps can never be remedied. The first ten years of their sojourn in the colony, the Scotch emigrants were almost the only settlers; the next ten years they were the majority; but the last ten, they have been the minority; and, by a combination of untoward circumstances, they can hardly now be said to retain their nationality, being as a mere fraction in the mass of the community. It is as if they had come to Red River merely to endure its hardships, and as trusty pioneers to bear the heat and burden of the day, where a people of less hardihood and perseverance must necessarily have succumbed.

CHAPTER XIII.

CONTENTS.—The windmill—Its history—Red River windmills—The watermill—The dam operations—Keg of rum—The contented master—Men at work—Result—New sheep speculation—Governor Simpson—Contractors—Broils—Going the wrong way to work—Paying for one's folly—The deadly grass—The effect—Marking the road to St. Peter's—The vote of thanks indoors—Murmuring out-doors—Result—Tallow trade—Object—The wolves—Winding up—General remarks—Winter road—The object—Result.

WE have noticed the progress of the building art, and the public edifices of the colony. The eye of the stranger would have been arrested also by the great number of windmills in the neighbourhood. One of these was sent out as a model by Lord Selkirk in the early period of the settlement; it had cast rollers, and machinery capable of working two pairs of stones, but for years no one was found able to set it in operation. It was even sent back to England and re-shipped. At length, ten years after its first arrival in the colony, Lord Selkirk's executors sent out one Mitchel, a millwright, from Scotland, expressly to set it in order, by whose exertions it commenced working in 1825, having cost altogether no less than 1,500*l.*; soon afterwards it was sold to Mr. Logan, a gentleman in the colony, for a fifth part of that sum, and he, having some knowledge of machinery himself, turned the mill to good account, especially as it remained for several years the only one in the settlement. It is going still, and ranks among the best in Red River. During the year of the flood its strong and lofty pillar resisted the high water, and afforded protection to many who sought shelter within its walls.

All the other windmills were made with the materials of the country, iron only excepted, and finished by the workmen of the settlement, at an average cost, everything included, of 150*l.* sterling. Their ingenuity has been equally successful in the construction of watermills, the first of which was built on Sturgeon Creek, a small tributary of the Assiniboine, nearly midway between the Forks and the White Horse Plains, by Mr. Grant, chief of the half-breeds, a gentleman who has already been mentioned in our history. To tell the truth, the history of the first water-wheel bears a very striking resemblance to that of the first windmill. The attempt was suggested by Mr. Logan's success with the windmill when it came into his possession. Stimulated by the prospect of gain, and fond of notoriety, Mr. Grant began the construction of a dam from bank to bank across the creek, a distance of some 240 feet, without considering that a man might be a good huntsman, and, at the same time, a very indifferent millwright. In due course the dam was made, the mill built, and the stores for grain finished; but the mill, after several trials, gave but little satisfaction—the dam still less. It gave way—gave way a second time—a third—a hundred times—gave way altogether: it was no longer a dam! At last the mill gave way also, and in less than three years all was abandoned, leaving Mr. Grant minus 800*l.* sterling. Everyone regretted the failure as a loss to the public, and still more on account of the projector himself, who was, on the whole, a generous and good-hearted fellow.

The history of Red River may be said to turn on a series of speculations. Notwithstanding the failure of his flax and hemp project, the Governor was still possessed with a desire to advance the interests of the colony, and at this period he again turned his attention to the introduction of sheep, which was always one of his most favourite designs. To this end he proposed the formation of a joint-stock association, in order to raise the sum of 1,200*l.*, to be laid out in the purchase of sheep from the United States, a plan which was embraced with great readiness, and the money as promptly raised. The Governor, on his part, generously offered to send Mr. Rae, a gentleman of the fur company, along with the adventurers, to superintend the business, and see the sheep brought safe to Red River; with him was associated, on the part of the colonists, Mr. Bourke, who has already been introduced to the notice of the reader, and the dissensions of these two leaders, as we shall see, ruined the undertaking.

These gentlemen, with only four men, crossed the wide desert to St. Peter's late in the fall of the year. From St. Peter's their course was directed to St. Louis, and from thence through the state of Missouri, where it was expected the sheep would be purchased, in which case the return home would have been comparatively easy. Here, however, the leaders quarrelled. Mr. Rae was young, high-minded, active, and full of enterprise, but destitute of the experience which qualified his sagacious and equally stubborn colleague, whose haughty and overbearing demeanour was more than he could brook. The occasion of their rupture was as follows. On arriving in Missouri, the price of sheep was found to be from 5s. to 7s. 6d. a head; but not being much of a sheep country, the people were so ill-advised as to demand of our travellers an advanced price of 10s. per head, it being rumoured abroad that they wanted as many sheep, perhaps, as the King of Moab rendered to the Israelites. Mr. Rae took offence at this attempt at extortion, as he considered it; and though the sheep were afterwards offered at 7s. 6d. a head, he refused to deal with the Missourians, and was resolved to push on for Kentucky, a further distance of 450 miles. Remonstrance was in vain. To all that Mr. Bourke could urge on the score of increased difficulty in the transport of the flocks, and other probabilities of mischance, Mr. Rae only whistled a reply, and went on his ill-starred course. After this little outbreak, Bourke scarcely interfered in the management of affairs during the whole journey.

After a variety of adventures and loss of time, the party reached Kentucky, where the price of sheep differed but little from that of the Missouri, being from 5s. to 7s. a head. Here the number required was completed, say 1,475. But on their way back, as Mr. Bourke had remarked, they had to pay for pasture and keep every night, and not unfrequently during the day, losing many sheep after all. On their way up the Mississippi, another instance of their good management transpired. At a certain place they halted to clip or shear the sheep, and agreed with a person to give him all the wool at a stipulated price. The following day, at an hour fixed upon, the money was to have been paid, and the wool delivered; but the individual not being able to raise the full amount agreed upon, the wool was ordered to be burnt on the spot, rather than sold for a cent less than the price bargained for. In the mean time a number of poor people had collected about the place, and made several offers for the wool, according to their means; their offers, however, falling short of the original valuation, were rejected with scorn, and the wool burnt.

By the time our friends got back to St. Peter's with their flock, they might, had they purchased on the Missouri, have been in Red River. The season was not only far advanced, but the weather excessively hot; and, under any circumstances, a journey of 1,500 miles must have been very trying for the poor sheep, who are so much the more difficult to manage, as they want that instinctive apprehension of danger so peculiar to the deer and goat species. Nor were the actual dangers of the way of a trifling nature. As the party advanced over trackless prairies, they had to force their way through oceans of thick and long grass, where a spark from a pipe, or the wad of a gun, would have sealed their doom. These parts likewise abound in a sort of grass, which, in its ripe state, has barbed and prickly points, like ears of barley; with these the sheep's hides got literally full, and by the action of walking, they even penetrated their bodies, and caused death. The destructive effects of this fatal grass, aided by fatigue and forced marching, caused the sheep to give up by tens and by twenties every day.

It is sickening to relate, that every sheep which gave up was doomed to have its throat cut, by order of the chiefs who had been so unhappily trusted with their safety. In one morning only, while the party were at breakfast, the bloody knife settled the account of forty-four on one spot! Every now and then one or other of the men had to ride up to the conductor, who kept a long way ahead, with the news that so many of the sheep had given up. "Cut their throats and drive on," was the reply, without ever stopping or turning round his head. And although harassed with fatigue, as well as disabled by the cause we have alluded to, an hour or two of rest was denied them. The managers were infatuated with the determination to get back with all possible speed to Red River, without the least regard to the lives of the sheep—nay, for one yard in advance, it mattered not if ten of those innocent lives were sacrificed. After all the cost and trouble, —when out of danger as we may say, and just on the eve of arriving,—these scenes of cruelty were persisted in, till at last, the men themselves becoming disgusted with the task, refused to use the knife any more; and the officials had to perform the delicate office themselves,

At length, early in the autumn, and long before the fall weather set in, the party reached Red River, their flock reduced to 251 in number, of which many died after their arrival. From St. Peter's to Red River the road was marked for future travellers by upwards of 1,200 carcases.

Notwithstanding the facts we have stated, the committee of management presented the two leaders of the expedition with a cordial and unanimous vote of thanks. The voice of the colonists was universally against them, and a vote of censure was demanded; but the Governor's pride was wounded, and without yielding to these murmurs, he brought the matter to a close by returning the people's money.

The next scheme projected by the Governor, who was as anxious as ever to promote the welfare of the colony, appeared to most people moderate, reasonable, and promising. It was another joint-stock concern, to be called the "Tallow Company." Its capital was to consist of 1,000*l*., divided into two hundred shares of 5*l*. each. The affairs were to be managed by a chairman and six directors. The shares, to the amount subscribed, were paid up at once in cattle, and six shares qualified any subscriber to be a director. The general principle of taking in cattle was their age— none taken under one, nor above five years old. Those of a year old were valued at 1*l*., two years old at 2*l*., three years old at 3*l*., and so on. The whole herd consisted of 473 head. The Governor, in a clear and lucid speech, recited the advantages that would accrue to the settlement from such an undertaking, if conducted with energy and judgment. The rich pastures and extensive range of plains in the colony and neighbourhood, led to a universal belief that cattle, in any numbers, like the wild buffalo of the prairies, might be raised, as in some parts of New South Wales, without the aid or trouble of hand-feeding in winter; grazing and stock, it was thought, might be increased to any extent, and tallow and hides become valuable as articles of export. The wild herbage and grasses which grow spontaneously everywhere throughout the boundless plains, far and near, were deemed equal to any wild pasture in the world; and in this view the bleakness and dreariness of the climate in our case was entirely overlooked.

The cattle, in fine, were received, branded with the initials T. T., signifying Tallow Trade, and, on the last of April, conveyed to a place of pasture some ten miles out of the settlement, along the pine hills, and placed under the care of two herdsmen. On the 6th of May there fell about eighteen inches of snow—a circumstance rather unusual at that advanced season. This fall of snow was followed by some very cold and stormy weather, and there being at the time scarcely any grass, twenty-six head died through cold and hunger—rather a discouraging circumstance at the beginning. In the earliest seasons there is no shoot in the grass before the 10th of May, and in late seasons it is the 20th or the 1st of June before the cattle can feed. During the summer, however, they did as well as could be expected, and the undertaking was viewed favourably by the colonists.

At the same time the cattle were not left to shift entirely for themselves during the bleak weather, but hay was provided for them, and a few roofless stockyards railed in for keeping them together at night, or rather preserving them from the wolves. Their average allowance was a third of the quantity of hay usually given to cattle regularly housed and fed; yet with all this care, the cold of forty-five below zero was too much for them. While pent up they kept as close together for warmth as sheep in a fold, and generally passed the night standing; hence, when turned out in the mornings, they were so benumbed with cold that they could scarcely walk, and of course were utterly unable to procure their food in deep snows during the day. In this half-dead-and-alive manner they passed the first winter, during which time thirty-two died of cold. The ears, horns, hoofs, and tails of many of them froze and fell off, and the cows lost their teats; besides which, fifty-three were killed by the wolves. Total loss the first year, 111. The carelessness of the herdsmen, perhaps, greatly contributed to this disaster; but the greatest share in it may fairly be attributed to the wolves, the dread of whose ravages led to the cattle being cooped up together in a torpid state all night.

During the second year of this experiment, the cattle were removed to a new and better grazing ground, at a greater distance from the settlement, and, withal, more sheltered. In place of roofless enclosures, sheds were built, and as much hay provided as they could eat; fresh herdsmen were also engaged, and the cattle were driven under shelter every night. As a further precaution against neglect, it was arranged that each director in his turn should visit the cattle at weekly periods; the Governor himself was the first to set the example, but some of our great men never once went to see them; and yet those were the very men who talked loudest at meetings—had most plans in their heads—the first to speak, the last to act. Under this defective system, the cold killed, during the second winter, sixteen, and the wolves twenty of our stock.

Finally it was arranged that the superintendence of the business should be vested in one director, and the appointment fell on the writer, who must confess that the task proved no sinecure. No plan, however, could be devised to prevent the destructive ravages of the wolves; the people were discouraged by every fresh loss, and the business, by mutual consent, was given up. The herd was then disposed of by auction; and as the proceeds fell short of the amount put in by 137*l.*, the Company paid this amount to the shareholders, whose only sacrifice was the interest of their money. The loss on the undertaking, however, could not have been less than 1,000*l.* sterling. The bones of the tallow cattle will mark their grazing ground for years to come.

One failure often causes another. During the progress of the various undertakings we have noticed, all entered upon with a view to produce some article of export, the Company, as sanguine as the colonists themselves, were busy in opening a winter road between Red River and York Factory. This road was formed by cutting down and clearing away the timber along the most direct line of communication, a tedious and costly undertaking, which, however, was attempted. The object was to facilitate winter travelling along the lakes and woods, and establish stations or resting places where hay, water, and shelter could be most conveniently obtained; also to shorten as much as possible the length of the land carriage, which it would have done by a hundred miles. In consequence of the failure of all the speculations we have described, this road, after the heavy cost it had entailed upon the Company, was abandoned as being, if not impracticable, more costly than the conveyance of goods by water.

CHAPTER XIV.

CONTENTS.—The petty trader—Change of men and change of measures—The rich and the poor—The shopping confusion—Steer a middle course—Company's tariff—Great promisers small performers—A petty trader behind his counter—Competition—Hints—The fur trade—Remarks—Indians—The awkward Cree question—Useful hints—Alarm—Patrols—The Saulteaux in Red River—Guns pointed—Mr. Simpson—General remarks—Sioux visits—Wannatah—Half-breeds—Physical demonstrations—Demagogues at work—Manœuvring—First-rank men—Results.

WE have now arrived at the year 1834, making ten years since the affairs of the colony were entrusted to the Company's officers acting for Lord Selkirk. Until then the practice had been, as shown in a former part of this history, to supply goods on credit; but now a ready-money system was introduced, the effect of which was to curtail the supply of goods to nearly one-half of the quantity formerly brought into the colony, in order to correspond with the amount of money in circulation. Consequently goods became all at once very scarce; and the sales being restricted to certain stated days, increased the evil. It was a time of rejoicing for the rich and of mourning for the poor, as the shops were emptied by those who had money at command before the poorer colonists could obtain half their supplies. The evil was greatly increased by the crowds of people collected from all parts of the settlement at the opening of the shops on the appointed days. To be in time, people travelled all night, and the rush in the morning to get admittance could only be checked by locked doors and a guard, and sometimes the guard would be knocked down and trampled under foot. Many had to dance attendance for days and nights together, cold, wet, and hungry; and at last return home, perhaps a distance of twenty miles, without obtaining their supplies.

The distress and confusion of this system had lasted for several years, when a few private individuals resolved on importing supplies for themselves; and this becoming the rage, at length every man who could muster twenty shillings became an importer. The Company, through their new Colonial Governor, Mr. Christie, who about this time succeeded Mr. McKenzie in the charge of the colony, afforded every facility to this new class of traders, allowing individuals to bring out what they pleased in the Company's ships, at the rate of 8*l.* per ton; storage and agency at the port of York Factory free. Thus encouraged, they who commenced by importing for themselves soon enlarged the field of enterprise, and sent for goods on speculation, obtaining for them money, produce, or labour, according to circumstances, but generally all upon credit. This little accommodating system, commenced at the right time, gradually diffused much comfort throughout the settlement, and gave a happy spur to industry and enterprise, as it afforded the settlers the means of obtaining supplies from the petty traders, which the Company's ready-money system denied. The first adventurers did uncommonly well; for when the Company's shops were empty they raised their prices, and made a good business of it. The corrupt system of taking advantage, however, could not last.

Repeated complaints were addressed to the Company, urging them to bring out a more ample supply of goods, which at length had the desired effect; their shops were kept full of goods all the year round, at the usual rate of 75 per cent. on the London prices. This new turn of affairs was severely felt by the petty traders, who raised a hue and cry against the Company, and accused them of a wish to monopolize all the trade in goods, as they did in furs. After all, the change has proved for their advantage, as it obliged them to contract the credit system, and eventually to sell their goods, like the Company, for ready money only. Since that change things go on much better; the petty traders are now doing a good share of business, live comfortably, and many of them have saved considerable sums of money.

We have now to trace upwards to the period at which we have arrived, another influence to which the colony was subject—that of the Indian tribes, who belong more immediately to the soil and neighbourhood. The colony, as already remarked, is not only a mere dot on the mighty map of the universe, but a dot on the map of Hudson's Bay: a mere speck, an isolated spot in the midst of a benighted wilderness, just entering on the career of civilization. It was only to be expected that a handful of civilized men thus set down in the midst of a savage population would be subject to considerable annoyance, either from their visits or their threats; yet the truth is, these tribes have given the colonists but little cause of complaint. It cannot, indeed, be denied that the settlers have passed many anxious nights and days in consequence of the proximity of such a people; but whatever danger may have existed, it has been diminishing in proportion as the whites have increased in numbers. At the present time, we may observe, the conduct of the savages generally—with only one exception, in fact—has but little influence on the colony either for good or evil. It will not be uninteresting, however, to speak more in detail.

The chief Indian tribes who inhabit this quarter, and who occasionally visit, and sometimes annoy the colony, are the Crees and Assiniboines on the west, the Saulteaux on the east, the swampy Crees on the north, and the proud and haughty Sioux on the south. All these are more or less friendly. The last-named has been for ages past the most warlike and powerful nation east of the Rocky Mountains—perhaps, at the present day, on the continent; but their physical condition is fast changing. They are now divided into many separate tribes and families, and every division weakens the national stem; their power is on the decrease, their progress is westward. They are, nevertheless, still formidable, and can, when united, muster 2,000 warriors.

But, paradoxical as it may appear, the greatest annoyance to the settlers has proceeded from the tribe most friendly to the whites, namely, the Crees on the west. To explain this is not difficult. The Cree nation always claimed Red River as their lands; but Lord Selkirk having found on the soil some Saulteaux as well as Crees, gave them an interest in the treaty, though, as they acknowledge to this day, they had no right to the lands, being originally foreigners. Errors of this kind cannot always be avoided, and the mistake having been made, the Saulteaux claim a sort of prescriptive right, rendered as valid, by mere lapse of time, as that of the Crees themselves. The latter, thus provoked, threaten to expel their rivals from Red River altogether, and the whites along with them, unless the names of the Saulteaux chiefs are expunged from the compact, and the annual payment be made to the Crees only. This matter, unless amicably settled, may one day cause much trouble, if not bloodshed; indeed, we have seen the whole settlement in an uproar more than once on this very account. It has even proceeded so far that the settlers, excited with fear, have sought refuge in the Company's forts; nay, we have seen the police and settlers too armed, and sent on scouting parties to scour the settlement from end to end, and watch for days and nights, in consequence of the threats held out by the Crees. Would it not, then, be an act of wisdom in the colonial authorities to remove this grievance, especially as the whole cost for its final settlement would not exceed at most 100*l.*? The settlers will be justified in not accepting their title-deeds until the question is set at rest, and their property secure.

We more than glanced at the character of the Saulteaux in the first chapter of this work. They are a turbulent and revengeful people. Many of them abide in the colony from one end of the year to the other, not as hunters, nor as labourers, but as vagrants and evil-doers; they beg, roam about, and annoy the settlers. To some of them the benefits of education have been extended; and yet, though fed, clothed, and nursed by the benevolent hand of charity, they are, after all, the most debased, vicious, and criminal of all the tribes. Nay, those who have received the benefits of instruction are, unfortunately, the worst. There are instances of their having been condemned for murder; they have been imprisoned for manslaughter; they have been whipped for cattle-killing, and punished in various ways for theft and robbery. They have violated, time after time, engagements, broken contracts, set the police at defiance, and menaced the civil power; and yet they are but a handful, and that handful still allowed to infest the settlement, and often to live at the expense of the industrious settler.

The Sioux are a bold and numerous race, whose very name has been the terror of every other nation. They are inhabitants of the open plains. War is their profession; horses, guns, and hunting, their delight. They occupy and claim, as their field of chase, all that extensive region lying between Pembina on the north and St. Peter's on the south, the centre of their lands being perhaps 300 miles distant from this colony. They are light, slender men, quick as thought in their motions, expert runners, fine horsemen, shy as the wolf, wild as the buffalo. In general they know nothing of the luxuries of life, but at Lake Travers a portion of them have lately been brought within the limits of civilization. Their improvement is encouraging, and it is to be hoped that something permanent will be effected for their good.

Distant as these Indians are situated, they frequently visit the colony. Their paramount object is generally curiosity and a romantic love of adventure, backed sometimes by the desire of gain; for in this country, it is customary, in addition to a welcome reception, to bestow on all strange Indians a few trifling presents. For a savage to travel a hundred miles, perhaps through an enemy's country, ostensibly in quest of a little tobacco or a few loads of ammunition, but really for the fame of the achievement, is a very common occurrence; and as soon as the adventurer gets back to his tribe, it is just as common for him to distribute freely the fruits of his daring among his friends and countrymen. It is not, according to Indian ideas, exactly the value of the articles, but to show his heroic courage, his daring hardihood, that he travels. All such adventures are associated with the national glory, and are rehearsed on all public occasions to stimulate others to imitate the example. An orator always commences his public harangues by running over such incidents, reminding his auditory of some glorious deed, some bold adventure. " Remember," he will say, " when such a scalp was taken, when such a foe fell under our tomahawks, when such a daring spirit eluded his enemies, travelled through their country, and brought us tobacco to smoke and ammunition to load our guns. Friends! imitate the glorious example."

Mr. Simpson, in his narrative, notices two visits from the Sioux during his residence in the colony in 1834 and 1836. On the first occasion, "A party of six-and-thirty men, headed by a daring chief, called the Burning Earth, arrived at Fort Garry. All went on pleasantly," Mr. Simpson relates, "till the evening, when a large party of Saulteaux galloped suddenly into the court. They were completely armed, and breathed fury and revenge, having lost forty of their relatives by an attack of the Sioux a year or two before. We instantly stationed a strong guard for the defence of the strangers, who had thrown themselves on our hospitality. The great difficulty now was how to get the strangers safely home again. We supplied them with provisions, some tobacco, clothing, and ammunition. . . . Perisien and his half-breeds undertook to conduct the Sioux safely out into the open plains, where they might set their bush-fighting foes at defiance. The party had no sooner crossed the river than a number of the Saulteaux threw themselves into their canoes on the Assiniboine, a little distance above, with a view to intercept their retreat. Observing this manœuvre, I ran towards them, followed by Mr. McKinlay and a few others, and, levelling our guns at the men in the canoes, ordered them to turn back. They angrily complied, when the principal man, seeing we were but a handful, began to vent threats against us; but a party opportunely riding up to our assistance, we carried the old fellow with us to the establishment, and his followers dispersed." This is

Mr. Simpson's account of the first visit, on which we have a few observations to offer.

First, " Perisien and his half-breeds undertook to conduct the Sioux." The number who crossed over the Assiniboine to escort the Sioux under Perisien was fifty-seven, making, with the Indians, ninety-three armed men. Indeed, seven or eight guns were all that remained among nearly 200 persons after the people crossed over, while more than a hundred Saulteaux, all armed *cap-à-pie*, stood in a group alongside of us.

Secondly, " The party had no sooner crossed the river." As soon as the Sioux landed on the opposite bank, twelve of the Saulteaux embarked in three small Indian canoes to cross over and have a parting peep at them; a movement, under all circumstances, not thought worthy of notice at the time till it derived importance from a foolish and imprudent act on our part. Viewing the Saulteaux' intention in a wrong light, Mr. Simpson and Mr. McKinlay, to render themselves more conspicuous than others, heedlessly " ran towards them, and pointing their guns at the men in the canoe, ordered them to turn back," or they would fire on them. The uncalled-for threat surprised and alarmed everyone present. Our people were thunderstruck, and called out, " Don't fire! For God's sake, don't fire!" In the bustle and confusion, the Saulteaux, mistaking our meaning, thought we were all the time calling on them to fire. Under this erroneous impression, in a moment a buzz and bustling of guns among the Indians indicated their intention in a language not to be mistaken. Had a gun gone off, in the surly mood manifested by the

Saulteaux at this critical moment, it would have been the signal for a general massacre, our party at the time being unarmed; fortunately, however, one of our friends stepped forward, and having struck down the muzzle of Mr. Simpson's gun, all was safe. We had still some difficulty to appease the chief. The rash and thoughtless gasconade of pointing the guns drew from him a pointed challenge. " If you are so fond of shooting," said he to the whites, " come on, and we will fight it out." After some coaxing and explanation, however, the chief shook hands with us, and we parted good friends.

On the second occasion, Mr. Simpson relates, " The Sioux came in double numbers, better armed, and led by Ulàneta, the greatest chief of their whole nation." Not " Ulàneta," we would remark, but Wannatah, was the name of this great Sachem. The party under Wannatah had approached the settlement, as we learned afterwards, in a rather suspicious manner. They were 250 strong; but to avoid giving alarm, the sagacious chief had left in ambush 180 of his followers, and reached the fort with only 70, and perhaps it was to the very friendly manner in which he and his men were received and dismissed, that we owed our escape from any further trouble. Since that time they have paid two other visits to the colony, of which we shall speak in another place.

Mr. Simpson goes on to observe, " It gives me sincere pleasure to say that a reconciliation has at length been effected between these lately inveterate and bloody enemies, the Saulteaux and Sioux nations."

Now we are extremely puzzled to comprehend what grounds Mr. Simpson could have had for supposing that a peace or reconciliation had "been effected." The impression, in our opinion, must have been purely ideal; for war and deadly animosity have ever existed between them, and every year widens the breach. Without further remark on this subject, we pass on to its kindred topic, the half-breeds or plain hunters—a class of people whom, like the Indians, we have already noticed from time to time in these pages.

At the commencement of the colony, and long after the irregularity and disorder which mark its early history were superseded, in some measure, by the better management of the Company, the half-caste children, or half-breeds, as they are more commonly called, were found extremely useful: and, according to their usefulness, they were indulged, pampered, and spoiled. They were then but few in number, and the produce of their hunts, consisting of dried buffalo meat and grease, was in great demand. According to the custom of the country, it was pounded and amalgamated into a strong and wholesome food, called pemican, and made up into bags of about 100 pounds weight, and sold by the freemen or hunters at 2$d.$ per pound. This food is generally used by voyageurs and trip-men, and though the buffaloes were numerous, the supply was never adequate to the demand; they who devoted themselves to the chase being but few in number. Proportionately great, therefore, was the encouragement always held out to the hunter. He was the man everyone looked up to— a favourite in every place he visited; and the fame he thus acquired drew thither, in addition to its natural increase, others of the same profession from the four quarters of Rupert's Land; so that the half-breed class in Red River soon multiplied and became a numerous and formidable party.

The hunters increased; not so the voyageurs and trip-men, who were the principal consumers of their produce; and at length, instead of inadequate supply, inadequate demand was the complaint. This want of a market or outlet was the cause eventually of a bad feeling on the part of the half-breeds towards their benefactors, the rulers of the country; and here it is necessary to bear in mind the fact, that these people were not regular settlers, but intruders, and had wedged themselves in among the settlers when they were not wanted, spoiling their market in fact. It was with just reason, then, the agricultural class complained.

In this state of things, the Company very properly raised its voice against the vagrant habit of going to the buffalo in such numbers, and overstocking the market; and their advice being disregarded by the half-breeds, they, in fine, absolutely refused to take the pemican off their hands. The half-breeds pleaded hard, and here was the point at which all the subsequent difficulties commenced. A bold and firm stand at this time, had the authorities known their position, would have settled the matter; but rather than push things to the extreme, the Company broke through the principle they themselves had laid down, by doling out favours to this one and that one, till the favour became a demand, and the demand grew to a threat. Time and numbers increased the boldness of the half-breeds, until it became their habit to bully the Company into their views.

Accustomed to depend on the Company, they seldom thought for themselves, and could never be persuaded to keep a supply of their own produce for the use of their families when the season was against them. Their usual resource, when starvation pressed hard on them, was to renew their threats. The writer has known them, in the fall of the year, to compel the Company to purchase the little grain they had raised, as well as their plain provisions, and the next spring force their rulers, with similar threats, to give them back again the grain for seed, as well as the provisions for food. They did not, indeed, resort to violence, for their demands, however unreasonable, were always complied with, rather than risk an outbreak, the consequences of which none could have told.

From what has been stated, it must appear evident that it required no ordinary forbearance on the part of the governing power to manage these people, so as to preserve peace and order; but, generally speaking, both were maintained till the period at which we have arrived (1834), when the inflammable materials took fire, blazed out, and we had the first hostile demonstration of the half-breeds. The exciting cause was a very trivial circumstance, alluded to in Mr. Thomas Simpson's narrative, who placed himself in the situation of an aggressor by chastising, on the spot, a half-breed named Larocque, who had provoked him by his insolent and overbearing conduct.

No sooner had the news of this daring act spread

abroad, than the half-breeds met in council, and in conclusion demanded that Mr. Simpson should be forthwith delivered up to them, to be dealt with as they might think proper, in retaliation for the pounding he had given their friend; or if this demand were not complied with, they would destroy Fort Garry, and take him by force. This threat was transmitted to the Governor of the colony, and almost at the same moment the war-song and war-dance were commenced in the fashion of the Indians. The whole half-breed race of French extraction were in motion, and a buzz of anxiety pervaded the settlement. Several messages now passed to and fro between the parties to no purpose, and it was finally resolved to send a deputation to the aggrieved party, if possible, to settle the dispute before it was too late. With this purpose, Mr. Governor Christie, Mr. Chief Factor Cameron, Robert Logan, Esq., and the writer, left Fort Garry at ten o'clock at night, and a cold and stormy winter night it was.

On arriving at the place where the hostile party were assembled, we were struck with their savage appearance. They resembled more a troop of furies than human beings, all occupied in the Indian dance. As the arguments upon which we entered would only tire the reader, we shall pass them by, simply remarking, that reason is but a feeble weapon against brute force. Nevertheless, after a two hours' parley, reason triumphed, and we got the knotty point settled by making a few trifling concessions, taking no small merit to ourselves for our diplomatic success. We must confess, however, that the bearing of the half-breeds became haughtier than ever, for the spring was no sooner ushered in than another physical demonstration took place at the gates of Fort Garry. This was the introduction of a new series of demands:—1. Not content with getting their provisions sold, they raised the price. 2. They demanded an export trade, although they had nothing to eat, much less to sell. And 3. They protested against any import duty on goods from the United States. Demand after demand now followed in close succession. These were all feelers sent forth covertly by designing and disaffected demagogues, who made dupes of the silly half-breeds to answer their own vile purposes, by always pushing them forward in the front rank to screen themselves; yet, during all these hostile attempts and foolish demands, no act of outrage was committed. Left to themselves, the half-breeds are credulous and noisy, but are by no means a bad people. As a proof of this, in what country, without even the shadow of power to control violence, would so many hostile movements have been made and no actual mischief? With all their threats, they harmed neither man nor beast. They touched not, tasted not, nor did they handle anything but what was their own. We shall, however, resume this subject again.

CHAPTER XV.

CONTENTS.—Political aspect of things—Colony changes masters—The costly child—Value of the colony—A step-mother's care—The political miracle—The Company's liberality—An overruling power—The mystery—Ground-work of law and order—Prefatory address—Constitution of first council—Law enactments—Their tendency—Presbyterians and their minister—The parson's justification—The Reverend Mr. Cockran—The Presbyterians renew their application—Mr. Governor Christie's policy — The English missionaries — Remarks — Change of opinions—More of form than reality—Emigration—The cause—The coincidence—Things as they are—Ariosto and his tempest, a type of parties in Red River.

WE have now arrived at the period (1835) from which the commencement of constitutional or legal rights may be said to date, and may therefore, in few words, sum up the previous history of the colony. For the first ten or twelve years, it was under the management of Lord Selkirk's authority, as lord paramount; and after that, in consequence of his death, it fell into the hands of his Lordship's executors, who found it convenient to transfer the government of its affairs into the hands of the Company, as noticed in the last chapter. This arrangement lasted about twelve years more, till the present time, when we have to regard it as the property of the Hudson's Bay Company by right of purchase.

Like the great Astor, with his Pacific Fur Company scheme, Lord Selkirk chose a very bad time for planting his infant colony. Astor's project was set on foot, not at the end, but at the beginning of a war, and that war thwarted his views and swept his grand project before it. The juncture chosen by his Lordship was equally sinister to his designs, for he began to establish his devoted colony in a time of lawless strife, which snapped asunder the cord of social intercourse, baffled his views, and opposed his best interests. We allude in particular to the lawless conduct of the North-West Company, as described in the earlier part of our history; but apart from that, the distance and other difficulties were almost insuperable. By the authority of his presence, and his unremitted devotion to the colony, Lord Selkirk must nevertheless have ultimately triumphed over all difficulties had he lived. It will be admitted there was reason enough for his solicitude in behalf of the enterprise, when it is considered that this favourite child of his Lordship's cost him, from first to last, no less a sum than 85,000*l.* sterling; an amount the colony would not have realized, had it been sold off at auction, even twenty years after it was founded.

The government of the colony under the agency of the Company, before it became their own, was far from satisfactory, as we have seen. Although the troubles arising from the opposition had long ceased, and peace throughout the length and breadth of the land had been restored, yet it was found that the colony, under their jurisdiction, experienced but the cool and languid care of a step-mother. Everything was attempted, but everything failed; chiefly, as we have seen, through the want of zeal and perseverance. Hence its general character remained as it was, without making one step in advance: as gloomy and as forbidding as ever. Such, then, were the prospects of the colony at this date, when it fell into the hands of the Company. But it is a common saying, that people take more interest in what is their own than what belongs to another; hence it was to be hoped, and the hope has been realized, that the colony would see better days under its new masters.

From a perusal of the preceding chapter, and other transactions up till the present year, the absence of laws and municipal regulations must appear but too evident. In a country without laws, there can scarcely be ordinary security; nor indeed have we ever seen so much as a camp of Indians with only their own moral sense to rule them; but always with certain laws and regulations for their government, and for the punishment of offenders. Yet, in this settlement, the contrary fact is remarkable. Up till the period at which we have arrived, the inhabitants may be said to have lived without laws and without protection, simply and solely depending on the good feelings and faith of the people themselves. This fact—we might call it, political miracle—may be regarded as a phenomenon in history: that any community, much more a colony, could have held together, morally and politically, in spite of itself, we may say, in spite of human measures, without protection and without laws, during a period of twenty-four years; showing, that whatever the state of society may be, the members soon learn that it is the interest of all to cultivate and preserve peace. It has been so in this remote and isolated spot. And the example may be worthy of imitation.

We ought, however, to repeat, what we have already noticed, that for several years past a few councillors, to assist the Governor, some few constables too, had been nominally appointed; and this little machinery of government had dragged along under what has been very properly called the smoothing system, or rather no system at all; yet for several years it worked more or less to the satisfaction of the people, which is the great end of all legislation and law. All points hitherto in dispute were settled by the Governor himself, or not settled at all—as often the one as the other—and yet peace was maintained. But the time having come, when the smoothing system would no longer work satisfactorily, other means were necessary, by the adoption of which law and order were for the first time established in the settlement.

During all these political changes the colonists were kept in the dark, never having been put in possession of their intellectual rights, by knowing what was going on, or to whom the colony belonged. Nor was it till many years after the settlement became virtually the Company's own property, that the fact was made known to the people, and then by mere chance. Till this eventuality, the people were under the persuasion that the colony still belonged to the executors of Lord

Selkirk, and were often given to understand so. By this political finesse, or shall we rather call it, political absurdity, the Company preserved themselves clear of all responsibility, whatever transpired. Did they remove any grievance or assist the colonists? It was looked upon as purely gratuitous on their part. Whereas, had the people known the relative position in which they stood to the Company, they would no doubt, as a matter of course, have insisted at an earlier period on what was their undoubted right, as subjects.

But to return. The first step taken by the Company after its new acquisition, was to organize something like local regulations, courts of justice, and a code of laws for the colony. To carry out these measures, new councillors, selected out of the more influential inhabitants in the colony, were nominated and commissioned by the committee in London, this year, and these officials, with the Governor-in-Chief at their head, were to constitute a legislative council, with power to make laws in criminal as well as civil matters. To give effect to the new order of things, a council was convened at Upper Fort Garry on the 12th day of February 1835, and here we shall present our readers with the opening address of the President of the Council, now Sir George Simpson, which will confirm all we have stated as to the real condition of affairs at that time.

"Gentlemen," said Sir George, "in order to guard as much as possible against misapprehension within doors, or misrepresentation out of doors, on the subjects which I am now about to bring under your consideration, I shall thus briefly notice them. From their importance, they cannot fail of calling forth due attention, and from the deep and lively interest you all feel in the welfare and prosperity of the colony, I am satisfied you will afford me the benefit of your assistance and support towards carrying into effect such measures as may appear to you best calculated, under existing circumstances, to answer every desirable object.

" The population of this colony is become so great, amounting to about 5,000 souls, that the personal influence of the Governor, and the little more than nominal support afforded by the police, which, together with the good feeling of the people, have heretofore been its principal safeguard, are no longer sufficient to maintain the tranquility and good government of the settlement; so that although rights of property have of late been frequently invaded, and other serious offences been committed, I am concerned to say, we were under the necessity of allowing them to pass unnoticed, because we have not the means at command of enforcing obedience and due respect, according to the existing order of things.

" Under such circumstances, it must be evident to one and all of you, that it is quite impossible society can hold together; that the time is at length arrived when it becomes necessary to put the administration of justice on a more firm and regular footing than heretofore, and that immediate steps ought to be taken to guard against dangers from abroad or difficulties at home, for the maintenance of good order and tranquility, and for the security and protection of lives and property."

Constitution of the First Council.

Sir George Simpson, Governor of Rupert's Land	President.
Alexander Christie, Governor of Assiniboine (the Colony)	Councillor.
The Right Reverend the Bishop of Juliopolis, now of the North-West..	Councillor.
The Reverend D. T. Jones, Chaplain to the Honourable Hudson's Bay Company	Councillor.
The Reverend William Cockran, Assistant Chaplain...	Councillor.
James Bird, Esq., formerly Chief Factor, Hudson's Bay Company...	Councillor.
James Sutherland, Esq..	Councillor.
W. H. Cook, Esq.	Councillor.
John Pritchard, Esq..	Councillor.
Robert Logan, Esq.	Councillor.
Alexander Ross, Esq., Sheriff of Assiniboine............	Councillor.
John Mc Cullum, Esq., Coroner	Councillor.
John Bunn, Esq., Medical Adviser	Councillor.
Andrew Mc Dermot, Esq., Merchant	Councillor.
Cuthbert Grant, Esq., Warden of the Plains............	Councillor.

Although the councillors thus appointed were undoubtedly the men of most influence in the settlement, yet their influence being all on one side, generally speaking, either sinecurists or paid servants of the Company, they did not carry the public feeling with them, consequently were not, perhaps, the fittest persons, all things considered, to legislate for the colony. Professional men, and old fur-traders, had but little experience in colonial affairs. The people knew this, and knowing it, they never placed that confidence in the council that they would have done had its members been taken from all classes, and not exclusively from the side of the ruling power.

The constitution and working of this council provoked the first desire of the people for representative government; and although we do not altogether approve of such a system, nor think it the best in the present state of the colony, yet it may be forced on the people as the best possible, by foolish and oppressive acts. To guard against such, the sooner the people have a share in their own affairs the better; for to repeat the oft-quoted political maxim, it is only fair that those who have to obey the laws should have a voice in making them. It is said, indeed, that a man who contributes, by his vote, to the passing of a law, has himself made the law; and in obeying it, obeys but himself. Whether or not this is a mere play on words, it is certainly fair play; and if order requires that a people should ask no more, they will of a certainty be contented with no less. Who is it that does not know, that laws and equitable justice, like men and money, are the elements of a country's strength—that strength on which constitutional liberty depends; whereas the contrary is the utter prostration of political freedom and moral independence. But to return to the council.

At this meeting a number of enactments were formed, and passed into law; most of which gave general satisfaction. We shall here enumerate a few of them.

1st.—That an efficient and disposable force be embodied, to be styled a volunteer corps, to consist of sixty officers and privates, to be at all times ready to act when called upon; and to be paid as follows:—commanding officer, 20*l.* per annum; sergeants, 10*l.*; and privates, 6*l*. sterling, besides extra pay for serving writs. When not so employed, their time to be their own. Of this corps the writer was appointed commanding officer.

2nd.—That the settlement be divided into four districts: the first to extend from the Image Plain downwards; the second from the Image Plain to the Forks; the third from the Forks upwards, on the main river; and the fourth the White Horse Plains, or Assiniboine River; and that for each of the said districts, a magistrate be appointed. That James Bird, Esq., be justice of the peace for the first district; James Sutherland, Esq., for the second; Robert Logan, Esq., for the third; and Cuthbert Grant, Esq., for the fourth. These magistrates to hold quarterly courts of summary jurisdiction on four successive Mondays; to be appointed according to the existing order of precedence, in the four sections; beginning with the third Monday of January, of April, of July, and of October.

3rd.—That the said courts have power to pronounce final judgment in all civil cases, where the debt or damage claimed may not exceed five pounds; and in all trespasses and misdemeanours, which, by the rules and regulations of the district of Assiniboine, not being repugnant to the laws of England, may be punished by a fine not exceeding the aforesaid sum of five pounds.

4th.—That the said courts be empowered to refer any case of doubt or difficulty to the supreme tribunal of the colony, the Court of Governor and Council of Assiniboine, at its next ensuing quarterly session, by giving a *viva voce* intimation of the reference in open court, and a written intimation of the same under the hands of a majority of the three sitting magistrates, at least one whole week before the commencement of the said quarterly session, and this without being compelled to state any reasons for so doing.

5th.—That the Court of Governor and Council, in its judicial capacity, sit on the third Thursday of February, of May, of August, and November; and at such other times as the Governor-in-Chief of Rupert's Land, or, in his absence, the Governor of Assiniboine, may deem fit.

6th.—That in all contested civil cases, which may involve claims of more than ten pounds, and in all criminal cases, the verdict of a jury shall determine the fact or facts in dispute.

7th.—That a public building intended to answer the double purpose of a court-house and gaol, be erected as early as possible at the Forks of the Red and Assiniboine Rivers. That in order to raise funds for defraying such expenses as it may be found necessary to incur, towards the maintenance of order, and the erecting of public works, an import duty shall be levied on all goods and merchandise of foreign manufacture imported into Red River, either for sale or private use, at $7\frac{1}{2}$ per cent. on the amount of invoice; and further, that an export duty of $7\frac{1}{2}$ per cent. be levied on all goods and stores, or supplies, the growth, produce, or manufacture of Red River.

At the close of the business, Governor Simpson intimated that the fur trade would make a grant of 300*l*., in aid of public works in Red River; on this being announced, a vote of thanks was returned to the Governor and Council of Rupert's Land, for their liberal grant. The Council then adjourned. The liberality of the Company to the colonists has already been shown in many instances; in the affairs of the Buffalo Wool Company; in the tallow trade concern; the winter road; sheep speculation; experimental farms; and a thousand other instances. But we have not yet done with the resolutions in council: a remark or two on them may be necessary.

First. The people looked with a rather jealous eye on the constitution of the new Council, by observing that the folks in power, Church and State linked together, were the only party represented.

Secondly. The heavy duty of $7\frac{1}{2}$ per cent. on all imports was aimed against the petty traders, and, in consequence, unpopular. The like duty of $7\frac{1}{2}$ per cent. on the exports of Red River was looked upon as a foolish and impolitic thing in itself; although at the time it could do neither good nor harm, there being virtually nothing to export; but if there had, the law was calculated to operate against the colony, against political economy, and against the best interests of the people.

There is in general a great and decided want of political unity among parties in Red River; arising from pursuits, interests, and feelings, totally different from each other. Three distinct parties may be named—the Company, the farmers, and the hunters, who all act on the principle of free agents; each for itself. The agricultural party, and the hunting party united, form the great body of the population; while the governing party or Company, as fur traders, are as widely separated from both, as one part of the population from the other. To have dealt out even-handed justice to all these conflicting interests, they ought to have been equally represented in Council. Nevertheless, the state of things was evidently improved, and as a whole, the present arrangements worked tolerably well. We here dismiss the subject for a season, and take up the all-absorbing and kindred topic of the Scotch settlers and their minister, of which we have almost lost sight.

The introduction of laws and regulations into the colony imparted a degree of confidence that all would now work well in Church as well as in State, and that the poor and neglected Presbyterians might, even at the eleventh hour, be put in possession of their rights. The current, however, still ran strong against them. The English missionaries were furious against every other creed but their own, and especially against the Presbyterians; knowing well that the introduction of a Presbyterian minister into the settlement would break down the stronghold of exclusiveness, and put an end to that undue influence which had so long deprived them of a clergyman of their own persuasion. Mr. Jones, we ought to observe, had been succeeded by another missionary, the Reverend Mr. Cockran, a man of pious character, indefatigable in his zeal for religion, but especially zealous as a Church of England man. He was possessed of many good qualities, but in religious matters wedded to the dogma of exclusiveness, and strongly prejudiced against everything that he regarded as sectarian.

On seeing that Mr. Jones, from a feeling of Christian charity, as well as motives of policy, towards his Presbyterian hearers, had deviated, in some small degree, from the Liturgy and Homilies of his church, Mr. Cockran felt uneasy, nor did he repress what he felt; although he, too, as we shall hereafter see, gradually fell into Mr. Jones's steps himself. The rule of action by which the latter was guided is admirably expressed in his own words: "We must," said he, "make ourselves useful; we must be guided by circumstances if we would do good. I have preached to the Presbyterians these many years now; I have done everything in my power, in every possible way, to gain them over to the simple and beautiful forms of our church service; but all in vain. These people brought their religion to the country along with them, and are conscientiously wedded to the rites and discipline of the Presbyterian form of worship; and nothing will make them forsake the church of their forefathers. Fourteen years' experience convinces me that any further attempt is utterly useless, utterly hopeless; for not one of them, either young or old, up to this hour, will use our prayer-book. They are obstinate in the extreme; yet as soon as I was made sensible that their obstinacy arose from conscientious motives, I did sympathise with them; I was constrained to relax a little in the outward forms of our Church, and I have never regretted it; for ever since all has gone on admirably well, and I hope I have done good by so doing. We must try and gain souls; we must follow the example of the Apostles—'Therefore to the weak I became weak, that I might gain the weak: I am made all things to all men, that I might by all means save some.' 1 Cor. ix., 22."

But Mr. Cockran at first thought otherwise. " I will preach to them," said he, with some warmth, " the truths of the gospel, and they must listen to me; they have nothing to do with our forms; I will not allow them an inch of their own will;" and sure enough he handled the Scotch settlers and their Presbyterian notions pretty roughly. Nevertheless, of all the English missionaries that ever came to Red River, he was for a long time the greatest favourite. This was due to his earnestness, his candour, and his zeal as a minister, qualities for which every one esteemed him, while it was obvious that his strong opposition to the Presbyterian party weakened his hands in the ministry, and made the Scotch settlers more and more anxious for a pastor of their own. In fine, the return to a stricter observance of the ritual, after the departure of Mr. Jones, kindled a new flame between the preacher and his hearers.

The Presbyterian party renewed the application for their minister through Mr. Governor Christie, a task which had always to be performed on the arrival of a new governor. The result was the same as heretofore; the applicants being coolly advised to apply to the executors of Lord Selkirk.

Mr. Christie was, nevertheless, a kind urbane man— nay, he was himself a Presbyterian; but allowed policy to rule his conduct, and went jogging on hand and hand with the men of the day, while the poor Scotch had to battle the watch themselves as they best could. Thus backed, as it were, by the man in power, the church folks took a bolder stand than ever, and smiled at our repeated disappointments. They now thought that all was secure, and on the strength of that security sneered at our efforts, and boldly told us that we should never see the day we looked for. Such mode of reasoning served rather to exasperate than to remove the existing difference, and we need not say that religious animosity, like civil war, demoralizes a community, by creating and mixing itself up with the worst feelings of our nature. In this case it paralyzed the energies of industry, and snapped asunder the chain which linked the social ties of society together. In the very year we are writing, no less than 114 persons, chiefly of the Presbyterian party, left the settlement for the United States, carrying along with them much valuable property; and others are preparing to follow their example. The effect of this movement will operate materially against those that remain, by reducing their numbers and weakening their efforts.

On the occasion just named, we were struck by a singular coincidence. The same number of cattle were carried off to the States by the emigrating party that the Americans brought into Red River some thirteen years before; but the Yankees had the upper hand of us in one respect, for they got from us more pounds sterling for theirs, than they gave us dollars for ours; and yet, on the whole, we were the greatest gainers by the speculation.

Mr. Cockran, after all, was not relentless, but being

a man of kind heart, and willing to do good, he finally relaxed in his forms, and, like his predecessor, met the people half way. The difficulty forcibly reminds us of Ariosto describing his tempest: he tried it sixteen different times, and as many different ways for aught we know, and the last was found the best. The Presbyterians of Red River, it would appear, have taken from him the familiar motto, "Try it again," which encourages them to persevere, hoping the last will be the successful effort; while those who oppose them seem actuated by a similar spirit, "To resist again." But we have not exhausted this subject, and shall in due time resume it again.

CHAPTER XVI.

CONTENTS.—First petty jury—The flogger flogged—Summer frosts—Crops destroyed—Chain of cross purposes—Preamble—The three imposing months—The stranger—Mosquitoes—Bulldogs—The black fly—The ramble—Canadians and half-breeds—Their mode of life—The man of consequence—Gossiping parties—Amusements—The effects of habit—Children in their infancy—Votaries of pleasure—Wood rafters—Squatters—Result—Scene changed—Europeans—Visit the Indians—Fish on dry land—Tea-drinking in the wilderness—Indians and the aurora borealis—Superstition—The Scotch in Red River—Domestic comforts—New habits—The Sabbath-day—The agreeable mistake.

THE new laws were not brought into operation without difficulty, as may be supposed, after crimes and misdemeanours had been so long committed with impunity. The first petty jury was empanneled on the 28th day of April 1836, in the case of a man named Louis St. Denis, a French Canadian, who had been tried, convicted of theft, and, besides some further punishment, sentenced to be publicly flogged: which sentence was carried into effect on that day. The police being all in attendance, the utmost order was maintained till the close of the scene, when the popular excitement assumed a somewhat threatening aspect.

The unusual spectacle of a white man being stripped

and flogged before the public gaze had raised a spirit of indignation against the poor flogger. His task being accomplished, he no sooner stepped outside the ring, or police circle, than one fellow called out, "Bourreau, Bourreau;"* another threw a chip at him; a third improved upon the example by throwing mud, while the bystanders, with one voice, called aloud, "Stone him! Stone him!" The poor frightened German, for such he was, ran, as he probably thought, for his life, and had not gone many yards before he stumbled and fell headlong into a hole, which gave rise to an uproarious burst of laughter, mingled with hisses. Here, however, the police interfered, and the bespattered official being dragged out of the pit, was locked up in the fort till the people dispersed. So strong was the public feeling against this mode of punishment, that some five years afterwards, when the same disagreeable service was required to be performed, not a person could be got to act out-doors. On this occasion, therefore, the flogging took place within the prison walls, the official being masked, and for further security, locked up till dusk, when he was dismissed unknown.

We have already more than once noticed the slow and uncertain progress of agriculture in the colony, and this year have to record as many failures, disappointments, and cross purposes, as ever befell the settlement; including the partial failure of diet from the plains, and the loss of the crops.

On the 7th of June we had a heavy fall of snow, and on the following day the ice was the thickness of a penny

* Hangman.

piece on the water; but still nothing serious happened to damp our hopes, till the 19th of August, when the severity of the frost blasted our fairest prospects, by destroying the crops. Misfortune, as often remarked, seldom comes in one single form at the same time, and the old proverb was verified by the defection in the same month of the half-breeds—or rather, that portion of them engaged as trip-men to York Factory—who now refused to perform a second trip, although engaged and paid for it as usual. After some delay, they were restored to order, without the serious results that were feared; but it was judged necessary that Mr. Grant, the under sheriff, and warden of the plains, should accompany them to prevent any further outbreak. The month indeed seemed fated to cross purposes; and before it expired, our annual ship was driven from her moorings at York by a storm, and the captain, without making any effort to regain his position, and without that hardihood and resolution which belong to his class, returned to England, carrying along with him the Red River supplies for the year.

The season continued cold, drizzly, and frosty, till the latter end of October, which added another item to the catalogue of evils by destroying the fall fisheries: after that, however, the weather became unusually mild and pleasant, insomuch that men were whistling at the plough on the 12th of November, and hauling with their carts, without snow, till the 14th of January 1837, a most unusual circumstance in the colony. With the introduction of this year, we may conveniently give our readers a picture of life as it is in Red River.

A stranger entering Red River in June would be dazzled at the prospect around him. June, July, and August, are the three imposing months, when nature appears luxuriant in the extreme. The unbounded pasture, cattle everywhere grazing without restraint, the crops waving in the wind, every species of vegetation rich in blossom, and fertile as imagination itself. To enjoy these scenes as completely as possible, the writer invited a friend newly arrived in the place to accompany him from one end of the settlement to the other. The summer picture of this colony is truly delightful and enchanting, but like others of the same kind, after the first burst of admiration, the senses tire of viewing the same objects over and over again, and one day's ride exhausts the store of novelty. For this pleasure, indeed, the traveller must sometimes pay dearly; for should he deviate ever so little from the public road, or saunter from the path, he is beset and tormented with the blood-thirsty musquetoes, rising in clouds at every step; surely the most unconquerable and fiercest people on earth, for though you kill a million, and but one remain alive, the fearless enemy never retreats, but advances either to conquer or die. In July also, the horse-fly,— called in Red River, bull-dog—are very numerous, and annoying to cattle in particular. In August, both musquetoes and bull-dogs disappear; and then the black house-fly takes their place, filling the dwelling-houses with their swarms, till the month of October, or the cold, removes them. Picture-frames, windows, tables, victuals, are not here the only objects of attack, but the owner's face and hands suffer also; while his ears are stunned with the perpetual hum, which can only be compared to the buzz of a disturbed bee-hive. These unwelcome visitors are destructive of all peace and comfort, whether sleeping or waking, during their continuance in the colony.

To return to my friend, I must here apologize for speaking in the first person as a matter of present convenience. Having taken a ramble on the highway, and satisfied his curiosity as to things generally, we halted at the Forks. This place, as has already been described, is the nucleus and chief rendezvous of the settlement—the division line between the Europeans and Canadians. Here the beaver hat and silken gown, the papered walls and carpeted floors meet the eye. Different this from what things were some ten or twelve years before, when I first visited the place!

From Fort Garry I invited my friend to accompany me on a visit to the upper part of the settlement, as he was anxious to know what kind of life the Canadians and half-breeds lead in this part of the world. We had not proceeded far before we met a stout, well-made, good-looking man, dressed in a common blue capote, red belt, and corduroy trousers; he spoke French, and was a Canadian. That, said I, pointing to his dress, is the universal costume of both Canadians and half-breeds, the belt being the simple badge of distinction; the former wearing it generally over, and the latter as generally under the capote. The stature of the half-breeds is of the middle size, and generally slender, countenances rather pleasing than otherwise. In manners mild, unassuming, not to say effeminate, and somewhat bashful. On the whole, however, they are a sedate and grave people, rather humble than haughty in their demeanour, and are seldom seen to laugh among strangers. The women are invariably fairer than the men, although at all seasons almost equally exposed. They are not, however, high coloured, but rather pale and sallow; resembling in their complexion more the natives of Spain, or the south of France, than the swarthy Indian here. I have, indeed, seen individuals as fair, and the tint of their skin as delicate, as any European lady.

The half-breed women are also slender, still more so than the men, but exceedingly well-featured and comely —many even handsome; and those who have the means are tidy about their person and dress. They are fond of show, and invariably attire themselves in gaudy prints, and shawls, chiefly of the tartan kind—all, as a matter of course, of foreign manufacture; but, like Indian women, they are very tenacious of the habits and customs of their native country. The blanket as an overall, is considered indispensable; it is used on all occasions, not only here, but throughout the continent, both at home and abroad; if a stick is wanted for the fire, or a pleasure party is to be joined away from home, the blanket is called for. This invariable habit gives them a stooping gait while walking, and the constant use of the same blanket, day and night, wet and dry, is supposed to give rise to consumptive complaints, which they are all more or less very subject to. At the age of thirty years, they generally look as old as a white woman of forty; perhaps from the circumstance that they marry young, and keep their children long at the breast.

We have noticed the extreme bashfulness peculiar to the half-breeds, or what might more properly be termed their false modesty or shyness, similar to what is observable among the Formosans. It is exhibited in almost every circumstance; for, although many of them understand and speak both French and English, yet they are averse to speak any other language than their mother tongue. And if the traveller chance to meet one of them on the road, she will instantly shroud her head in her blanket, and try to pass without speaking. Speak to her, and she looks to the ground. Stop, and she turns to one side, and ten to one passes without answering you. For one of her own countrymen, however, a smile, a " bon jour," and a shake of the hand is always ready.

Such is the roving propensity of these people that they are never in their proper element, unless gossiping from house to house. Like a bird in the bush, they are always on the move; and as often in their neighbours' houses as in their own. It is not uncommon for a woman getting up in the morning, to throw her blanket about her and set off on a gossiping tour among her neighbours, and leave her children foodless and clothesless among the ashes, to shift for themselves; yet, like most Indian women, they are generally tender mothers. We hope the ladies alluded to will take a useful lesson from these remarks. And likewise reform their shopping propensity and love of fineries, which do not bespeak industrious habits, or a great desire to manufacture their own clothing. These are blemishes not easily removed.

Canadians and half-breeds are promiscuously settled together, and live much in the same way, although we shall be able to point out some differences. They are not, properly speaking, farmers, hunters, or fishermen; but rather confound the three occupations together, and follow them in turn, as whim or circumstances may dictate. They farm to-day, hunt to-morrow, and fish the next, without anything like system; always at a nonplus, but never disconcerted. They are great in adventuring, but small in performing; and exceedingly plausible in their dealings. Still, they are oftener more useful to themselves than to others, and get through the world the best way they can, without much forethought or reflection. Taking them all in all, they are a happy people.

The men are great tobacco-smokers, the women as great tea-drinkers; but they seldom indulge in the luxury of sugar with this beverage. Debts may accumulate, creditors may press, the labourer may go without his hire, the children run naked, but the tea-kettle and tobacco-pipe are indispensable. We have already observed that they are passionately fond of roving about, visiting, card-playing, and making up gossiping parties. To render this possible, they must of course be equally hospitable in return; and, in fact, all comers and goers are welcome guests at their board. The apostle recommends hospitality; but we cannot give the name of hospitality to the foolish and ruinous practice we are speaking of: strictly following the

Indian principle, " Divide while anything remains," and beg when all is done. This habit is carried to excess among them, as most things are, the false indulgence of which reduces them to misery and want; and when there is nothing left at home, they live abroad at their neighbours' till they are generally all reduced to the same level. Far be it from us to find fault with a people for attachment to their own ancient usages; but all men must condemn a practice that not only fosters poverty in the individual homes, but is, in its consequences, injurious to society.

We have to notice a marked difference between the Europeans and the French. In the spring of the year, when the former are busy, late and early, getting their seed into the ground, the Canadian is often stuck up in the end of his canoe fishing gold-eyes, and the half-breed as often sauntering about idle with his gun in his hand. At the same time, if you ask either to work, they will demand unreasonable wages, or even refuse altogether; preferring indolence to industry, and their own roving habits to agricultural or other pursuits of civilized life. Their own farms, if farms they may be called, point them out as a century behind their European neighbours. Harvest time shows no improvement on sowing time, for they are to be seen anywhere but in the neighbourhood of their proper work. In short, they do all things out of season, and in the multiplicity of their pursuits oftener lose the advantage of all than accomplish one; verifying the old proverb of too many irons in the fire. While they are planning this and that little labour, the summer passes by, and winter threatens them often with their crops unsecured, their houses unmudded, and their cattle unprovided for. They live a ragged life, which habit has made familiar to them. Knowing no other condition, they are contented and happy in poverty; and, perhaps we may add, contentment in this life is everything.

Continuing our tour of inspection, we visited the houses of these people, and here truth compels us to draw a line of distinction. The Canadian of any standing is tidy in his dwelling: the floor is kept clean; the bed neatly made up, and generally set off with curtains and coverlet; the little cupboard, if there is nothing in it, is still orderly and clean; in short, everything else just as it ought to be. On the contrary, the half-breeds, generally speaking, exhibit more of the discomforts that attend a mere encampment in their dwellings. When anything is wanted, everything in the domicile has to be turned topsy turvy to find it, and the inmates sleep as contented on the floor as in a bed—a sort of pastoral life, reminding us of primeval times. Among this class, the buffalo robe is more frequently to be seen than the blanket in their dwellings. The better sort, however, have their houses divided into two rooms; but they are all bare of furniture, and ornament never enters, except occasionally a small picture of the Virgin Mary, or a favourite apostle, hung to the wall in a little round frame. Variety or taste is, of course, out of the question, and a multiplied sameness characterizes everything about them.

But what pleased and interested my friend most of

all,—he being a young man and fond of novelty,—was their winter amusements; the fine horse, the bells, the ribbons, the gay painted cariole, trotting matches, fiddling, dancing, and gossiping parties. The gaiety of their carousals ought, indeed, to be mentioned. When met together on these occasions, they are loud talkers, great boasters, and still greater drinkers and smokers; they sing vociferously, dance without mercy, and generally break up their bacchanalian revels with a sort of Irish row. The constant tide of cariole comers and goers, Sundays and week-days alike, would lead to a belief that the Canadians and half-breeds were all official men, did all the business of the colony, and settled affairs of state into the bargain. And yet, what is the fact? All this heyday, and hurrying to and fro, is mere idleness and gasconade. A Canadian or half-breed able to exhibit a fine horse, and gay cariole, is in his glory; this achievement is at once the height of his ambition, and his ruin. Possessed of these, the thriftless fellow's habitation goes to ruin; he is never at home, but driving and caricoling in all places, and every opportunity; blustering and bantering every one he meets. The neighbourhood of the church on Sundays and holy days has all the appearance of a fair; and whether arriving or returning, the congregation is deafened by the clamour, and shocked by the vagaries of these braggarts.

While we were enjoying the scenes around us, a fellow with a showy horse and gay cariole shot past us on the glib ice like lightning, with a lustre that threw us completely into the shade.

" Who is that?" said my friend, staring with surprise: " he must be a person of some consequence!" Could he believe that this glittering Phaeton was not worth a shilling in the world? That only a day or two since he possessed a house, a snug little farm, an ox, and a cow; and gave all for the tempting horse and cariole?

Soon afterwards I asked my companion to accompany me to a dwelling near by; and as we were driven out of doors again by the cold and discomfort, he truly remarked, " What a miserable hovel! Not a blanket on the bed, the children are naked, not a stick to put on the fire, and the poor woman, with her little ones, like a hen with her brood of chickens sitting in the ashes!" " It is all true, too true," said I; " yet the man who dazzled you so amazingly a short time ago dwells here! This is your man of consequence; this is his family." When I told him so, he stood confounded. " These things," said I, " are not uncommon here; folly and idleness all!" How these people bring up their children from infancy is almost a mystery. No special care, as in other countries, is here taken to feed a child; it is constantly stuck at its mother's breast like a leech, till it can sprawl about or walk and feed itself, and then it fares as its parents do; it eats strong meat and drinks strong tea, breakfast, dinner, and supper, the same—always meat, and nothing but meat, washed down, as the general custom is, with tea, strong and bitter as tobacco juice. Healthy children, indeed, with strong stomachs, thrive well; but the puny and delicate soon sink under such treatment, and relieve their parents of all further trouble on their behalf.

The destitution in which the indulgence of their idle fancies soon leaves them, never disconcerts a people so fertile in expedients. When the husband is in want of tobacco, or his wife of tea; when the children are naked, and all their own resources are dried up, they resort to the petty traders, or any one else among the settlers, from whom they can beg or extort some advance. The only field here, for speculators of this description, is wood-cutting, wood-rafting, and domestic labour. The principle that anything is better than nothing buoys up the giver and the taker. One contracts to cut and raft down fire-wood; another building-wood; another fencing; some this, some that. On the strength of these undertakings, they take up advances, generally heavy, considering their small means; so that before the work is begun, the wood speculators are involved over head and ears in debt; especially as the value put on the articles thus advanced is generally in proportion to the risk. In these arrangements, the fool and the knave often come in contact, or just as frequently knave is set against knave. Each party to the bargain tries to outwit the other; and, after all, a fifth of the contracts agreed upon is never fulfilled. Still, necessity compels the colonists to employ these men, as they are in general allowed to be able axe-men, and the only available class of people that can be got for such duties in the colony. But there is still a part of their character to notice, which is especially provoking to the industrious settler.

The reader is aware that the half-breeds are not of the emigrant class; but rather squatters and intruders, who have from time to time dropped off from the fur-trade, or come in from the Indian camp, and set down among their countrymen on the first vacant lot they find handy, which they make no scruple of calling their own. On this spot they remain, and burrow like rabbits, or rather freebooters, till the last stick of timber on it is cut down, and sold or destroyed; the wood being the only article on the lands which such people can turn to advantage. When the lot is stripped bare, they remove to another, and reduce it to the same condition. Thus the upper and best wooded part of the settlement has been entirely ruined, and rendered treeless. This alone might prove, if proof were necessary, not only the absence of all law, but the weakness or rather indifference of the government which permits the waste of a useful and indispensable article. Within the boundary of the colony, wood is already scarce; and unfortunately the country affords no substitute. Of all those squatters, there is not at this day half a dozen to be found on their original lots.

A singular result of this system remains to be noticed. When any settler is induced from the quality of the soil, situation, or some other advantage, to select one of those timberless lots, the squatter claims, and is, according to the existing regulations of the place, entitled to, remuneration for what he calls his improvements! When sitting on the lot, the occupier generally builds a log-hut, and sometimes cultivates a few roods of the land for his convenience, till he finishes destroying the timber; and this is what he calls his improvements, and what he claims remuneration for. Thus he is virtually paid, not for improving, but for destroying the lot! And yet the farce is carried still farther: the squatter may be on his second lot; the first, having become useless to him, is thrown away; nevertheless, the new comer has to pay him for his improvements.

All these people of French extraction are of the Roman Catholic religion; and the vernacular of both Canadians and half-breeds is a provincial jargon of French and Indian mixed up together. My companion would often remark, "Your half-breed women, although pale, are fairer in complexion than the Canadian women, but their extreme bashfulness deprives them of that graceful address peculiar to white women."

Having finished our promenade, and satisfied the curiosity of my friend, we hastened back to the Forks again, when I asked him how he liked the customs and habits of the people above; but he answered me with a significant shrug of the shoulder, and I could read in the expression of his countenance no very lively satisfaction. "If," said he, "the lower part of the settlement affords no more valuable information to the stranger than the upper, I am done with Red River; but, as I have seen the one, I should have no objections to visit the other." Having made some arrangements to that effect, we set out accordingly on our journey below. It happened to be the harvest season; all hands were at work in the fields. Men in their shirt-sleeves, women in their white jackets, and boys and girls everywhere busy in cutting and gleaning, or frightening away the blackbirds and wild pigeons, which at this season are very destructive to the crops. These people, with all their industry, and though their farms are large, cultivate but small patches; for which two reasons may be assigned—the limited market, and the scarcity of servants. Another inconvenience is fast growing up. The country not being suitable for back or second concession of lands, as the young marry, the lots become divided; and there are now, not only one establishment, but sometimes two, and even three on the same lot, giving them a ribbon-like appearance. The time cannot be far distant, therefore, when the Scotch themselves, if they wish to keep together, must remove to some other part of the colony, in order to have elbow room. The scarcity of wood and hay will likewise render a flitting soon necessary. But to return to our journey.

After travelling on the public road for about seven miles, to a place called the middle church, my friend made a halt, and turning to me observed, "This part of the colony we have just passed, is the thickest settled I have yet seen; and, if we may judge from outward appearances—houses, corn-yards, parks, and inclosures, the hand of industry has indeed been busy." "Yes," said I, "these are the Scotch settlers, the emigrants sent hither by Lord Selkirk; the people who have suffered so much, and to whose fortitude and perseverance the colony owes that it is what you see it at this day." "This spot," he rejoined, "is really full of interest."

Thus talking we journeyed on some fourteen miles further, till we reached the Stone Fort. Here the aspect is somewhat gloomy, yet deeply interesting; and beyond this point, with the exception of the Cree Indian village, there are no settlers. My friend, however, wished to prosecute the journey further in order to visit the lakes and the Indians of the neighbourhood; so, indulging his curiosity, we journeyed on, and before we got back to the Stone Fort winter had set in. This gave us an opportunity of comparing the pursuits of the people below with those above during that season, upon which we may have a word to say when we have reported our visit to the Indians.

The weather had been very dry and sultry for some time before we started, but all at once a heavy thunderstorm from the north-west burst out, and poured down such a torrent of rain, that in a few minutes rivulets ankle deep were running in all directions over the barren surface. After this deluge fell, the direction of our journey lay over a high ridge, and our party got separated for a time some distance from each other. In the evening we all met again and camped together, when two of the men brought us several small fishes, from one and a half to three inches in length, scarcely yet dead, which they averred they had found on the open plains, where no lake, river, creek, or water of any kind was to be found, but what had fallen during the late storm. In answer to our queries on the subject, they replied, " Where we found the fish there was, in two or three places, some gallons of them together, as if left by the torrent of the day before." We afterwards mentioned this rather curious circumstance to several persons, some of whom assured the writer they had more than once seen the same thing after a great storm and heavy fall of rain, and they had no doubt on the subject, but were firm in the belief that they were the fruits of the storm we had encountered, and had fallen with the rain. The probability of such a phenomenon was subsequently confirmed by a friend, who assured me that in crossing the wide plains between St. Peter's and Red River, after a storm of this kind, he had himself seen fish of a similar description, some of them yet alive, half a day's journey from any water, and lying in considerable numbers on the ground. We have seen it stated, after the land-slip called " Rosenberg," that live fish had been thrown to an immense distance out of the Lake " Lawertz ;" but here was no Alpine land-slip, but a torrent-slip from the clouds. Query— had the fish been carried thither by a waterspout, or had they fallen from the clouds?

Proceeding in a north-westerly direction, but more intent on hunting than despatch, it took us some time before we made the rocky and romantic shore of Lake Winipeg. There we fell in with a small camp or two of Cree and Saulteaux Indians, the chief men of which pressed us hard to pass a night with them, which we agreed to do, and soon learned their motives; for, as it proved, they were all out of tobacco. After putting our little camp in order, we went, accordingly, and smoked and talked with the Indians. During our parley with them, we noticed a fellow busy heating stones in the fire and then throwing them, ashes and all, into a wattappe kettle, or a kettle made of small willows, by which means he soon made the water boil; we then observed him taking something out of a dirty black bag and putting it into the kettle; we expressed a wish to see it, and the chief having laid the bag before us, behold! what was there but tea! tea imported from England. After the process we have described, they strained it through a dirty mat, and drank it, smacking their lips after the delicious beverage. Tea is now nearly as common in the Indian camp as in the settlement; but the half-breeds surpass everything yet heard of in the article of tea-drinking. In a small camp last winter, among the buffalo, there were thirty-eight adults, men and women, and forty-six children; and this small community, in the course of seven months, with the addition of a few Indians, consumed the enormous quantity of 3,528 pounds of tea! equal to forty-two pounds a head, young and old. This equals the Uzbeks themselves—surpasses Mrs. Flammond, the jolly hostess already noticed, and all other tea-drinkers of whom we have read, either ancient or modern.

We had agreed, as already mentioned, to pass the night with the Indians. Soon after we had retired to rest, we were aroused in the night by a great buzz in the camp; and on our going out to learn the cause of it, we found the Indians all assembled, and a fellow going through his juggling or conjuring performances. Almost immediately a shot was fired in the air; and on our inquiring the reason, our hosts pointed to the heavens, where the aurora borealis presented a most brilliant appearance, shifting and dancing about with all the resplendent colours of the rainbow; they added with a serious air, " Don't you see that? It is the

Indian's custom to shoot to keep the ghosts at a distance, or they might in their anger kill us." The aurora borealis they call " chee pye," or ghost. After firing, according to the Indian tradition, the ghosts disperse, or remain passive and harmless. We know that they resort to a similar mode of self-preservation on the approach of a thunder-storm—that is, they fire off a gun in the direction of the dark and ominous cloud; but to have the desired effect, the gun must be loaded in a peculiar manner, and fired off by a man who is entitled to carry a medicine-bag; after this ceremony is gone through, they apprehend no danger either from the thunder or the lightning. What idle fancies will not superstition give rise to?

Yet the people we are now describing have, perhaps, a less number of vile practices or acts of barbarity among them than most other savages. They neither deform the head nor pierce the septum of the nose for ornament. Infanticide is not even mentioned among them, nor do they abandon their sick and infirm to die unassisted or unpitied. Here my friend wished to know if all the Indian tribes were as superstitious as those people? " Some much more so," said I. " They are," said he, " a sad specimen of the fallen race, as far as wretchedness and superstition goes." But to return to the aurora borealis. It has been doubted by many, and is still doubted, whether or not, in their evolutions, these lights make a noise. It may be useful to state, therefore, that on the present, as well as on many other occasions, we all heard the whizzing noise, clear and distinct; as if a person kept waving a silk handkerchief on the end of a pole rapidly through the air in a calm night.

In this quarter, idolatry and superstition reign unmolested. These children of nature, we may with truth say, have not to this hour heard, except at a distance, of revealed religion, nor the sound of the gospel, although living in the vicinity of the settlement. Neither Roman Catholic priest, nor Protestant minister, though stationed in Red River for nearly twenty years, has ever visited these wretched beings at their camps. Could they draw nearer the settlement and find the means of living, they would no doubt be taken by the hand and receive instruction; but hitherto, with the exception of any advantage derived from the Hudson's Bay Company, they have remained a hopeless and friendless race. Where then are the thousands and tens of thousands subscribed by the liberal and charitable hand of benevolence for instructing the heathen? Is this the return that boasted England is to make the natives of Rupert's Land for impoverishing their country and draining off its riches during the last 200 years? But we have wandered from the story of our journey, which it is time to resume.

The season being now far advanced, and the piercing storms of winter at our heels, we proceeded from lake to lake, and from one camp to another, without seeing anything that the fancy or eye of curiosity could delight in; we therefore hastened our return to the colony. The lower district of the settlement, we may remark, is peopled with a mixture of all races, settled promiscuously together, like those above the Forks. On reaching the middle church, my companion intimated to me a desire not to return, as we had come, by the public road, but by the houses, in order to have a peep at the Scotch settlers and their domestic comforts; for the Scotch occupy the centre of the colony, and are mostly all together. This plan being agreed upon, we kept winding our way among the dwellings, where we spent a few days, and were warmly received and kindly treated by my countrymen with all the good things of the place, according to their usual hospitality. These people surpass in comfort those of the same class in most other countries. Rich in food and clothing, all of them have likewise saved more or less money. Abundance on every hand testifies to their industry and economy, and this within doors and without in the same profusion. The evidence of domestic happiness everywhere meets the eye. No want of blankets here on the beds; the children well clothed, and the houses warm and comfortable. The barns teeming with grain, the stables with cattle, and all classes wearing more or less of their own manufacture, which bespeaks a fair prospect for the future. My companion was often gratified by the scenes of industry around him, so different from the conduct of the people at the upper end of the settlement. Everything here is exactly as it ought to be. Every man minds his own business— every woman may be found in her own kitchen. The flail and spinning-wheel are ever at work. Such things, cheering in any country, are doubly so in Red River, which would else be a wilderness indeed.

A certain moral and religious discipline, of course, lays the foundation for the habits we have described. Every morning and evening the Bible is taken off the shelf, and family worship regularly observed. "We see no carioling, gossiping, card-playing, or idling here," observed my friend. "Not to any extent," said I; "the idler has no encouragement here." In their social relations, the Scotch are sober, shrewd, and attentive to their several duties, both as Christians and subjects; yet they are not altogether free from the influence of local habits. Their customs and habits have changed not a little with the change of country, as we have noticed before: they cariole, and go about too, on a small scale; nor is it likely they could be so near neighbours as they are to the good people above, without imbibing more or less of their habits and foibles. They often imitate the French, but the French never imitate them. The blue capote and red belt, so peculiar to those of French origin in this quarter, have become favourite articles of dress among the rising generation; and although this whim cannot be called a great deviation or fault, it may soon become so; for if we encourage foreign manufacture, it shows we lightly esteem our own. One false step often leads to another. There is likewise a strong infusion of French notions among the youngsters, notwithstanding all their whining and twaddle about the French not keeping the Sabbath-day holy. Carioling on Sunday is, perhaps, an instance in point. With the Canadians and half-breeds, every day is alike; but with the English community, Sunday is almost the only day for the practice of this worldly enjoyment. Although in the neighbourhood of the church, they take no small pleasure in assuming an air of importance, and aping manners which ought to be foreign to them. The fine horse and gay cariole may be seen gliding over the ice on the Sabbath morning, not going moderately, much less in that solemn and devout manner befitting the day or the occasion, but driving like Jehu of old, contesting the honour of arriving first at church. On such occasions they are not over civil either to strangers or superiors, nor will they give the road to any one with the easy and familiar politeness of a Frenchman. Indeed, it is not uncommon for "young Scotland" to enter the church whip in hand, and his tobacco-pipe stuck up in his pocket. We hardly need say that it was necessary to come to Red River to learn such practices.

The French, as already stated, make the church on Sundays and holydays a thorough fair; and now what is the practice of the English? It cannot be pronounced worse; but assuredly it is but little, if anything, better. All those on foot, on leaving the church, have to leave the road also, until the last horse and cariole has passed; or they must run the risk of being run down and trampled in the snow. Such is their observance of the Lord's day. These irreverent and wild freaks of horsemanship, however, it must be remembered, have their light as well as their dark aspect. During winter, almost the only indulgence of the population, whether French or English, consists in carioling—a pastime as innocent as it is amusing.

To conclude this somewhat lengthened chapter. Although we dwell on the outskirts of Christendom, holding as it were a middle course between refined civilization on the one hand, and gross darkness on the other, we live in all moderation and good fellowship in our semi-barbarous and semi-civilized state. The expressions used by my fellow-traveller when we reached the Forks, may be taken as a fair representation of the state of society amongst us, viewed at its best. " I have," said he, " travelled much in my time, and have seen many countries ; but, under all circumstances, I have seen no part of the world where the poor man enjoys so many privileges, and is more happy and independent than in Red River, and I regret I cannot prolong my stay to inform myself a little better on the subject of your laws and institutions ; but judging from what I have seen," you seem, said he to me, " to live almost without laws, and yet enjoy in that primeval condition more real happiness, comfort, and contentment, than any other people I ever saw; but I must hasten my departure, and take my leave of you, assuring you, and all my friends behind, that wherever Providence may destine my lot, I shall always cherish with fond recollection the kind and hospitable people of this colony." My friend and I then parted.

CHAPTER XVII.

CONTENTS.—Another experimental farm—Remarks—Views of the people at home—Comparisons—The half-pay officer—Great promises—Small performances—The first experiment—The grand operations—Stock—How far for the benefit of Red River—Quality of the hands—The hay party—Captain Cary—Result of the undertaking—Anecdote—The proposition—British Government—Civilization—The Scotch and their minister—The two zealots—Viewing things through a false medium—Mr. Cockran—Observations—Change of system—New laws—Judge Thom in Red River—Opinions of the people—Mr. Simpson, of the Arctic expedition—Subject continued—His death—North American half-breeds—Remarks—Subject concluded.

HAVING arrived at the commencement of the year 1838, we propose to conduct the reader through the operations of another experimental farm, set on foot with the same ostensible object in view as the former one, namely, the benefit of the settlement. We have often before remarked, that the people of Red River delight in novelty, and however great may be their failures and disappointments, they soon take courage again, and are ready for a new enterprise. It is not likely that our readers have forgotten the experiments already made under this familiar name; nor do we think they will easily forget the one of which we are about to give some account; for each of them has had its characteristic mark. In Red River these farming bubbles have been designated the " three unfortunate sisters," in allusion to their results.

The difficulties to be overcome in a first experiment are usually much greater than in a second, or a third, of the same kind. In the present instance, however, we derived little or no advantage from past experience, since the plan was now dictated by a committee in London, some 4,000 miles from the scene of operations, whose orders had to be implicitly followed. To prevent, as they thought, a repetition of the ruinous results of the former experimental farm, the London committee, in place of appointing a fur trader to the office of manager, sent out from England, at a high salary, a half-pay officer of the army, who was accompanied by people of little, if any, experience in agricultural pursuits.

Behold, then, Captain George Marcus Cary, the gentleman alluded to, and his experimental squad, some twenty in number, men and women, commencing operations on that point of rich alluvial soil where the Assiniboine enters the Red River, adjoining the site of old Fort Garry! Here a grand establishment was got up, and a full supply of the most costly implements imported on a scale far beyond anything we had yet seen in the colony. In short, nothing was wanting that money could procure. The new comers delighted to expatiate on the advantages of skill and system combined together, the prodigies contemplated, the experiments to be made, and the results that were to follow, compared with our manner of doing things in the settlement hitherto. The interest excited, made all listen in silent admiration, with eyes and ears open. A new era was about to commence; and the Captain himself, full of theory, and big with projects, raised expectation to its highest pitch, so that there was but one opinion, "The Company have hit upon it at last!" Nevertheless, though men and implements were set to work, two years had passed by before twenty acres of mellow soil were under cultivation; nor at the end of ten years more had this grand farming scheme extended another acre! The whole farm enclosed did not much exceed eighty acres, and a fourth part of that was never under cultivation.

On this contracted spot, Captain Cary and his operatives exercised their agricultural talents in raising wheat, barley, potatoes, and turnips—articles which every one in Red River had for sale, and for which there was no market. In this manner they kept going round and round, like the blind horse in the mill, always finding themselves, in the evening, where they had started from in the morning; till the spot was ruined, and themselves bewildered with the painful result. They barely succeeded in feeding themselves, and therefore had no spare produce to return to the Company.

The only benefit the settlers derived from the example of the experimental farmers, and what they had not learned of themselves before, was to mow down their fields of grain with the scythe, in place of cutting it with the sickle; and to gather it with rakes in lieu of tying it into sheaves. With this practice, by the way, we had little reason to quarrel—the model farmers were really playing our game; because what was left or lost by the slovenly process on the fields, required no market. This was the first, the last, and the only experiment they exhibited for our benefit; and because we would not follow their example, they swore they would show us no more; and they kept their word. The dairy served to keep the Governor's tea-table in milk; but his butter and cheese were still furnished by the settlers: this part of the experiment proved a complete failure. For a year or two, a few quarters of flax seed were cultivated; but, as in the former experiment, it grew up only to rot without further notice. Hemp was equally a dead letter. During a year or two, a flock of some two or three hundred sheep were attached to the farm, but they soon dribbled into the hands of the settlers; and the wool which was not allowed to rot, got also into their hands, at a shilling the pound. A herd of swine was also kept up; but the poor creatures were generally so famished, as to render it prudent in the wayfarer to keep at a respectful distance from them. Geese, hens, and turkeys, also adorned the princely farm during the days of its sunshine.

All this profusion of good things was consumed at the farm establishment. Was such a project, then, we may ask, calculated to benefit the settlers, who had themselves similar articles for sale—nay, taking the aggregate, had them in ten times the profusion required to supply the limited market. We trow not. Rather, it was shutting up so far, if it had succeeded, the only market that existed for colonial produce. Every ounce or shilling's worth supplied to the Company by their own experimental farm, would lessen the settlers' market. It still may be argued as beneficial to the settlement in the way of example; for had not the influence of system, the rotation of crops, and the general working of the plan, a good effect on the farmers of Red River? We answer, no!

Bad as the system or want of system in the colony may have been, it was in every respect superior and better adapted to the country than the experimental farm methods. The settlers had always the better crops, both in quantity and quality. The most ordinary farmer in the place sowed as well, ploughed as well, did three times as much work, and kept his fields, his grain, and his cattle in better order, than was the case at the experimental farm; much of this, however, depended on the quality of the hands employed; they were awkward, ignorant, and stubborn. The most simple of Tusser's "five hundred points of good husbandry" they had yet to learn, and they also forgot they were in Red River; for they could neither work nor eat without the beer pot at their lips; they slowly moved at the sound of the bell. Before six in the morning, or after six in the evening, they would scarcely budge, had the house been on fire about their ears. Seed time and harvest time, summer and winter, was all one to them. Still it is not with the good or bad qualities of the farm-servants that we have to deal; and have only touched upon them to show, that had they come out for the benefit of the colony, the good derived from their skill, conduct, and exertions, would have been small indeed. Take the following as an example:—

The article of hay was very scarce one year in the neighbourhood, so that the Captain had a place examined some ten miles off, where it was to be had in abundance. To this spot the settlers, in years of scarcity, generally resort, for the same purpose as was the case this year; and hither our model farmer despatched seven of his best mowers, provisioned for a month. Of course, these pampered gentlemen were not disposed to go haymaking, as the settlers do, with a piece of dry pemmican for their food, the swamp water their only beverage. No, indeed, they must have their douceurs, their tit-bits, their dainties; and the Captain being an indulgent master, fitted them out with all the luxuries of a more favoured country—their beef, their mutton, their butter, their cheese, tea, coffee, and something stronger into the bargain, with all the apparatus and cattle necessary for carrying on their work to the best advantage. After some days' preparation, the hay party, along with a squad of the settlers, took its departure; it was a Monday morning, as we recollect. The latter got to the ground at 9 o'clock in the forenoon, and before night, had averaged five loads a-piece of cut hay; while the experimental boys, who only reached the field of their labours at 1 o'clock in the afternoon, spent the rest of the day in putting up their tents, and making themselves comfortable. Tuesday, they spent the day in gossip, and boasting what they could do. On Wednesday, they did not like their encampment, shifted to another, and prepared for the following day.

Thursday they commenced work. Friday their oxen strayed away, and they spent the day in getting them together. Saturday, they turned their faces towards the settlement, and resolved on home! Two of them returned late in the evening; but the other five made for the beer-shops, where the mortified Captain had hard work to find them out, and only got them home on the following Tuesday. Various were the reports they made to their disappointed master; but when the truth became known, the seven experimental lads had, during the week they were absent, cut the enormous quantity of ten loads of hay!

Captain Cary, the chief manager of the experimental farm, was a person of active business habits, sober, intelligent, and prepossessing in his manners; in all respects a gentleman of amiable qualities; but his agricultural knowledge consisted in theory alone—the practical qualifications were wanting. He had read a great deal, and was possessed of much general information; but was, in point of fact, more of a florist than agriculturist. After dragging on for about ten years, without advancing a step, or doing a farthing's worth of good to the colony, the prodigal experiment was wound up; and the stock, implements, &c., being sold off, left the experimenters minus 5,500*l*. The zealous Captain was so disgusted with the whole affair, that he left the colony in a pet, and removed with his family to Canada.

The object of the Company was probably not very clear to themselves; but if we may judge from circumstances, it was far from a sincere purpose towards the settlement. Captain Cary often remarked on this point to the writer, in terms which we may here quote: "When I left London," said he, "the Committee held out the fairest prospects; and so deeply did that body appear to be interested and sincere in the success of their plan, that I was promised, in addition to my salary, a certain share in the profits; but when I came to Red River, the feeling about its success, among the Company's officers, seemed to be the very reverse; cold water was thrown on the whole project, and all my plans and movements were fettered, as if the officials were perfectly indifferent about its success." It has been stated, but whether true or false we know not, that 6,000*l.* had been laid aside for the speculation, and the feeling was, the sooner it was got out of hand the better; that, at least according to this story, was all the Company cared about it. If this statement be true, there must have been a *mal entendre* or mystery in some quarter. We have already noticed in our experience of things here, that the Company in London and the Company in Red River are two different things; and here we have before us a practical illustration of the fact. This we know, that Captain Cary and the Company in Red River seldom pulled together. He always said, he was entitled to a tenth share of the profits. "If," said he, "the business has failed, it is the fault of the Company, not mine." On repeating this one day, the writer observed to him, he had better hold his tongue, and say nothing on that head, or he might be brought in for a corresponding share of the loss. One thing we know—his appointment proved a profitable sinecure to him.

Before taking leave of the Captain, we might mention the following anecdote. On the arrival of his party in the colony, I happened to join the Captain as he stepped on shore, and as we walked along, we had to cross a ploughed field, on seeing which, the Captain stopped short, and turning suddenly round to me exclaimed, " What! the people of Red River know how to plough!" "Yes," said I, "we do a little in that way, and sow too." If the ploughed field astonished the Captain, his remark no less surprised me; as it showed how little he knew of our history.

We have stated over and over again, and in most instances proved by a variety of circumstances, that neither this nor the other experimental farms could have been designed for the benefit of the settlers. A question then arises, if not for the benefit of the settlers, for whose benefit were they? And what could have been the Company's motives for their introduction? It could not have been, at least in a pecuniary point of view, for the Company's own benefit. At first view it is, we must confess, a subject that might appear to many as mysterious as the " handwriting on the wall;" but to those who penetrate a little below the surface of things, and weigh impartially the state of affairs in this quarter, the Company's motives for making such a sacrifice as this venture proved, are not absolutely impenetrable. It is a common saying here, "When the Company deal in furs, they work for money; but when they farm, they work for fame!" Now, as success attending the experimental farm would have more and more embarrassed the limited market here, everything seemed to be so calculated as to ensure its failure; and if that was virtually the object, no better plan than the course pursued could have been devised.

A gentleman of long standing in the colony, talking over these matters one day, expressed himself thus:— "You don't seem to understand the matter right. The fact is, that the colony, on a small scale, is favourable to the Company's interest, in order to ensure its supplies on the spot, and give a tone to its proceedings at home; but were it to increase in numbers, wealth, and power, the colony, in the nature of things, must soon have a voice of its own, and that voice would render allegiance extremely doubtful: even the existence of the great monopoly itself might receive a shock from a thriving settlement in Red River. And this mode of reasoning," said he, "is applicable to the export trade question, as well as the experimental farms, and many things else in this quarter; so that we can very easily and reasonably account for their failures, on the same principle—a principle inherent in all governments, to pursue that line of policy best suited to their own aggrandizement."

This reasoning, we must confess, hardly appears to us as conclusive. It might have been just a century ago, when the country was rich in furs; but at the present time, when the wild animals are completely swept away, the country ruined, and the Company, in a manner, as much occupied everywhere in farming operations as in the pursuits of hunting, it cannot hold good. Their business is said to be a losing game; and the Company, it is rumoured, are anxious to get it off their hands. Civilization at length dawns far and wide throughout Rupert's Land. The plough is at work in almost every valley, and the missionary threads almost every wild. The door, as it were, stands open; the time is come for the full tide of emigration to pour in; and we hope the day is not far distant, when the British Government will say to the Hudson's Bay Company, "Relinquish your chartered rights, not without their just value, indeed, and we will take the country to ourselves." This is what the Company is looking for; and we hope, for the sake of the redundant population of the British isles, the bargain will be speedily and finally closed.

At the period we have reached, the Scotch settlers and their minister again court our attention. It will be remembered that we left them in some degree contented with the endeavours of Mr. Cockran, to accommodate the service of the Church of England to their spiritual wants; and so long as that gentleman was left to the exercise of his own judgment, things went on as well as could be expected. Unhappily it was not long before this good understanding was again disturbed, by the arrival of two new labourers in the missionary field. The great good that such men have done, and are doing in many parts of the world, claim our admiration; yet it cannot be denied, that they have often injured their own cause by uncalled for interference with other sects. It was so in Red River during Mr. West's time, when he could not rest without experimenting on the Roman Catholics. In the like spirit, his successors have continually agitated the Presbyterians, with no better result than a mere waste of time and money. No sooner had the holy zealots alluded to entered the settlement, than they began to find fault with Mr. Cockran for what they considered a deviation from the ordinary forms and ceremonies of the English church. In an evil hour, the minister gave way to their counsel; and in so doing, he revived the smouldering embers of contention between himself and the people.

The two new comers took no small merit to themselves for having thus, by their interference, restored the fallen church to her orthodox purity. We willingly recognise their claims to this distinction; for, in speaking of Mr. Cockran, notwithstanding he has often raised his voice against the Presbyterian party, it is but justice to acquit him of so much bigotry and imprudence. Of all the missionaries sent to Red River in our day, none has laboured more zealously in God's vineyard than he; none has accomplished so much good; and as a Christian at the bed of sickness, or as a friend to the helpless poor, no minister of the Gospel ever surpassed him. Deeply it is to be regretted that the services of such a man should not have been secured for the poor neglected Indian.

We have recorded the first introduction of constitutional laws into this settlement; now five years ago. During all this period they worked remarkably well, and gave general satisfaction, *without the aid of lawyers*, with the exception, as already noticed, of the $7\frac{1}{2}$ per cent. on imports, which being found obnoxious and oppressive, was rescinded by an order of council, and reduced, first to five, and then to four per cent; which, remains unaltered to this day. In other respects, no complaints were made; in no instance were the decisions of the magistrates questioned or disobeyed; no collision of interests or parties disturbed the peace. So much confidence was placed in the simple and straightforward course pursued, that the good will of the people always backed and strengthened the hands of justice. Thus peace and order were thoroughly maintained throughout every part of the settlement; the laws were respected, and life and property was everywhere secure.

To let well alone has always been a maxim with us; but with this course some are not satisfied. In order to give a more legal tone to our judicial proceedings, and lend strength, as they supposed, to the arm of justice, the Company introduced a professional man into the colony this year, under the title of Recorder of Rupert's Land, and placed him as judge in Red River. As Recorder of Rupert's Land there could have been no objection raised; but as judge in the colony, the appointment raised up a formidable host of objections. Its legality we do not pretend to discuss, but simply to remark upon it as a disturbing cause; since, in place of the simple honesty which marked our proceedings hitherto, it has a tendency to substitute the quibbles and technicalities of law, which few but lawyers themselves comprehend. Besides this, a professional judge on the bench, without a professional lawyer at the bar, is an anomaly in judicial proceedings; not to mention that this high functionary is a paid servant of the Company's, drawing a liberal salary of 700*l.* sterling per annum. In the nature of things, a paid servant must have a special eye to his employer's interest, above that of all others.

Intellectually considered, Judge Thom is a gentleman of talent and high attainments in his profession; but under all the circumstances, whether such a man would be any advantage to the settlement was very problematical. On this point, public opinion was divided. Mr. Thom being a Company's man, the people observed, "He cannot be the man for us;" and they added, that as the Company had got a legal adviser, the people ought to have another, in order to keep the equilibrium of justice on a fair balance. "A lawyer on either side," said the people, "or no lawyer at all;" this was their creed; and whether law or no law, it was certainly common sense. Others, again, objected to Mr. Thom on the ground that he could not speak French, which, nevertheless, was the language spoken by the majority of the population. Some of these might have had less weight, had it not been noised abroad on the arrival of Mr. Thom, that during the Papineau troubles in Canada, he was no favourite of the French. "Will he," said the Canadians and half-breeds here, "be more favourable to us than he was to our countrymen in Canada?" In short, the dislike became a fixed prejudice, which time only served to strengthen.

It must be admitted that the fundamental objection against Mr. Thom was not unreasonable. All the affairs of the colony, politically and judicially, as in other countries, lay between the rulers and the ruled, with the exception of trifling occurrences between man and man; and as a matter of course, in all such cases, whether civil or criminal, the person appointed must preside as judge. A man, then, placed in Mr. Thom's position, liable to be turned out of office at the Company's pleasure, naturally provokes the doubt whether he could, at all times, be proof against the sin of partiality. Is it likely he could always take that impartial view of a case that might involve in its results his own interest, or deprive him of his daily bread? Mr. Thom might be the most upright man in the world; yet human nature is weak, and gifts too often corrupt those who profit by them. In every case, then, where Mr. Thom sat as judge, to decide between the Company and the people, or in which the former were directly or indirectly concerned, he sat as it were in his own cause—being, from what has been stated, more or less interested in the result; and for any man to sit as judge in a case wherein he himself is concerned, is as contrary to law and justice as to common sense. In this respect, the law, in its anxiety to do justice, looks on all interested parties as partial. Such was the common sense opinion of the people on the arrival of their judge in 1839; and having now stated the facts, we shall reserve the working of this system for future notice.

With feelings of deep regret we now come to a subject already associated with the affairs of Red River. We have, in the course of our remarks, had occasion to mention the name of Mr. Simpson of the Arctic expedition. We now resume that painful and somewhat mysterious subject, with the view of following it up till the final catastrophe which closed the earthly career of that bold and adventurous traveller; and likewise to clear up some mysterious points as to the manner in which he came by his death.

It is stated in the "Memoir" that " on the 6th of June 1840, Mr. Simpson left Red River Settlement for the purpose of crossing the prairies to St. Peter's on the Mississippi, and thence making his way to England. On starting from the colony, he was accompanied by a party of settlers and half-breeds. Eager to reach England, he got tired in a very few days of their slow movements, and went on ahead in company with a party of four men. He pursued his journey with much rapidity; for, on a chart which was found with his other papers after his death, we trace his day's journey on the 11th of June to have been forty-seven miles in a straight line.

" Subsequent to that date every circumstance is involved in mystery. All that can be ascertained with certainty is, that, on the afternoon of the 13th or 14th of June, Mr. Simpson shot two of his companions; that the other two mounted their horses and rejoined the larger party, a part of which went to the encampment where Mr. Simpson was alone, on the next morning; and that Mr. Simpson's death then took place.

" Whether he shot these men in self-defence, and was subsequently put to death by their companions; or whether the severe stretch to which his faculties had been subjected for several years, brought on a temporary hallucination of mind, under the influence of which the melancholy tragedy took place, is known to God, and to the surviving actors in that tragedy.

" But it must be noticed, in support of the former supposition, that the depositions of those who pretend to describe the manner of his death are contradictory in the extreme. Moreover, the North American half-breed is, of all races in the world, that which retains the *odium in longum jaciens*. Mr. Simpson had five years before incurred the animosity of the half-breeds of Red River, by inflicting a chastisement on one of them who had grossly insulted him, and they then threatened his life. Three of his companions were of this race. They saw Mr. Simpson returning to England, after having achieved an object important in itself, but of which they even exaggerated the importance; their long-treasured animosity was likely to have shown itself in threats and insults, if not in actual attack; and hence, it is the opinion of many intelligent men who have examined the circumstances, and are acquainted with the character of the half-caste natives, resulted the events which cut short the career of this enterprising young traveller."

Such is the account of the circumstances given in Mr. Simpson's Memoir. A more exact review of the particulars, however, will place them in a different light, and account for the discrepancies in the affidavits. On the 10th of June, Mr. Simpson left the main party and shot ahead with three men and a boy. For two days they forced their march, and pursued their journey with unusual rapidity; Mr. Simpson himself keeping at times far ahead, and at other times turning back to meet his men, and then dart off again ahead, as if impatient at their delay, without saying a word, but apparently in great uneasiness and anxiety of mind. At last the men observed to him, that if he continued to proceed thus, their horses would soon get worn out, and they would find themselves awkwardly situated in the midst of an enemy's country. "Well, then," said he, abruptly, "let us turn back!" and, without waiting for a reply, wheeled round at full speed, to retrace his steps. The men, thinking he was in jest, stood still for some time; but seeing him nearly out of sight, and still going on, they spurred their horses and followed in his track. On observing this, Mr. Simpson turned back as if to meet them; but suddenly changing his mind, went off again at the gallop on his former course, without saying a word.

However painful the conclusion, conduct like this admits of only one explanation. For some days previous, also, Mr. Simpson showed great absence of mind, looked wild, and spoke but little; would stand among his people, contrary to his usual habit, without saying a word; and would often rise in the night, and walk about stark naked. From the time he left Fort Garry, and even before, his words and actions betrayed symptoms of aberration of mind; but this passed for mere anxiety about his journey, without any special notice being taken of it at the time.

On the third day after turning back and pursuing this zig-zag course, for they did not follow any direct path, they crossed the track in rear of the main party. His men pointed out the fact, but Mr. Simpson exclaimed, "It is not true," and then added, "You wish to humbug me!" At the same time, the unfortunate man pointed out a spot a little on one side where he declared his intention to encamp, but after reaching the place, he selected another, and there they put up for the night.

We now come to the tragedy. The moment the party alighted from their horses, Mr. Simpson placed all their guns together by the cart, a circumstance quite unusual. It was already late; the moon shone bright; and as two of his men were in the act of putting up his tent, Mr. Simpson suddenly laid hold of his double-barreled gun, and without a word being uttered on either side, shot them both dead. This happened on the evening of the 14th. He then said to Bruce, "I am justified by the laws of England in killing these two men; for they had conspired to kill me this night, and carry off all my papers!" Hereupon, also, he demanded of him, if he knew the road back to Red River? Bruce turning round to hear what he was saying, he made signs to him with his hand, exclaiming, "Keep off! keep off!" and then added, "Go and bridle the horses, and if you conduct me back to Red River, the Company will give you 500*l*." Bruce and the boy each seized a horse and galloped off to rejoin the main party; for at this time, Mr. Simpson was about twenty-two miles behind. The sun had been up some time when they reached the spot.

An hour or two after their arrival, it now being the morning of the 15th, a party of six men, including Bruce, mounted their horses and returned to the fatal spot. "When about 200 yards off, seeing nobody stirring about," says Bruce, "we made a halt, and called to Mr. Simpson by name, but received no answer: we then went round, and took up another position, about the same distance off, and hailed Mr. Simpson again, but still no reply. After a few minutes had elapsed, we saw him distinctly get up in a sitting or leaning posture, and presently a shot was fired from the spot, and we heard the ball whistling in the air. At first we supposed the ball to have been fired at ourselves, but afterwards concluded that it was shot at random as a warning for us not to approach nearer. Gaubin, one of our party, then fired a shot, and hit the cart. Richotte fired another, and wounded a dog belonging to the camp. The rest fired off their guns in the air. After a pause of some minutes, we resolved to approach crawling through the grass on our bellies; but finally agreed, as the better plan, that one man should mount a swift horse, throw himself flat on his back, and pass the camp at full speed, to see what he could discover. The signal being made by the man on horseback, we all approached the spot. Mr. Simpson was lying stretched at full length, with his face on the ground, the body warm, and the butt-end of the gun between his knees, the muzzle in a line with his head where the shot took effect, one barrel empty, and his right hand with the glove off, along the guard: his night-cap blown some yards off, in a line with the position of the gun. The left hand, with the glove on, was on his breast. The body, in the position it lay, almost covered the gun." With these facts before us, there can be no doubt as to the manner in which Mr. Simpson came by his death.

It is remarkable, that during the night, Mr. Simpson had covered the two bodies, one with his tent, the other with the blankets, and had laid his own pillows under their heads; from the beaten path it was apparent that he had passed the night walking to and fro between them. The party having buried all the bodies, returned to the camp on the same day.

It is stated in Mr. Simpson's memoir "that the depositions of those who pretend to describe the manner of his death are contradictory in the extreme." This may be the case, and we can easily account for it. Till the party reached St. Peter's, nearly a month after the tragedy took place, no one ever thought of drawing up a statement of the facts as they occurred; questions were then asked when no one was prepared by anticipation to answer them with the necessary exactness; the scrutiny itself was too much of the kind dictated by curiosity—hurried, imperfect, and contradictory; besides which, Bruce alone could have given the information correctly. All these contradictions, however, were subsequently corrected. With reference to the affidavits, four of the depositions were taken by the writer, as magistrate of the district of Assiniboine, copies of which are now before him; and although taken at different periods, there is scarcely any discrepancy observable. They not only agree on the main point, but on all minor points also. The facts, indeed, were compared and confirmed by examining the spot afterwards. Bruce, one of the deponents, travelled with Mr. Simpson from the hour he left Red River, till the moment the two unfortunate men fell.

The memoir goes on to say :—" Moreover, the North American half-breed is, of all races in the world, that which most retains the *odium in longum jaciens.*" This may or may not be true; but for my own part, I have travelled and lived with the North American half-breeds for nearly half a century now, and quarreled with them too; yet I found them neither more vindictive nor revengeful than South American half-breeds, or the half-breeds or whole breeds of any other country. They are, in short, much like other people—*aliqui boni aliqui mali;* but I might say more: the North American half-breeds, are by no means a people who treasure up animosity long, if they can resent it soon; they are rather a fickle people, who act according to the impulse of the moment, give free scope to their passions, quarrel this moment, and become friends again the next. This disposition is more peculiarly the case with those of French extraction, and Mr. Simpson's quarrel " five years before," was purely with the French half-breeds; men in whose power he had frequently been, by day and night, since his quarrel with them, had they set their hearts on revenge. The truth is, on the contrary, that they respected him for his daring hardihood, and loved him for his generosity.

Apart from these considerations, the French half-breeds could certainly have had no hand in the present melancholy affair. Mr. Simpson's travelling companions were Antoine Legros, a pure Canadian; John Bird, an English, and James Bruce, a Scotch half-breed: the fourth was a boy—Legros's son. But a conclusive argument still remains to be adduced. On receiving the intelligence of Mr. Simpson's death, a medical gentleman, with a party of men, was sent from the colony to the scene of the tragedy, and having disinterred the bodies, and examined them, his report fully confirms the truth of the above statement. It may be added as a curious fact that, although the deed was committed within two days' travel of Pembina, the account of it had time to reach the remotest parts of the earth, before we heard of it in the colony; it not having reached us before the party returned from the States, in the month of October following.

CHAPTER XVIII.

CONTENTS.—Half-breeds in Red River—Parents and children—Company's policy—Relative position of the Company and half-breeds—Steps against interlopers—The French half-breeds change—The cause—The English half-breeds join them—Influence of Papineau's rebellion—Mob-meeting—Half-breeds demand an export trade—Governor Simpson's reply—Foreigners at the buffalo-hunts—Influence of buffalo-hunting on the colonists—The outfit and start—Pembina camp—Number of carts—Dogs—Anecdote—Camp regulations—Honesty of the half-breeds—Officials—Council—Stroll in the camp—Two sides to the picture—First sight of the battle-field—The half-breeds in their glory—Sky darkened—Casualties—Fruits of the chase—Comparison—The risks—The duties—Vallé and the Sioux—Speedy revenge—Pleasures of the chase—Question and answer—Chamois hunter—The mêlée—Perplexing scene—Remarks—The conflict—The waste—Camp raised again—Descent to the Missouri—Tariff—Uncertain travelling—The Sioux chief—Indian telegraphs—The fatal storm—The battle—Loss of life—Sioux warriors—Reflections—Expedition arrives—Effect—Provisions—Result of expedition.

WE have already had frequent occasion to allude to that portion of our community called the half-breed class, and have given a somewhat particular account of their social relations and domestic habits. We now come to regard them as an integral part of the community, whose pursuits affect, more or less, all the great interests of our colonial life. We shall describe, in short, their hunting expeditions while in the plains, their mode of carrying them on, and the general result, both as regards themselves in particular and the settlement at large. The unceasing succession of whims and changes which characterize the operations of this class throughout the year, cannot indeed be given in detail; but an outline of their proceedings will not be without its interest.

First, then, the class of which we are speaking may be considered, in a general sense, as the children of the Hudson's Bay Company—at any rate as their adopted children; that Company having, at the period of the coalition with the North-West Company, become by law the rightful owners of their parents' inheritance. The question then arises, whether the Company, as the common parent of these people, have done all that parents could or ought to have done for their children?

From the manner in which these people were brought up about the Company's establishments, as hunters and plain-rangers, it was natural to expect that they would show a decided preference for such pursuits, and cling to their early habits. When, therefore, they began to flock into Red River in crowds, and turn their attention to the plain and to buffalo-hunting, it was the proper business of the Company to direct their energies into some useful channel, and not suffer them to be frittered away in desultory operations. Experience could not but have taught them, that however insignificant and powerless these people were while scattered by twos and threes about their distant parts, yet, assembled together in one place with one common interest, one common object in view, they must soon become formidable either as friends or as foes. The course which the Company pursued towards the half-breeds on their arrival is sufficient to prove that they were guided by a due sense of this responsibility. They were not, indeed, united together by the Company's aid into one joint association as buffalo-hunters, which, under all circumstances, might have been the best plan; yet individually they were taken by the hand the moment they arrived. Those who wished to settle were allowed lands on their own terms; others were taken into the service and employed in every possible way they could be made useful; while such of them as were able hunters received every encouragement, got advances, and were fitted out with everything necessary for the plains, to be paid for at their own convenience. Here is the language in which they were addressed by the Company on their arrival:—" My friends! in coming to Red River you evince a laudable feeling, a determination to throw off your savage customs, follow the habits of white men, and cultivate civilization. If these are your views, the Company will hold out to you the right hand of fellowship, and give you every encouragement; but, remember, there is no field here for the pursuits of savage life; your hunting and roving propensities cannot be indulged; you must settle down, cultivate the soil, and become Christians."

The fairest promises were made in answer to this

appeal; but notwithstanding all the advantages before them, it was soon evident that the habits of a lifetime were not to be overcome easily. Those who took lands, after destroying the timber, abandoned them; those who made choice of the service soon left it, and drew into the colony again: the plains had too many attractions for men trained up in the school of idleness and wild freedom. All eyes, all hearts, were directed to the buffalo; and the plains became the favourite haunt of all the half-breeds. The Company, nevertheless, still sympathized with and assisted them, more or less; but as they increased and became formidable in numbers, their filial duty began to cool, their allegiance became doubtful, until, as we have before observed, what at first was asked as a favour was at last boldly demanded as a right, and every refusal was met on their part by a menace or threat. In this state of things, it required but a spark to set the combustible materials into a living flame, and that spark soon fell among them.

In their vagrant mode of life, the half-breeds, frequently crossing and re-crossing the line, had tampered with the Company's rights, contrary to the regulations of the colony. This conduct was not altogether overlooked at the time, for they were distinctly warned of the line of conduct they were to pursue in future; yet their apparent impunity served as an invitation to others, who could not plead the same ignorance. In restraining these interlopers, the Company's officers went a step too far themselves. A Canadian, by the name of Registe Larant, having, as was alleged, been guilty of infringing the Company's chartered rights, his house was forced open, and the furs it contained forcibly seized by the Company's officers. A similar act was committed on another Canadian; and a third seizure was made at Manetobah Lake, and the owner of the furs made prisoner, conveyed to York Factory, and threatened with deportation to England. These acts greatly enraged the whole Canadian population; and as that class exercised considerable influence over the French half-breeds, chiefly their own offspring, they delighted to aggravate their hatred against their superiors. From this moment both parties united in sentiment and ill-will against the rule of the Company.*

The English half-breeds for a while remained staunch, but they also at length considered themselves aggrieved by the following circumstance:—One of the Company's officers, residing at a distance, had placed two of his daughters at the boarding-school in the settlement. An English half-breed, a comely, well-behaved young man, of respectable connections, was paying his addresses to one of these young ladies, and had asked her in marriage. The young lady had another suitor in the person of a Scotch lad; but her affections were in

* We may here remark, by the way, that these acts were at the time considered heedless and impolitic, inasmuch as there was no proof that the furs thus seized were to have been sent out of the country through any other channel than that of the Company. The Company at home, indeed, took this view of the case by reprimanding its officers and indemnifying the parties injured; and so effectual was their policy, that for the last twenty-five years only one solitary instance of trespass against the Company's rights has occurred. Subjects in Red River enjoy great freedom under the Company's sway.

favour of the former, while her guardian, the chief officer in Red River, preferred the latter. In his zeal to succeed in the choice he had made for the young lady, this gentleman sent for the half-breed, and reprimanded him for aspiring to the hand of a lady accustomed, as he expressed it, to the first society. The young man, without saying a word, put on his hat and walked out of the room; but being a leading man among his countrymen, the whole fraternity took fire at the insult. " This is the way," said they, " that we half-breeds are despised and treated." From that moment they clubbed together, in high dudgeon, and joined the French malcontents against their rulers; so that for years afterwards this spirit of combination and hatred gave rise to plots, plans, and unlawful meetings among them, which threatened, and threatens, in a more or less degree, to this moment, the peace and tranquillity of the settlement. As we could not avoid mention of this love-story, we may add that the Scotchman carried off the prize.

The Papineau rebellion which broke out in Canada about this time, and the echo of which soon reached us, added fresh fuel to the spirit of disaffection. The Canadians of Red River sighed for the success of their brethren's cause. Patriotic songs were chanted on every side in praise of Papineau. In the plains, the half-breeds made a flag, called the Papineau standard, which was waved in triumph for years, and the rebels' deeds extolled to the skies.

Such was the spirit of the times when the collision between Mr. Simpson and the half-breeds took place, and we have had two or three disturbances since. Last spring upwards of 300 of them assembled at Fort Garry, demanding a higher price for their plain provisions; but their request was no sooner complied with, than they were loud in their demands for an export trade. The Governor-in-chief, being on the spot, answered this demand by one of his own. "What," said he to them, "have you got for sale?" well knowing that at the time they had nothing to eat, far less to sell. "What," repeated he again to them, "have you got for sale?" They looked at each other, but uttered not a word. Continuing the subject, the Governor observed again, "My friends! if you can load a ship, half a ship, or a quarter of a ship, I shall furnish you with that ship for nothing I will do more for you; if you can furnish even a boat's load of any exportable article, I shall take it off your hands immediately, and pay you down the London price for it!" It may be imagined how sheepish they looked, with this brilliant prospect before them, and not an ounce of anything for sale. Their mouths being thus completely shut, they dropped away, one by one, without saying a word.

When any threat or demand is contemplated, which may lead to a disturbance, the Canadians never fail to act as prompters, and push the half-breeds forward in the front rank, while they themselves are slyly lurking behind the curtains. This is always their mode of attack; and the half-breeds, from their ignorance and simplicity, are invariably made the silly tools of their more designing confederates. It is never any definite grievance they complain of; but sometimes one thing, sometimes another. The minds of the ignorant are poisoned and inflamed by restless and disaffected demagogues, who wish to put down the existence of all social order, law, and subordination in the settlement. Nor is this deplorable state of things to be much wondered at, considering the mixed and discordant elements of our population, and our situation in a country so remote, with no protection but the good will of the people.

With these general remarks, we turn more particularly to our proposed subject—the plains and plain-hunters. Buffalo-hunting here, like bear-hunting in India, has become a popular and favourite amusement among all classes; and Red River, in consequence, has been brought into some degree of notice, by the presence of strangers from foreign countries. We are now occasionally visited by men of science as well as men of pleasure. The war road of the savage, and the solitary haunt of the bear, have of late been resorted to by the florist, the botanist, and the geologist; nor is it uncommon now-a-days to see Officers of the Guards, Knights, Baronets, and some of the higher nobility of England, and other countries, coursing their steeds over the boundless plains, and enjoying the pleasures of the chase among the half-breeds and savages of the country. Distinction of rank is, of course, out of the question; and, at the close of the adventurous day, all squat down in merry mood together, enjoying the social freedom of equality round Nature's table, and the novel treat of a fresh buffalo-steak served up in the style of the country —that is to say, roasted on a forked stick before the fire; a keen appetite their only sauce, cold water their only beverage. Looking at this assemblage through the medium of the imagination, the mind is led back to the chivalric period of former days, when chiefs and vassals "took counsel together." It may be trusted, that the moral influence will eventually lead to the elevation of the savage, and add a link to the chain of his progress in civilization.

The half-breeds, from their intermarriages and other connections with the Indians, form, at least when united together, nearly a half of the settlement; certainly a striking fact, when it is remembered what a gipsy-like class they are, holding themselves above all restraint, and well knowing the defenceless state of the colony. In other countries property gives strength, and the want of it weakness; but here the case is reversed. Not to be unjust, and considering the risks and hazards they run in acquiring a livelihood, the half-breeds are by no means an ill disposed people—on the contrary, they possess many good qualities; while enjoying a sort of licentious freedom, they are generous, warm-hearted, and brave, and left to themselves, quiet and orderly. They are, unhappily, as unsteady as the wind in all their habits, fickle in their dispositions, credulous in their faith, and clannish in their affections. In a word, of all people they are the easiest led astray and made the dupes of designing men.

With the earliest dawn of spring, the hunters are in motion, like bees, and the colony in a state of confusion, from their going to and fro, in order to raise the wind, and prepare themselves for the fascinating enjoyments of hunting. It is now that the Company, the farmers, the petty traders, are all beset by their incessant and irresistible importunities. The plain mania brings everything else to a stand. One wants a horse, another an axe, a third a cart; they want ammunition, they want clothing, they want provisions; and though people may refuse one or two they cannot deny a whole population, for indeed over much obstinacy would not be unattended with risk. Thus the settlers are reluctantly dragged into profligate speculation—a system fraught with much evil, and ruinous alike to the giver and receiver of such favours.

The plain-hunters, finding they can get whatever they want without ready money, are led into ruinous extravagances; but the evil of the long credit system does not end here. It is now deeply rooted, and infused into all the affairs and transactions of the place. Nor, indeed, is this the worst. The baneful influence of these wild and licentious expeditions over the minds and morals of the people is so uncontrollable, that it unhinges all their ideas, and draws into its illusive train, not only the hunters, but almost every class of our population. So many temptations, so many attractions are held out to the thoughtless and giddy, so fascinating is the sweet air of freedom, that even the offspring of Europeans, as well as natives, are often induced to cast off their habits of industry, and leave their comfortable homes to try their fortunes in the plains; there, however, disappointment and ruin never fail to convince them of their error, and dearly at last do they repent their folly.

The practical result of all this may be stated in few words. After the expedition starts, there is not a man-servant or maid-servant to be found in the colony. At any season but seed time and harvest time, the settlement is literally swarming with idlers; but at these urgent periods, money cannot procure them. This alone is most injurious to the agricultural class, and if so, to every other in the settlement; but we will now also look at the subject in another light—by calculating the actual money value expended in one trip, estimating also their lost time as follows:—

STATEMENT.

	£	s.	d.		£	s.
1,210 carts, number to the plains this year...............	at 1	10	0	each,	1,815	0
620 hunters, 2 months or 60 days	,, 0	1	0	per day,	1,860	0
650 women, two months	,, 0	0	9	,,	1,462	10
360 boys and girls...............	,, 0	0	4	,,	360	0
740 guns...........................	,, 2	0	0	each,	1,480	0
150 gallons gunpowder.........	,, 0	16	0	per gallon,	120	0
1,300 pounds trading balls......	,, 0	1	0	per pound,	65	0
6,240 gun flints.....................	,, 0	0	0½ each,		13	0
100 steel dagues..................	,, 0	3	0	,,	15	0
100 couteaux de chasse.........	,, 0	3	0	,,	15	0
403 buffalo runners (average good and bad)	,, 15	0	0	,,	6,045	0
655 cart horses	,, 8	0	0	,,	5,240	0
586 draught oxen	,, 6	0	0	,,	3,516	0
1,210 sets of harness	,, 0	8	0	,,	484	0
403 riding saddles	,, 0	8	0	,,	161	4
403 bridles and whips	,, 0	10	0	,,	201	10
1,240 scalping knives	,, 0	0	6	,,	31	0
448 half axes......................	,, 0	2	6	,,	56	0
Sundries. Camp equipage, such as tents, tent furniture, culinary utensils, too tedious to be enumerated					1,059	16

£24,000 0

Hence the variety of articles and the large sum required for the outfit of one expedition; one half of the whole amount is generally on credit, depending on the uncertain and doubtful returns of the trip, to liquidate the debt.

To illustrate the subject further by this year's expedition. On the 15th of June, 1840, carts were seen to emerge from every nook and corner of the settlement, bound for the plains. As they passed on, many things were discovered to be still wanting, to supply which a halt had to be made at Fort Garry shop; one wanted this thing, another that, but all on credit. The day of payment was yet to come: it was promised. Many on the present occasion were supplied, many were not: they got and grumbled, and grumbled and got, till they could get no more; and at last went off, still grumbling and discontented.

From Fort Garry the cavalcade and camp-followers went crowding on to the public road, and thence, stretching from point to point, till the third day in the evening, when they reached Pembina, the great rendezvous on such occasions. When the hunters leave the settlement, it enjoys that relief which a person feels on recovering from a long and painful sickness. Here, on a level plain, the whole patriarchal camp squatted down like pilgrims on a journey to the Holy Land, in ancient days; only not quite so devout, for neither scrip nor staff were consecrated for the occasion. Here the roll was called, and general muster taken, when they numbered, on this occasion, 1,630 souls; and here the rules and regulations for the journey were finally settled.

The officials for the trip were named and installed into office; and all without the aid of writing materials.

The camp occupied as much ground as a modern city, and was formed in a circle; all the carts were placed side by side, the trams outward. These are trifles, yet they are important to our subject. Within this line of circumvallation, the tents were placed in double, treble rows, at one end; the animals at the other in front of the tents. This is the order in all dangerous places; but where no danger is apprehended, the animals are kept on the outside. Thus the carts formed a strong barrier, not only for securing the people and their animals within, but as a place of shelter and defence against an attack of the enemy without.

In 1820, the number of carts assembled here for the first trip was 540
In 1825 680
In 1830 820
In 1835 970
In 1840 1,210

From this statement it is evident that the plain-hunters are rapidly increasing. There is, however, another appendage belonging to the expedition, and to every expedition of the kind, which we might notice *en passant*; for the reader may be assured they are not always the least noisy. We allude to the dogs or camp followers. On the present occasion they numbered no fewer than 542; sufficient of themselves to consume no small number of animals per day, for, like their masters, they dearly relish a bit of buffalo meat. These animals are kept in summer, as they are, about the establishments of the fur-traders, for their services in winter. In deep snows, when horses cannot conveniently be used, dogs are very serviceable animals to the hunters in these parts. The half-breed, dressed in his wolf costume, tackles two or three sturdy curs into a flat sled, throws himself on it at full length, and gets among the buffalo unperceived. Here the bow and arrow play their part, to prevent noise; and here the skilful hunter kills as many as he pleases, and returns to camp without disturbing the band.

Many a curious and amusing incident occurs at buffalo-hunting, one of which may be noticed by way of example. A friend of the writer's, about this time, went to enjoy a few weeks' sport in the plains, and often repeated, with a comic and serious air, a scene which took place in his own presence. Some of the hunters who were accompanying him were conveying their families across a large plain, intersected here and there with clumps of wood. When in the act of rounding one of those woody islands, a herd of buffalo suddenly burst into view, causing two dogs who were drawing a sled, on which a child and some luggage were being conveyed, to set off at full speed in pursuit, leaving the father and mother in a state of despair for the safety of their only child. The dogs soon reached the heels of the buffalo, and all were mixed pell-mell together; the dogs running, the sled swinging to and fro, and the buffalo kicking. At length a bull gored one of the dogs, and his head getting entangled in the harness, went off at the gallop, carrying the dog on his horns, the other suspended by the traces, and the sled and child whirling behind him. The enraged animal ran a good half mile before he shook himself clear of the encumbrance, although pursued by a large party, by whom many shots were fired at him without effect. The state of the parents' feelings may be imagined; yet, to their utter astonishment, although both dogs were killed, the child escaped unhurt!

But now to our camp again—the largest of the kind, perhaps, in the world The first step was to hold a council for the nomination of chiefs or officers, for conducting the expedition. Ten captains were named, the senior on this occasion being Jean Baptiste Wilkie, an English half-breed, brought up among the French; a man of good sound sense and long experience, and withal a fine bold-looking and discreet fellow; a second Nimrod in his way. Besides being captain, in common with the others, he was styled the great war chief or head of the camp; and on all public occasions he occupied the place of president. All articles of property found, without an owner, were carried to him, and he disposed of them by a crier, who went round the camp every evening, were it only an awl. Each captain had ten soldiers under his orders; in much the same way that policemen are subject to the magistrate. Ten guides were likewise appointed; and here we may remark, that people in a rude state of society, unable either to read or write, are generally partial to the number ten. Their duties were to guide the camp, each in his turn—that is day about—during the expedition. The camp flag belongs to the guide of the day; he is therefore standard-bearer in virtue of his office.

The hoisting of the flag every morning is the signal for raising camp. Half an hour is the full time allowed to prepare for the march; but if any one is sick, or their animals have strayed, notice is sent to the guide, who halts till all is made right. From the time the flag is hoisted, however, till the hour of camping arrives, it is never taken down. The flag taken down is the signal for encamping. While it is up, the guide is chief of the expedition. Captains are subject to him, and the soldiers of the day are his messengers: he commands all. The moment the flag is lowered, his functions cease, and the captains' and soldiers' duties commence. They point out the order of the camp, and every cart, as it arrives, moves to its appointed place. This business usually occupies about the same time as raising camp in the morning; for everything moves with the regularity of clock-work.

All being ready to leave Pembina, the captains and other chief men hold another council, and lay down the rules to be observed during the expedition. Those made on the present occasion were:—

1. No buffalo to be run on the Sabbath-day.

2. No party to fork off, lag behind, or go before, without permission.

3. No person or party to run buffalo before the general order.

4. Every captain with his men, in turn, to patrol the camp, and keep guard.

5. For the first trespass against these laws, the offender to have his saddle and bridle cut up.

6. For the second offence, the coat to be taken off the offender's back, and be cut up.

7. For the third offence, the offender to be flogged.

8. Any person convicted of theft, even to the value of

a sinew, to be brought to the middle of the camp, and the crier to call out his or her name three times, adding the word " Thief," at each time.

Having mentioned their honesty, we might state an instance in point: before reaching Pembina, on one occasion, a gentleman on his way to the States forgot, in his camping place, a tin box containing 580 sovereigns in gold, and in silver and bills the amount of 450*l*. more. The following night, however, a half-breed named Saint Matte happened to encamp on the same spot, picked up the box, followed the gentleman a day's journey, and delivered box and contents into his hands to the utmost farthing, well knowing it was money. Considering their poverty, we might well speak of Saint Matte's conduct in the highest strains of praise. And this act might be taken as an index of the integrity of the whole body, generally speaking. This virtue is fostered among them by the mildest means; for what have such a people to fear from a breach of the penal code? Punishments here are scarcely more than nominal; and may well suggest the question to a more civilized community, whether it is always the severest punishments that have the best effect in reclaiming offenders.

On the 21st, after the priest had performed mass (for we should have mentioned that a Roman Catholic priest generally accompanies these expeditions), the flag was unfurled, it being now six or seven o'clock in the morning. The picturesque line of march soon stretched to the length of some five or six miles, in the direction of south-west, towards Côte à Pique. At

2 P.M. the flag was struck, as a signal for resting the animals. After a short interval, it was hoisted again; and in a few minutes the whole line was in motion, and continued the route till five or six o'clock in the evening, when the flag was hauled down as a signal to encamp for the night. Distance travelled, twenty miles.

As a people whose policy it is to speak and act kindly towards each other, the writer was not a little surprised to see the captains and soldiers act with so much independence and decision, not to say roughness, in the performance of their camp duties. Did any person appear slow in placing his cart, or dissatisfied with the order of the camp, he was shoved on one side *sans ceremonie*, and his cart pushed forward or backward into line in the twinkling of an eye, without a murmur being heard. But mark: the disaffected persons are not coerced into order, and made to place their carts in line themselves—the soldiers do it for them, and thus betray their lack of authority; or rather it is their policy so to do, for it would be impossible, in such cases, to proceed to extremes, as in civilized life. The moment the flag was struck it was interesting to see the rear carts hasten to close up, the lagging owners being well aware that the last to arrive must take the ground as it happens, however inconvenient. In less than twenty minutes all was in order.

The camp being formed, all the leading men, officials and others, assembled, as the general custom is, on some little rising ground or eminence outside the ring, and there squatted themselves down, tailor-like, on the grass in a sort of council, each having his gun, his smoking-bag in his hand, and his pipe in his mouth. In this situation the occurrences of the day were discussed, and the line of march for the morrow agreed upon. This little meeting was full of interest; and the fact struck me very forcibly, that there is happiness and pleasure in the society of the most illiterate men, sympathetically if not intellectually, as well as among the learned: and I must say, I found less selfishness and more liberality among those ordinary men than I had been accustomed to find in higher circles. Their conversation was free, practical, and interesting; and the time passed on more agreeably than could be expected among such people, till we touched on politics.

Like the American peasantry, these people are all politicians, but of a peculiar creed, favouring a barbarous state of society and self-will; for they cordially detest all the laws and restraints of civilized life, believing all men were born to be free. In their own estimation they are all great men, and wonderfully wise; and so long as they wander about on these wild and lawless expeditions, they will never become a thoroughly civilized people, nor orderly subjects in a civilized community. Feeling their own strength, from being constantly armed, and free from control, they despise all others; but above all, they are marvellously tenacious of their own original habits. They cherish freedom as they cherish life. The writer in vain rebuked them for this state of things, and endeavoured to turn the current of their thoughts into a civilized channel. They are all republicans in principle, and a licentious freedom is their besetting sin.

Here, for a moment, I cannot avoid continuing my narrative in the personal form. Having left my friends in council, I took a stroll through the camp; and was not long there among the tents and children, before I discovered that there was a dark side to this picture. Provisions were scarce; scarcely a child I met but was crying with hunger, scarcely a family but complained they had no food. How deceiving outward appearances are! Had I judged of things by the lively conversation and cheerful countenances I saw on the little council bluff, I had been greatly deceived indeed. The state of the families in the camp revealed to me the true state of things: the one half of them were literally starving! Some I did see with a little tea, and cups and saucers too—rather fragile ware, for such a mode of life—but with a few exceptions of this kind, the rest disclosed nothing but scenes of misery and want: some had a few pounds of flour; others, less fortunate, a little wheat or barley, which they singed, and were glad to eat in that state. Others, again, had no earthly thing but what chance put in their way—a pheasant, a crow, or a squirrel; and when that failed they had to go to bed supperless, or satisfy the pangs of hunger with a few wild roots, which I saw the children devour in a raw state! A plain hunter's life is truly a dog's life—a feast or a famine. To judge of these people's circumstances, it is necessary to look a little below the surface—to see the inside of their dwellings, their wives and their children. Mixing with the men only, the false side of things is always uppermost. Their improvidence and want of forethought has become a proverb. They live by the chase, and at times wallow in abundance; but, like Indians, never provide against a bad day. Every year, every trip, sad experience teaches them this useful lesson, "In times of plenty provide against scarcity;" but yet, every year, every trip, finds them at this season in the same dilemma. Every summer they starve themselves over again going to the plains. Reason is thrown away on them. All that can be said on the subject is, that it is "their way," and it would be as easy to change their nature.

Early in the morning of the 22nd, the flag was hoisted; but reports from various parts of the camp prayed delay. Horses had wandered, oxen could not be found: a hundred horsemen were out in search of the missing animals; some of them, during the night, had returned to Pembina, and before they got back, and all the strayed animals found, many were so exhausted with fatigue that it was judged proper not to resume the march that day. So the flag was hauled down, and strict orders issued for the next morning. In the then starving condition of the camp a day's delay was a serious consideration; but it was unavoidable. When animals are allowed to stray, the turmoil and hallooing about the camp and environs is deafening; and the pursuit in search of them, as well as the harassing work bringing them back again, is far more destructive to the animals, on expeditions of this kind, than the regular march itself. Hence the necessity of guarding them well at night, apart from the risk they run of being stolen by the enemy when out of sight of the camp.

Of late years, the field of chase has been far distant from Pembina; and the hunters do not so much as know in what direction they may find the buffalo, as these animals frequently shift their ground. It is a mere leap in the dark, whether at their outset the expedition takes the right or the wrong road; and their luck in the chase, of course, depends materially on the choice they may make. The year of our narrative they travelled a south-west or middle course; being the one generally preferred, since it leads past most of the rivers near their sources, where they are easily crossed. The only inconvenience attending this choice is the scarcity of wood, which in a warm season is but a secondary consideration.

Not to dwell on the ordinary routine of each day's journey, it was the ninth day from Pembina before we reached the Chienne river, distant only about 150 miles; and as yet we had not seen a single band of buffalo. On the third of July, our nineteenth day from the settlement, and at a distance of little more than 250 miles, we came in sight of our destined hunting ground; and on the day following, as if to celebrate the anniversary of American independence, we had our first buffalo race. Our array in the field must have been a grand and imposing one to those who had never seen the like before. No less than 400 huntsmen, all mounted, and anxiously waiting for the word, " Start!" took up their position in a line at one end of the camp, while Captain Wilkie, with his spy-glass at his eye, surveyed the buffalo, examined the ground, and issued his orders. At 8 o'clock the whole cavalcade broke ground, and made for the buffalo; first at a slow trot, then at a gallop, and lastly at full speed. Their advance was over a dead level, the plain having no hollow or shelter of any kind to conceal their approach. We need not answer any queries as to the feeling and anxiety of the camp on such an occasion. When the horsemen started, the cattle might have been a mile and a half ahead; but they had approached to within four or five hundred yards before the bulls curved their tails or pawed the ground. In a moment more the herd took flight, and horse and rider are presently seen bursting in among them; shots are heard, and all is smoke, dust, and hurry. The fattest are first singled out for slaughter; and in less time than we have occupied with the description, a thousand carcasses strew the plain.

Those who have seen a squadron of horse dash into battle, may imagine the scene, which we have no skill to depict. The earth seemed to tremble when the horses started; but when the animals fled, it was like the shock of an earthquake. The air was darkened; the rapid firing at first, soon became more and more faint, and at last died away in the distance. Two hours, and all was over; but several hours more elapsed before the result was known, or the hunters reassembled; and who is he so devoid of feeling and curiosity, that could not listen with interest to a detail of the perilous adventure.

The moment the animals take to flight, the best runners dart forward in advance. At this moment a good horse is invaluable to his owner; for out of the four hundred on this occasion, not above fifty got the first chance of the fat cows. A good horse and experienced rider will select and kill from ten to twelve animals at one heat, while inferior horses are contented with two or three; but much depends on the nature of the ground. On this occasion the surface was rocky, and full of badger-holes. Twenty-three horses and riders were at one moment all sprawling on the ground; one horse, gored by a bull, was killed on the spot, two more disabled by the fall. One rider broke his shoulder-blade; another burst his gun, and lost three of his fingers by the accident; and a third was struck on the knee by an exhausted ball. These accidents will not be thought over numerous, considering the result; for in the evening no less than 1,375 tongues were brought into camp.

The rider of a good horse seldom fires till within three or four yards of his object, and never misses; and, what is admirable in point of training, the moment the shot is fired, his steed springs on one side to avoid stumbling over the animal; whereas an awkward and shy horse will not approach within ten or fifteen yards, consequently the rider has often to fire at random, and not unfrequently misses; many of them, however, will fire at double that distance, and make sure of every shot. The mouth is always full of balls; they load and fire at the gallop, and but seldom drop a mark, although some do to designate the animal.

When the runners leave the camp, the carts prepare to follow to bring in the meat. The carters have a bewildering task to perform; they have to make their way through a forest of carcasses, till each finds out his own. The pursuit is no sooner over than the hunter, with coat off and shirt sleeves tucked up, commences skinning and cutting up the meat; with the knife in one hand, the bridle hanging in the other, and the loaded gun close by, he from time to time casts a wistful look around, to see that no lurking enemy is at hand watching for the opportunity to take a scalp. The hunter's work is now retrograde: the last animal killed is the first skinned, and night, not unfrequently, surprises him at his work; what then remains is lost, and falls to the wolves; hundreds of animals are sometimes abandoned, for even a thunder-storm, in one hour, will render the meat useless. The day of a race is as fatiguing for the hunter as the horse; but the meat once in the camp, he enjoys the very luxury of idleness. Then the task of the women begins, who do all the rest; and what with skins, and meat, and fat, their duty is a most laborious one.

We have stated, that when skinning the animals late, or at a distance, the hunters often run great risks. Many narrow escapes are reported on such occasions. It was while occupied on this duty, in an unfortunate moment, that Louison Vallé, as already noticed, lost his life by some lurking Sioux, who had concealed themselves among the long grass. Vallé had his son, a young boy, with him, who at the time happened to be on his father's horse keeping a look-out. At the critical moment, he had shifted his ground a few yards, and the enemy rushing in upon him suddenly, he had just time to call out to the boy, " Make for the camp, make for the camp!" and instantly fell under a shower of arrows. But the deed was not long unrevenged. The boy got to the camp, the alarm was given, and ten half-breeds, mounting their horses, overtook the murderers in less than an hour. The Sioux were twelve in number; four got into the bushes, but the other eight were overtaken and shot down like beasts of prey. One of the half-breeds had a narrow escape, an arrow passing between his shirt and skin; the others got off scot free, and all returned to the camp in safety.

Buffalo-hunting is called a sport, but the most miraculous and hair-breadth escapes sometimes occur, while at others no escape is possible: the hunter getting alongside an enraged animal, it makes a sudden thrust sideways, gores the horse, and occasionally kills the rider. It is with buffalo as with rabbits, whether from the situation of the eyes, or some other cause, they see better sideways than straight forward. The writer was one of a party once, running buffalo, and while making our way through a herd, looking here and there, as the custom is, for the fattest animal before firing, a bull, hard pressed, turned suddenly round on one of my companions, who happened to be near me at the time; to avoid the thrust in this dilemma, the horse made also a sudden start to one side, when the saddle-girth gave way, and the rider, saddle and all, were left between the bull's horns, which so surprised the sturdy brute, that with one toss of his head he threw the man high up in the air. Strange to relate, he fell on another bull passing a few yards off, and yet escaped with the fright alone, having received no other injury.

This class, in the whole tenor of their lives, resemble the chamois-hunters of the Alps—those, at least, of former days. "It is the chase itself which attracts these people, more than the value of the prey; it is the attraction of hope and fear—the continual excitement—the very dangers themselves, which render the chamois-hunter indifferent to all other pleasures. The very few individuals who grow old in this trade, bear on their countenances the traces of the life which they have led. They have a wild and somewhat haggard and desperate air, by which they may be recognised in the middle of a crowd." It is so with the buffalo-hunter: he encounters many dangers, so that his physical powers are often put to the severest trials; but it has been said, and with truth, " that there are few things beyond the reach of human energy."

A chamois-hunter, vaunting of his love for the chase, observed one day to Saussure the naturalist, "My grandfather was killed in the chase of the chamois; my father was killed also; and I am so certain that I shall be killed myself, that I call this bag, which I always carry hunting, my winding-sheet. I am sure that I shall have no other; and yet, if you were to offer to make my fortune upon the condition that I should renounce the chase of the chamois, I should refuse your kindness." This, too, is precisely the case with the hunters of the buffalo. There is no earthly consideration would make them relinquish the pursuit. They see the steady and industrious farmer indulge in every necessary and luxury of life, without risk, happy and contented; they may even envy his lot, and acknowledge their own poverty; and yet, so strong is their love for the uncertain pursuit of buffalo-hunting, that when the season arrives, they sacrifice every other consideration in order to indulge in this savage habit. Wedded to it from their infancy, they find no pleasure in anything else.

Of all the operations which mark the hunter's life, and are essential to his ultimate success, the most perplexing, perhaps, is that of finding out and identifying the animals he kills during a race. Imagine four hundred horsemen entering at full speed a herd of some thousands of buffalo, all in rapid motion. Riders in clouds of dust and volumes of smoke, which darken the air, crossing and re-crossing each other in every direction; shots on the right, on the left, behind, before, here, there, two, three, a dozen at a time, everywhere in close succession, at the same moment. Horses stumbling, riders falling, dead and wounded animals tumbling here and there, one over the other; and this zig-zag and bewildering *mêlée* continued for an hour or more together in wild confusion; and yet, from practice, so keen is the eye, so correct the judgment of the hunter, and so discriminating his memory, that after getting to the end of the race, he can not only tell the number of animals he had shot down, but the position in which each lies—on the right or on the left side—the spot where the shot hit, and the direction of the ball; and also retrace his way, step by step, through the whole race, and recognise every animal he had the fortune to kill, without the least hesitation or difficulty. To divine how this is accomplished bewilders the imagination. To unriddle the Chinese puzzles, to square the circle, or even to find out the perpetual motion, seems scarcely more puzzling to the stranger, than that of a hunter finding out his own animals after a buffalo race.

The writer asked one of the hunters how it was possible that each could know his own animals in such a *mélange?* He answered by putting a question remarkable for its appropriate ingenuity. "Suppose," said he, " that four hundred learned persons all wrote words here and there on the same sheet of paper, would not the fact be that each scholar would point out his own handwriting?" It is true, that practice makes perfect; but with all the perfection experience can give, much praise is due to the discriminating knowledge of these people; quarrels being rare indeed among them on such occasions.

When the buffalo are very numerous, as was the case this year, they run several times in succession, and then a day or two is set apart for drying and manufacturing the provisions, which is done on low stages by the heat of the sun. All provisions, however, keep the better if made a little crispy with the heat of the fire. In the early part of the season the bulls are fat and the cows lean; but in the autumn the case is the reverse, the bulls are lean and the cows fat. A bull in good condition will yield 45 lbs. of clean rendered tallow; cows, when in good order, will produce, on an average, 35 lbs. Flesh and bones, however, boiled down and consumed, will yield fully double that quantity.

A word of advice will not be deemed out of place here perhaps. On every expedition of this kind, we would recommend a race given gratis, for the benefit of the poor and helpless, for they are often many. The half-breeds need only be told this duty, and they will cheerfully do it, for they are in general a kind and generous people. During a summer expedition, the average number of general races—that is, the whole hunters to run at once—may be about ten or twelve; but there are many small or sectional races. When the buffalo are in small bands, only a few horses run in turn; these should be left for the poorer party, who have but indifferent horses; but this is not the case. Although the half-breeds are generous, yet their vanity is greater than their generosity; were only ten to run, those ten would be the best horses. Their regulations do not always guard against injustice. A feeling for the poor of their own people is often overlooked; hence they not unfrequently return back as empty as they went.

Every movement, according to the existing system, is exceedingly well regulated; but the system is altogether a bad one, and far from producing that profitable result which a well-regulated business, under proper management, might do. How many of these people had a kettle to melt their fat in? For want of this simple and cheap article, much of it was lost. They had even to borrow axes, knives, and awls from each other for the duties of the camp. And after the first week, many of them had scarcely a ball to put in their guns, except what might be required for self-defence. There is a manifest conflict of want and waste in all their arrangements. As a proof of the most profligate waste of animals, after all their starving, we might mention, that during the first and second races, it was calculated that not less than 2,500 animals had been killed, and out of that number only 375 bags of pemmican and 240 bales of dried meat were made! Now, making all due allowance for waste, 750 animals would have been ample for such a result. What, then, we might ask, became of the remaining 1,750? Surely the 1,630 mouths, starving as they had been for the month before (not forgetting a due allowance for the dogs), never consumed that quantity of beef in the short space of four or five days! The food, in short, was wasted; and this is only a fair example of the manner in which the plain business is carried on under the present system. Scarcely one-third in number of the animals killed is turned to account.

Abundance now caused every countenance to smile with joy, and the profligate waste of to-day obliterated all remembrance of the starvation of yesterday. The regulations of the camp not permitting us to remain longer than three days in one place, and the animals having left us, we raised camp to follow them, which led us far south to the elevated plateau, which divides the waters that debouch into Hudson's Bay, from those that flow into the Missouri. On the 16th we encamped on the bank of the latter river, when about forty of our hunters went on a visit to the American trading post, called Fort Union. Here they were kindly received, and bartered away furs and provisions for articles they either fancied or were in actual need of; and, among other good things, the prohibited article of whisky, at four pounds sterling the gallon, abating nothing for what the Missouri had contributed to it. Our people, however, avowed it was the best liquor they ever drank, for it made no one drunk.*

After passing a week on the banks of the Missouri, we turned to the west, where we had a few races with various success. We were afterwards for some time led backwards and forwards at the pleasure of the buffalo, often crossing and re-crossing our path, until we had travelled to almost every point of the compass.

While in this quarter, one of the Sioux chiefs, called the "Terre qui brule," or Burnt Earth, and his band, visited our camp. The affair of Vallé, and the eight Sioux who had been killed, was the subject of their mission. Among other things, the chief accused the half-breeds of wanton cruelty. "Only one of your friends fell," said he, "and for that one, you murdered eight of my countrymen." After some time, however, the affair was amicably settled. An Indian chief is always well received and kindly treated by the half-breeds. These people have a lively sympathy for the Indians, unless their half civilized, half barbarian blood is raised; and then they are worse than the worst of savages, for their cruelty and revenge have no bounds. A small collection was made and given to

* The tariff of the Missouri traders is very high compared with ours in Red River. A knife costs 5s.; a pound of coarse plug tobacco the same; and a common blanket 25s.; being considerably more than the double of our prices for similar articles.

the chief, according to Indian custom, and we parted good friends, as far as outward appearances went. We, nevertheless, kept a strict watch day and night; and this was rendered the more necessary as we had noticed several suspicious parties on the distant hills.

We may notice in this place a fact not generally known — that the Sioux have their telegraphic communications and signals, as well as the whites. A smoke is raised on some height, it is answered on another, and so on from height to height, from party to party, and from one camp to another; so that in half an hour's time, intelligence may be communicated a hundred miles off. The nature of the intelligence is explained by the number of fires raised. For example:—two smokes got up within a few yards of each other, simultaneously, is a signal that enemies have been seen; three, that some misfortune has happened. Smoke in the evening conveys good tidings; in the morning, bad news; and so forth. From the very level nature of the country, these people are very expert in communicating telegraphic intelligence to each other. Every other day we were annoyed with signals of this description. No man, the most intelligent politician, can be more keen and watchful of his national interest, than a Sioux chief: nothing escapes him. However uncultivated his mind may be, the fire of his eye, the expression of his countenance, shows that in many instances there is but a short link wanting between the cultivated and the uncultivated understanding. The phrases, the thoughts, and ideas of these men, are highly natural and appropriate. As a nation, they are proud and sensitive. To the half-breeds they are annoying and formidable.

But the day is fast approaching, nor can it be far distant, when the transient glories and fears of the plain-rangers must arrive at their end. The buffalo, the exciting cause, once extinct, the wandering and savage life of the half-breed, as well as the savage himself, must give place to a more genial and interesting order of things; when here, as in other parts of the world, the husbandman and the plough, the sound of the grindstone, and the church-going bell, will alone be heard. Things are fast verging to this end. Buffalo, the only inducement to the plains, are falling off fast. They are now like a ball between two players. The Americans are driving them north, the British south; and there is no space unmolested in which they may find an abiding-place. The west alone will furnish them a last and temporary retreat.

After a few more rambles and buffalo-hunts, we turned our backs to the south, and came gently down the smooth and undulating hills and dales, shrubless and bare, that lead to the north. The place being rather suspicious, scouts and armed parties were sent out to reconnoitre, and to occupy the heights; viewed from which, the line of carts, several miles in extent, presented an interesting and somewhat imposing aspect. Here Wilkie, with the officials grouped around him, stood viewing the different parties as they drew up to camp with as much dignity and self-satisfaction as Wellington could have marshalled his victorious army after the battle of Waterloo.

But we had not long enjoyed these pleasing reflections, when one of the reverses so common in these parts darkened the sunshine of our happiness. In the morning of the 22nd, the atmosphere became suddenly overcast; the lightning flashed in vivid gleams, and presently two of our horses were struck dead. There was then a lull till about 2 o'clock in the afternoon, when suddenly one of the most terrific storms ever witnessed, perhaps, burst upon the camp. Thunder, lightning, wind, and rain, contended violently for the mastery. Our camp was pitched on a high rocky ground, and yet, in the course of ten minutes' time, the deluge of rain that fell set everything afloat. The camp was literally swimming. Several children were with difficulty saved from drowning; and so fierce and overwhelming was the wind, that the tents were either flattened to the ground, or fluttering like ribbons in the air. During this distressing scene, three of the lodges were struck by lightning, in one of which a Canadian named Courchaine was killed, and a gun which stood by him melted in several parts like lead; in the second, an Indian, his wife, and two children, being all that were in the tent, shared the same fate; two dogs were also killed. The inmates of the third tent escaped. Thunder-storms are of common occurrence at this spot, and we heard that two Indians were killed there the year before.

Storms of hail of uncommon size are often experienced in the plains: one of these passed over our camp on the Missouri heights, in which the hailstones were composed of solid angular pieces of ice, measuring from four to five inches in circumference, and wounded several of our people who had been exposed to their violence. During storms of this kind, when the camp is in disorder, the Indians approach for the purpose of horse-stealing, and of doing more serious injury, if in their power. A hunter's life is, therefore, at best, but a precarious one, and seldom free from extreme anxiety and danger.

On the 25th, as we drew near the Chienne River on our way home, while the hunters were busy drying their provisions for a fresh start, between forty and fifty Saulteaux, attached as camp-followers to the expedition, went off a distance of some ten miles to surprise and destroy a small camp of the Sioux, which had been discovered the day before. All the caution, craft, and finesse of these savages did not prevent them being discovered when within a mile or two of the tents; but the Sioux taking them for strangers on a friendly visit, went out to the number of fifteen or twenty to welcome them.

At the place where they met, the two parties were divided by a small tract of water, which the Sioux were preparing to swim, when the treacherous Saulteaux fired a volley among them, and three of the party fell. The volley was instantly returned, and at the same moment three smokes were seen to rise as a signal to the Sioux camp, signifying what had happened; at the camp the signal was repeated to warn another at a still greater distance; while they, not to lose time, were observed to advance in great haste on foot. The Saulteaux now retreated, but the Sioux swam across and pursued; and if the night had not fallen before the reinforcement could arrive, every Saulteaux present would have been scalped. Seven Sioux were killed, and three wounded. Of the Saulteaux, three were killed and four wounded: the rest got back to the camp a little before day. We ought to have mentioned, that as soon as the Indians set off to find the Sioux, six of the half-breeds mounted their horses, made a circuit to reach a neighbouring height, and there remained smoking their pipes, and looking at their friends during the whole time of the combat.

This affair was like to have caused serious troubles. The Saulteaux and half-breeds, be it remembered, are mostly all related, either by marriage, or other kindred ties; and but for this it might have fared ill with the assailants guilty of such treachery. The half-breeds themselves, indeed, were greatly to blame, for not punishing them; since it is clear, if the camp had not secured to the Saulteaux a safe retreat, they had never ventured on such a step as to attack the Sioux in the middle of their own country. But this was not all. It was proved afterwards that a half-breed named Parisien was with the Saulteaux in the fight, and had actually fired the first shot. Had the half-breeds done their duty, they would have bastinadoed him, at the least. The Sioux, however, soon took ample revenge.

On the day following, 300 Sioux, armed cap-a-pie, appeared in front of the half-breed camp, and challenged the Saulteaux to turn out, man to man, and fight it out; but the Saulteaux begged to be excused, and the half-breeds acting as mediators between them, a sort of peace was patched up, and the Sioux returned—we may be sure, far from well pleased. This affair imposed on the camp the necessity of additional vigilance; the camp by night was watched by a double guard, and armed parties were kept constantly on the patrol. The Sioux had set the plains on fire in various directions, the animals were scared off, and had these steps been taken as early as they were late in the season, no hunt could have been made; which shows how circumspect the hunters ought to be, in order to retain the friendship of the Indians. Generally speaking, the half-breeds are sufficiently on their guard; but it is bad policy to allow so many bands of the Saulteaux to accompany them into their enemies' country, and on this occasion, they certainly showed too much lenity.

On leaving the river Chienne, Parisien, the same fellow who joined the Saulteaux against the Sioux, got into the dumps, and forked off to take a road of his own, contrary to the regulations of the camp, when Hallett, one of the captains, rode after him, and with a crack or two of his whip, turning his horses, brought them back to the camp. The fellow said nothing, but sat down in gloomy mood; after some little time, thinking better of it, he got up and followed his carts. Here, again, we have another instance of the want of proper discipline. In place of compelling Parisien to return with his carts, the captain, as on a former occasion, had to bring them back himself. A day or two afterwards, however, when getting out of danger, and within a short distance of the Côte à Pique, several small bands forked off under various pretences, and were allowed to go. The main party, however, kept on its course till it reached Pembina. Here all the functions of the men in office ceased, the camp broke up, and the different parties, as they got ready, threaded their way to the settlement, where they arrived on the 17th of August, after a journey of two months and two days.

We remarked at the time how much the settlement was relieved when the hunters left it for the plains; their return was the renewal of our troubles. The regular order of things is reversed: industry is almost at a dead stand, and everything turned, as it were, topsy-turvy again. Here once more the farmer is placed in an awkward position. In the midst of harvest his people are diverted from their labour, their fields, and their homes. Nor is this the only evil he experiences. The moment the people arrive from the plains, and provisions become abundant, servants' wages rise 50 per cent. So long as they can obtain plenty to eat, idlers will not work. Not only is labour interrupted, but the market is overstocked; and the husbandman, in the midst of this untimely superabundance, is unable to sell his produce.

The carts having now got back to the settlement, and the trip being a successful one, the returns on this occasion may be taken as a fair annual average. An approximation to the truth is all we can arrive at, however. Our estimate is 900 pounds weight of buffalo meat per cart, a thousand being considered the full load, which gives 1,089,000 pounds in all, or something more than 200 pounds weight for each individual, old and young, in the settlement. As soon as the expedition arrived, the Hudson's Bay Company, according to usual custom, issued a notice that it would take a certain specified quantity of provisions, not from each fellow that had been at the plains, but from each old and recognised hunter. The established price at this period for the three kinds over head, fat, pemmican, and dried meat, was 2*d.* per pound. This was then the Company's standard price; but there is generally a market for all the fat they bring. During the years 1839, 40, and 41, the Company expended 5,000*l.* on the purchase of plain provisions, of which the hunters got last year the sum of 1,200*l.*, being rather more money than all the agricultural class obtained for their produce in the same year. The reader has already been advertised of the fact that the Company's demand affords the only regular market or outlet in the colony, and, as a matter of course, it is the first supplied.

The Company being served, there is really no sale except to a few private individuals—unless, indeed, the crops fail, in which case the plain-hunters find a ready market; yet, before they have paid their debts in part, got their supplies in part (for everything they do is by halves), the whole of their provisions, one way or other, is dribbled off. In less than a month, therefore, they have to start on the second trip, as destitute of supplies, as deeply in debt, and as ill provided as at first. Such was the result of the expedition we have described in detail, and such is the result of every expedition. The writer is not acquainted with a single instance, during the last twenty-five years, of one of these plain-hunters being able to clear his way or liquidate his expenses, far less to save a shilling by the chase; the absence of a proper system, and the want of a market, render it impossible.

CHAPTER XIX.

CONTENTS.—First steps to civilization—Habits change—Influence of the Scotch emigrants—Gospel planted in Rupert's Land—Mr. West—Bishop's visit—Mr. Cockran and the Swampies—Indian settlement—The parson's mistake—Rules for missionary enterprise—Mr. Cockran takes leave of the Swampies—Their character—The Roman Catholic mission of St. Paul—Rev. Mr. Belcourt—Wabassimong mission—Wesleyan mission—Religious opposition—Baie des Canards mission—Partridge Crop mission—Protestants versus Catholics—Sagacious chief—False impressions of Red River abroad — Churches and missionaries — Liberality of the Hudson's Bay Company.

DURING the severe struggles and multiplied difficulties which agitated the colony in the days of its infancy, the Indians passed and re-passed, taking but little interest in our affairs, unless to look down with contempt on our slow and painful drudgery, or, it might be, interrupt and annoy us; but no sooner had perseverance and industry overcome the difficulties opposed to us, than these children of the wilds began to edge themselves in; not indeed to labour themselves, but to partake, if possible, in the fruits of our toil. This, however, was the first step gained towards civilization that exercised any degree of influence over the Indian character in

Red River. Their attention was riveted, their minds were receptive of a new idea. Convince the Indian, and you have him. As time rolled on, our Indian brethren drew nearer and nearer to us by slow degrees; one here and one there attached himself to the whites, so that the friendly intercourse acquired more and more strength every day. The Scotch emigrants had not been long in the land of their adoption before this friendly feeling became manifest.

It was invariably observed, however, that of all the different tribes that visited the settlement, the members of one only looked favourably on civilization, or showed any attachment to the whites. This was a tribe of the great Cree nation, called Swampies, from the low country or sea-coast. At the period of the coalition between the two rival fur companies, many of their servants and hangers-on were turned adrift, and not a few of these had formed connections with Indian women. These persons, on coming to Red River with their families, left their Indian relatives behind; and the latter, it may be supposed, longed to follow them, in order to taste of the good things which they knew only by report. From time to time these friendly Indians have visited and sojourned for a short time in the settlement; but it was not till the present year that any Swampy took up his permanent abode in the colony. One of this tribe came all the way from the swamps of Oxford-house, a distance of 500 miles, with the intention of visiting a daughter and step-son he had in Red River, and returning back the following spring; but he passed the winter with a family of his former acquaintance, who made every effort to convert him from his wandering and heathen habits. The result was, that he sent one of his children to school, and remained with them and the whites. Everything must have a beginning, and had the example of industry thus set been directed in the proper way, civilization might, ere now, have spread itself through the length and breadth of Rupert's Land.

Six years after the Scotch settlers reached the colony, they were followed, as we have before noticed, by Canadian emigrants of French origin; and two years later, Mr. West, an English missionary, came to the settlement. Slow and uncertain as was the progress of agriculture here in those days, yet the soil produced enough to keep hope alive; and on the strength of that hope a few Indian children were collected together by Mr. West, and put to school among the children of the whites. This was all that was or could well be done at the time; for everything was regulated by the prospect of the crops, the labour and success of the husbandman.

Here it becomes our duty to correct an error in a matter of some historical interest. It is stated in *Hochelaga*, p. 156, that " In the year 1820, Mr. West, a missionary, first preached the pure Gospel on the banks of the Red River." Now, what is the fact? For eight years before Mr. West crossed the Atlantic, baptism was administered, marriages solemnized, prayer-meetings established, and the pure gospel proclaimed on the banks of Red River, both by Presbyterians and Catholics. Let the reader compare this fact with the statement of a venerable prelate, which we here subjoin:—" It is the Episcopal Church of England," says his lordship, " which took the lead, and gave the impulse to other parties in whatever has been yet done, of any note, for planting and extending any of the forms of Christianity in that land." (*Bishop of Montreal's Journal,** p. 169.) This puff of his lordship is soon exploded; for should he not admit Mr. Sutherland's functions to have been in strict accordance with the established form of the Presbyterian Church, he will allow, perhaps, that the Catholic Bishop of the North-West acted strictly according to rule, and that he had laboured there for years before any English missionary entered the colony. We maintain, in short, that the pure Gospel was planted in Red River by the first emigrants; that they were next followed by the Catholics, and last of all by the Episcopal Church of England. At the same time we are willing to give all men their due. With the force of money and force of patronage, the Church Missionary Society has certainly effected the most; and having stated the facts, we shall gladly give it full credit for all the good it has done, and impartially explain that good as we proceed.

For twelve years after Mr. West came to the settlement, no step beyond what we have mentioned was taken to civilize the Indians. At the close of that period, however, many of them had got so attached and familiarized to the whites, in consequence of the intercourse we have mentioned, that Mr. Cockran, one of the Protestant missionaries at Red River, caught the happy

* Now the Bishop of Quebec.

idea of turning this favourable disposition to account; and from that day he laboured hard and zealously to collect a few Indians together in order to induce them to throw off their savage habits, and lead a settled life, with a view to their moral and religious improvement. It adds still more to the merits of Mr. Cockran, that his labours were purely gratuitous, occupying his own private time, and added, like task work, to his other ministerial duties. At this time, Mr. Cockran's allotted station was at what is called the Grand Rapids. He had there gathered round him a considerable number of Europeans and half-breeds, whom, in addition to his purely professional ministrations, he was successfully training to agriculture by his skill, energy, and liberality. It was probably the result of these labours that encouraged him, as it was entirely the experience thus acquired that strengthened him to induce the aborigines to " trouble" the ground—not to become mere settlers, for that at first would have been a hopeless task, but to blend tillage and pasturage with the avocations of the chase.

In the spring of 1832, Mr. Cockran had so far succeeded in his pious endeavours, that three families yielded their consent, and were located as settlers at the extreme lower end of the colony. This was the first step of a permanent nature taken by the Church Missionary Society either to civilize or evangelize the heathen in this quarter. The undertaking was encouraged in every possible way by a respectable and intelligent half-breed of the country, named Cook, who, feeling much for his kinsmen, morally and religiously, did everything in his power to aid Mr. Cockran in ameliorating their condition. It is but justice to Mr. Cook's memory to say that he was highly instrumental in the accomplishment of whatever good has been done to the Swampies. From this time forward others kept joining the three families, till at last they formed a village and became a distinct community, having also a church, a school, and a missionary of their own. This result, we repeat, was due to the instrumentality and benevolence of Mr. Cockran, whose zeal and unwearied perseverance in the work cannot be too highly eulogized. To this village of new converts, as a portion of the settlement, we invite the attention of the reader.

But to return. After much anxiety and labour in forming, training, and evangelizing this interesting little village, now called distinctively the Indian Settlement, Mr. Cockran rejoiced to see the fruits of his labour in so thriving and prosperous a state, and believed in his own mind, as would any other man with the same limited experience of Indian life, that his little community were all, in truth and verity, real Christians. A mill was built, houses erected, plots of land cleared ; and, to crown all, they had not a few domestic cattle among them. It was like a picture that looked well at a distance, but could not bear examination. Everything had been done too hurriedly, and the converts were still Indians in their wild state. Some with a resolution would begin to build, but ere long, changing their minds, their task would be left unaccomplished. Others, completing their building enterprises, would abandon all when finished, and take to the chase again. " It is easier," one would say, "to hunt than to dig." "A bow and arrow," another would say, "are lighter than a spade." They neither knew themselves nor their duties in the new sphere of life to which they were called: they had many queries to put, and would often halt between two opinions. This was to be expected. But, in the midst of all these conflicting scenes, Mr. Cockran would tell them, "You must not look back; you must look forward and persevere;" perseverance was his one peremptory word. Nor was Mr. Cockran's liberality less conspicuous than his care and anxiety. He not only assisted them with money to build, but his own hands were the first to set the example; he assisted them with cattle also, and often fed and clothed them to hurry and encourage their tardy operations.

This excellent minister was not only a pulpit man; but the plough, the spade, and the hoe, were all familiar to him; few men could be more persevering, more zealous, or more indefatigable. While he kept everyone busy, himself was the busiest of all. One moment called here, another there, handle an axe for one, a hoe for another. Show this one how to dig up a root, another which hand to put foremost; cut a sapling for one, lay a log for another, and a thousand things we cannot name. The next moment, perhaps, spades, hoes, axes, were all thrown aside, and everyone would be seen with his book in his hand; too soon the hour would be up, and twelve long miles to ride in a given time, urged his departure. But, alas! for the results. His back was no sooner turned than this multiplicity of operations were all at a stand. The humble converts became wild

Indians till he returned next day, or the day following; so that more was actually lost than gained by the system pursued. Nor could Mr. Cockran derive much consolation from the appreciation of his toils. The Swampies would grumble, and think they had made a bad exchange to barter away their idle life for one of toil and hard labour; nay, they imagined that Mr. Cockran was too worldly a man to be heavenly minded. Hard labour in their eyes degraded him; for they thought, with the Scriptures, that a minister ought to live by the gospel. From such results it must be evident that all this work and fuss cannot be consistent with the duty of a clergyman, and that missions of this kind ought to be established by quite another class of persons.

Civilization, however, ought certainly to precede evangelization, as the writer proposes to show more at length in a subsequent chapter on missionary proceedings. Another rule for the conduct of missionary enterprise is not less in importance, namely, that the missionary's hopes ought to centre in the young, not the old. The labourer in this field is too apt to imagine that he is dealing with a civilized population while he endeavours to Christianize them, and with a Christian people while he endeavours to civilize them; and this must always be the case until the savage is located, and in a manner trained or civilized, before the missionary interferes or takes him under his care. It is no part of the missionary's duty to be subjected, as Mr. Cockran was, to manual labour, and all the drudgery and hardships attending the first stage of such things. A practical farmer would be far more eligible to such an office than a clergyman; and the latter, when he enters on a mission of this kind, has duties enough to attend to regarding things spiritual, without dividing his attention and distracting his mind at all hours of the day with temporal matters. The more these points are considered, the more surprising it will appear that Mr. Cockran's converts made such progress as they did, the record of which must be admitted to form one of the brightest pages in Red River history. He was sadly missed by his little flock when he delivered over the mission to the Rev. Mr. Smithurst, a brother missionary, in 1839. Nor can we add, that the period of ten years which has since elapsed has much improved the Indian converts' condition, either temporally or spiritually.

Here a short description of their character and social condition, after a settled life of twenty years with the advantages of religious instruction, may not be uninteresting. Before they came into the colony, and while attached to the Company's posts, the Swampies were universally allowed to be a docile and teachable class of people, and for some time afterwards they were looked upon as obliging in their manner, and honest in their dealings. So much were the settlers prepossessed in their favour, that in those early days every farmer was anxious to have a Swampy about his house: their sole study, as it appeared, was to make themselves useful to their employers; and it was naturally supposed that a people so easily led would have rapidly improved under instruction. But time developed their true character. When they had become, as it were, naturalized, and got accustomed to our people and their ways—especially when they were taken by the hand, baptized, confirmed, and told they were Christians—they quietly threw off the cloak of hypocrisy, began at once to compare themselves with the whites, and to have a great itching for dress and finery. The blue coat, frilled shirt, scarlet belt, and attendance at church, were no sooner adopted than they became saucy, tricky, and dishonest; and in place of their former docility, they now showed themselves as proud and selfish as they were ignorant and superstitious. There was withal a dulness of comprehension, a positive stubbornness and contumacy of disposition in their character, which resisted the kindest treatment, and left but little hope of either moral or religious improvement during the present generation. Perhaps, if no other cause could be assigned for such a change, their being dragged through so many new phases in so short a time might well suffice to turn the head and distract the heart of the simple savage. Vice is soon learned. To crown all, they soon became notorious beer-drinkers.

This lamentable fact is alluded to by Mr. Simpson in his *Journal of the Arctic Expedition* (page 16). " Nothing," says that interesting writer, " can overcome their insatiable desire for intoxicating liquors; and they too often contrive to gratify that debasing inclination, to which they are ready to sacrifice everything they possess; and while they lose the haughty independence of savage life, they acquire at once all the bad qualities of the white man, but are slow, indeed, in imitating his industry and virtues." We must here observe, however, that of late years the Swampies are a little improved in this respect, while they have shown the old disposition for backsliding in another. If they have become less notorious for their drinking propensities, in short, they are now proportionately expert in cheating right and left most persons with whom they have any dealings. " As great a cheat as a Swampy" is now a byword in the colony.

It would be unfair, perhaps, to decide upon the average morality of a people from their criminal statistics; yet we may here mention a fact of some importance. During the last twenty years, there have been six cases of murder committed by Indians brought up in the colony, and five out of the six were by persons taught in our schools. It is sad to believe, that the preponderance of crime is to be found on the side of civilization; and especially as the Indians we refer to are of both creeds Catholic and Protestant. The fact may pass for what it is worth; and with the other points we have mentioned, may serve to correct the statements of travellers who had little time to study their character.

From the efforts of Mr. Cockran and the Protestants at the lower end of the settlement, we proceed to detail, briefly, the proceedings of the Catholics at the upper. The first Roman Catholic mission was founded about thirty miles up the Assiniboine, at a place named Saint Paul's, under the auspices of his Lordship the Roman Catholic Bishop of Juliopolis, now North-West. At the head of this infant mission was placed the Rev. Mr. Belcourt, a Roman Catholic priest from Canada—a man of active habits, intelligence, and enterprise; and to these qualities he had also the advantage of understanding and conversing with the natives, without the aid of an interpreter; which was a very important point in his favour. Paradoxical as the statement may appear, Mr. Belcourt understood the language of the savages better than the savages understood it themselves. With characteristic ingenuity and perseverance, he so far availed himself of the peculiar character of the Chippeway tongue, as to enrich it with compounds, which faithfully and vividly expressed, as far as possible, the foreign ideas of civilization and Christianity. In this respect, Mr. Belcourt had an incalculable advantage over his Protestant rivals, who, generally speaking, rely implicitly on native interpreters of very inadequate qualifications. For the benefit of this mission, Sir George Simpson, acting with his usual liberality, on behalf of the Hudson's Bay Company, made a grant of a very valuable tract of land on the Assiniboine River, fully five miles in length.

Here, then, Mr. Belcourt collected a sufficient number of Indians, chiefly Saulteaux, to found a village, erected houses, and built a church. In all this work he was himself the chief labourer, being assisted only by his hearers, whose help was small indeed. The Catholics here, we may remark, have no funds, at least their means are very slender. As proof of this, the Bishop's own cathedral in the colony has been for the last seventeen years left in a half finished condition, although the venerable prelate has made two trips to Europe, and one to Canada, for the purpose of collecting funds to complete it.

To return to Saint Paul's. Mr. Belcourt, with other priests to assist him, from time to time, laboured here for a number of years very zealously so far as the use of books went; but this was all. It is no wonder, therefore, that he laboured without results. Religion alone had no attractions in it for hungry savages. Rather than cling to it as a good, they turned from it as an evil. Had there been one or two good practical farmers attached to the mission, they would have done more real good in keeping the Indians together, and forwarding the work, than all the piety and books in the country could effect by themselves. When the Indians had anything to eat, they heard mass, sent their children to school, and attended church; but the moment a new supply of food was required, they dispersed in all directions, according to their usual habits, leaving Mr. Belcourt to read and pray alone, and months frequently elapsed before they could again be reassembled. In this way, we should not exaggerate to say, whole tribes are baptized and forced through the church forms, as it were at the gallop, and then given to the world as good Christians, although still running through the wilderness like beasts of prey. Mr. Belcourt must know better than we, whether or not this was the course pursued at Saint Paul's. After fifteen years' experience, therefore, the mission was broken up, the church demolished, and the houses abandoned. The Indians, thrown back again upon their native woods and plains, were as wild and ignorant as ever—indeed, worse than ever in a religious point of view; for, as the apostle says, " It had been better for them not to have known the way of righteousness, than after they have known it, to turn like the dog to his own vomit again, and the sow that was washed to her wallowing in the mire."

The next Catholic mission, established shortly after that of Saint Paul's, was on the river Winipeg, some 200 miles south-east of Red River, at a place called "Wabassimong." This mission was on the line of communication leading to Montreal, and had just began to take root, when the Wesleyans from Canada, under Mr. Evans, reached Lac la Pluie. Now, although this place is a long distance from the site of the Wabassimong mission—yet the Catholics claimed it as a part of their mission, on the ground that they had already been frequently there among the natives, for the purpose of converting them—and we certainly think, as they were the first, they had the best right; but, notwithstanding all this, at Lac la Pluie the Wesleyans commenced their mission in opposition to the Catholics, and here the work of strife began between them, as if the country had not been wide enough for both, without interfering with each other. Here, then, a system of proselytism was carried on by the rival parties, the labourers in the Lord's vineyard, trying who could draw most converts to his own way of thinking, by traducing the creed of his opponent. The opposition between the rival fur-traders of former days was not more virulent. Notwithstanding, a considerable establishment was formed at Wabassimong by the Catholics; a church was built, houses also, as at Saint Paul's, and cattle were sent thither from the settlement. For ten years the priests persevered in their efforts; children were catechised, baptisms administered, and several attempts made to form a school; but without success. The Indians at length absolutely refused instruction, and abandoned the mission. Everything was then demolished or cast away; and the melancholy recollection of their disappointment is all that remains of the French mission.

The success of the Wesleyans at Lac la Pluie was not greater than that of their rivals. Mr. Jacobs, one of the last Wesleyan missionaries stationed there, was one day conversing with the writer on the subject. "We have," said he, "been labouring there for the last eleven years, according to the usual system, without being able to form a school, or make a single convert." Such were the laurels they gained by their interference and opposition. To give the Wesleyan mission its due, however, few such instances as we have mentioned occur. In its own sphere, it is persevering, indefatigable, and generally successful in its operations. The members of that body require no false colouring to screen their doings; yet we find writers of high standing sending forth statements to deceive and mislead public opinion. It is stated that the Wesleyan Mission of North-West America consists of eight stations; one of which is said to be at Ross Ville, one at Norway House, one at Lake Winipeg, Moose Factory, one at Lac la Pluie, and one at Fort Alexander, and Edmonton and Rocky Mountains.* Now what is the fact? The one at Lac la Pluie we have already noticed; and with the exception of the one at Ross Ville, at Edmonton, and Moose—the

* R. M. Martin, page 136.

latter two have been abandoned—we know of no other that is, or ever was, at the places mentioned. However well meant, the harm such statements do is incalculable.

A third Catholic Mission was set on foot about 150 miles west of the colony, at a place named "Baie des Canards," on the Manetobah Lake. Its commencement dates a year or two after the Wabassimong Station, already noticed. A good deal of the country in that direction had previously been visited by the Catholic party, and the glad tidings of the Gospel announced to the natives, who occasionally began to assemble at the station finally selected for the mission. At length, a church, parsonage, and school were built, and hopes were entertained that a flourishing establishment would be called into existence. Unhappily, here, as at Lac la Pluie, the mission had scarcely been formed before its progress was interrupted by a missionary of another creed, in the person of the Rev. Mr. Cowley, of the Church Missionary Society, who had entered the field. The Catholics now began to feel that they were doomed to be the pioneers of the Protestants in every direction; but, loth to lose what they had gained, it was several years before they abandoned the contest in favour of their opponents, who were doing less good, if possible, than themselves.

We have remarked that the Catholics in this quarter are poor; and, perhaps, if it were not so, their prolonged efforts would have tended still more to demoralize the Indians. This, their poverty, however, must be admitted to redound much to their honour. Where a new mission is contemplated and the missionary named, the bishop allows him 10*l.* to fit himself out, then adds his benediction, and the thing is settled; the missionary, with his crosier in his hand, and his cross on his breast, sets out, like the apostles of old, without money in his purse or scrip for his journey. The mission at Wabassimong was not a fortunate one in any way; but the one at Baie des Canards proved still more unfortunate, for the first priest stationed there, a Mr. Derveau, met with his death in rather a mysterious manner, by drowning, and the last was threatened by the Indians, and had to make a precipitate retreat. The place was then abandoned by the Catholic party, as we have stated, and the fruits of nine years' labour were no better than dust and ashes.

The mission of Mr. Cowley, formed in opposition to the Catholics, was established at "Partridge Crop," situated, like that of the Catholics, on Manetobah Lake. Accustomed to opposition in trade, the Indians went to him who treated them best; and, as we have said before, the last creed with them is always the best. The Protestant mission had also funds at its command, with the aid of which Mr. Cowley could feed and clothe his converts, while the poor priest had nothing to offer them but instruction. This made all the difference in the eyes of the savages, who went from the one to the other till they had got for nothing all they could get in the way of temporal things, and then gave their reasons for abandoning both, as regarded spiritual things.

Their reasons, indeed, are too good to omit. A sagacious and wary chief, speaking on the subject of religious instruction, thus explained himself to Mr.

Derveau, the Catholic priest:—" You tell us," said he, " there is but one religion that can save us, and that you have got it; Mr. Cowley tells us that he has got it: now which of you white men am I to believe?" After a long pause, smoking his pipe, and talking with his people, he turned round and said, " I will tell you the resolution I and my people have come to; it is this— when you both agree, and travel the same road, we will travel with you; till then, however, we will adhere to our own religion; we think it the best." Here the matter ended; and as, from that day forward, the people would hardly join either communion, the chief was probably in earnest.

The Catholics, feeling sore for the loss of Manetobah, determined, by way of wreaking their wrongs on their opponents, to oppose the Protestants in another quarter, and take advantage of a blunder they had committed. Had the Protestant Church, in place of sending Mr. Cowley to wrangle with the Catholics at Manetobah, sent him direct to the Saskatchewan, where they had only a native catechist, they would, in all likelihood, have secured to themselves that important station. This field, by a mistaken policy, was left open to their opponents; and Mr. Cowley had no sooner troubled their proceedings at Baie des Canards than the Catholics sent off two active missionaries to the Saskatchewan, where they have now been located the last seven years. Here they are said to be very successful, and to dislodge them from that quarter will cost the Protestants a pound for every shilling it took to drive them from Manetobah. On the other hand, Mr. Cowley's mission at Partridge

Crop is certainly a failure, as the attendance of a few poor children at school, induced by the occasional offer of food and clothing, can afford little ground for hope of permanent success.

To clear our statements of any obscurity, we here insert a view of the foregoing missions in chronological order:—

1. Indian settlement commenced .... in 1832
2. Saint Paul's mission commenced .... in 1833
    ,,   ,,   abandoned .... in 1848
3. Wabassimong mission commenced............... in 1838
    ,,   ,,   abandoned .... in 1847
4. Lac La Pluie mission commenced............... in 1840
    ,,   ,,   abandoned .... in 1850
5. Baie des Canards mission commenced .... in 1841
    ,,   ,,   abandoned .... in 1850
6. Partridge Crop mission commenced .... in 1842

We have now briefly stated all that has been done for the Indians, first and last, in this quarter; not only in Red River, but within 200 miles of it on all sides. Missionaries have been here now for a period of more than thirty years, and during that time we have had, of Catholics and Protestants, no less than twenty-seven labourers at different times stationed among us, at an expense little short of 50,000*l.* sterling. Nay, more, the Company have thrown open one of the finest countries on the face of the earth for missionary labours; sacrificed their trade for the sake of the Gospel; and offered, in every possible way, every facility that either wealth or power could give, in order to facilitate inter-communication with the natives, and assist the pious missionary to come and go when and where he pleases for carrying on the great and benevolent work of salvation. Well may we here repeat, that the system pursued by missionaries for civilizing and evangelizing the heathen is defective, and that the results produced neither correspond to the means employed, nor to what might be accomplished on an improved system.

Of all the Indian tribes that hover about this settlement, Sioux, Saulteaux, Assiniboines, Crees, and Swampies, amounting to many thousands, each tribe branching out into numerous detached bands, and still more numerous detached families, how many individuals, we would ask, have been emancipated from the iron yoke of barbarism during the last thirty years? To find even one we must go back to the little "Swampy" village at the Indian settlement; and there how many shall we find? Should we plead as hard as did Abraham for Sodom and Gomorrah, we shall not find ten! Nevertheless, we find one of the missionaries of New Zealand addressing his hearers in these terms:—"Let us, my friends," said he, "follow the example of Red River; let us imitate the great and glorious success the missionaries there have met with in converting the heathen." And Warburton, author of the *Hochelaga*, page 155, states the case thus, "The many thousands of Indians scattered over the vast regions of Hudson's Bay afford a wide field for the efforts of Christian men; and the Red River settlement is a happy example of the invaluable advantages, temporal and spiritual, afforded them by the missionaries." The Bishop of Montreal, impressed with the immense good that has been done in the colony, remarks in his *Journal*, page 167, "That the day will arrive when the example of the Red River settlement must be followed in other portions of the territory."

In connection with this subject, we may here offer a few remarks on the Church establishment in Red River, in order to show the reader how comfortable people can be in a colony planted in the snowy regions of Hudson's Bay; and how much better provided with churches, and with ministers too, than most other countries more favoured by nature, and in the full sunshine of civilization.

In the colony, then, there are six churches, three built of stone and lime, and three of wood and lime, all by private subscription, at a cost of about 6,500*l.* sterling. Besides these, there are three meeting-houses, making in all nine places of public worship, which, in the aggregate, hold 5,500 persons. Other two churches are being provided for, and will probably be in existence before these pages meet the reader's eye. Now, according to the census of 1849, the population of the colony amounted only to 5,391; of which number there are, non-residents, 1,511,* leaving permanently in the colony a population of only 3,880 souls of all grades. One-half of the number, say 1,940, may be supposed to attend church regularly every Sunday, which would give to each of the places of public worship, Catholic and Protestant, a congregation of 215, or to each clergyman 161 persons. The spiritual staff provided for this snug

* Of this number, 636, according to the *Minnesota Register* of August 11th, 1849, crossed the line and became American subjects; and the remaining 875 regularly pass the summer in the plains, and the winter among the Indians and the buffalo.

little flock consists of one English bishop and five Church of England missionaries, who are equally balanced by one Catholic bishop and five French priests. At the same time, the Presbyterian party, although a large body, and the first settlers in the colony, are still without either church or minister of their own, notwithstanding their repeated calls for justice in this respect.

We have seen the time when people were fully satisfied with two or three clergymen in the settlement, and that when the population were little less than what they are at present; and we are still of opinion that were there any great anxiety manifested to convert the heathen, Red River could very comfortably and conveniently spare eight out of the twelve missionaries, and leave enough behind to satisfy the people. No settler in the colony can doubt, nor ought it to startle the ears of others to be told, that four active and well-paid clergymen are amply sufficient for all Gospel purposes in Red River; that is, two Protestants and two Catholics. We are not questioning the inexpediency of the missionary proceedings generally by these observations; our object is simply to repeat the fact we have stated in support of our argument: that were there any great anxiety to convert the heathen, the number we have stated could very well be spared for the work. This phalanx of officiating clergymen, in a little isolated nook like Red River, would imply a vast and rapid increase in our population, when the reverse is the fact; for during the last ten years the population has not increased 400; and from 1843, census 5,143, to 1849, census 5,391, inclusive, a period of seven years, our population has only increased

248. This is, however, accounted for by parties emigrating to the United States.

The Catholics out-number the Protestants, and are scattered over a much wider surface; yet they are satisfied with one cathedral and a parish church, whilst the Protestants within the settlement have five permanent stations: one at the Indian settlement, one at the Rapids, the middle church, Upper Stone church, and the Assiniboine. Well, then, might the stranger who visits the colony exclaim, in the language of surprise, " Red River for missionaries and churches!" But what must be his astonishment when he sees the heathen by hundreds wandering about within the sound of the church-going bell, and living and dying in the settlement without religious instruction. In this state of things, is the object of the Church Missionary Society forwarded and sustained as it should be? or is the Company rewarded, not merely for the liberal encouragement and support they give to the missionaries, but for the loss of their trade? It is denied by many, nor do we pledge ourselves to the fact, that the Company ever contemplated such a sacrifice for the sake of the Gospel; but this we know, and so may others who are in the least conversant with the nature of their trade know, that the introduction of Christianity to Rupert's Land was destructive of its very sinews. Granting that this fact was known to them, and that they were at all inimical to the progress of the Gospel through their territories, they might, as lords of the soil, have resisted its introduction with at least as good a grace as the lords of Scotland resisted and opposed the spread of the Free Church through their territories, by refusing sites after the disruption. Let those who deny that the Company are favourable to the spread of Gospel light, or that they have not in a more or less degree sacrificed their trade to it, answer this argument. So far, however, from being able to deny the facts we have stated, they must frankly acknowledge that the Company received with open arms all religious denominations, Jew and Gentile, that have come into their territories with the intention of instructing and converting the heathen. Indeed, had the long-neglected Presbyterian party in Red River, like other sects, made a pretence of introducing a minister to convert the heathen, they would not now, in all likelihood, have been without a church and a minister of their own. If the Indians have not benefited by the introduction of Christianity into Rupert's Land, the fault cannot justly be said to rest with the Hudson's Bay Company.

What effect, we might here ask, has the presence of so many more missionaries of the same creed, so many more places of worship, had on the mass of the population? Has it improved the religious feelings of the people, or the tone of society generally? or have the ties of affection between members of the same family been strengthened by it? Surely not. From two or three congregations on the Lord's-day, they are now multiplied to eight or nine. One member of a family runs above, another saddles his horse and gallops below; one here, one there. Every house is divided into factions; novelty is so attractive, that the Sabbath-day is spent in riding about from church to church to see and be seen, and the evening passed in discussing the merits of the preachers and the dresses of the hearers. Contrast with this the former practice, when, after divine worship, each family, young and old, invariably passed the evening of the Lord's-day at home in the exercise of religious duties, or attending in some measure to their domestic affairs. Few, we think, will venture to say that the change which has taken place is for the better.

Let us say in conclusion, therefore, it had been far better in all respects if the missionaries, who do, in fact, profess to come out for the heathen, had at once ranged themselves on the side of the poor and degraded natives. This conviction is the sole cause of our earnestness in taking up the subject, seeing it is one in which every friend to humanity, every Christian, must feel a deep and lively interest. If we have one wish at heart above every other, it is that the Gospel light, which we so liberally enjoy, may be more widely diffused, so as to dispel that thick and heavy cloud of darkness among those by whom we are surrounded. At the same time, remembering the facts we have stated, and the causes we have pointed out which present so many impediments to the success of the missionary, we would earnestly appeal against any measures tending to plunge the native Indians into temporal distress, unless the signs of spiritual benefit were unmistakeable and positive. To be gathered about the missions, without first providing for their subsistence in the new mode of life to which they are entitled, can have nothing but evil results. If the missions fail, as the greater number of them have hitherto done, the poor Indians are ruined: their hunting habits destroyed, and other cravings excited, nothing but wretchedness and poverty thenceforth await them. In the next chapter, however, we shall develope our views on this subject somewhat more in detail.

CHAPTER XX.

CONTENTS.—New missionary system—Introductory remarks—The text—Neglect of the heathen in Red River—The general principle—Three important conditions—Missionary difficulties—The first stage of progress—Staff of labourers—Governor Kempt's observations — The boon — The converts located — Second stage—Total of expenses—Comparison with the present cost — The missionary qualified — The success of the trader compared—Missionary station in the United States—Rev. Mr. Hunter—The Saskatchewan mission — Rivalry of sects — Coterie of Protestant missionaries in Red River — Crusade against idols—Church privileges—The Bishop of Rupert's Land—Sir George Murray's hints—Concluding remarks.

HAVING in the preceding chapter pointed out some of the errors and defects in the missionary plan for civilizing and evangelizing the Indians, and its almost universal failure, we proceed now to offer some practical suggestions, the adoption of which would greatly improve, as we think, the existing system, and facilitate the work of salvation. Without presuming that the plans we propose are suitable, without change, for universal application, we have long been satisfied that the course proper to be pursued among heathen tribes generally, may with some obvious alterations be applicable here, due attention being paid to the natural state of the people to be evangelized.

The first point to which we would more particularly call attention is the union of temporal and spiritual matters, which, as we have shown by examples sufficiently marked, ought not to be under the management of the same individual. This reform makes the preparatory part of our plan, which places the heathen, while he learns the first step of civilization, entirely under secular guidance; except, perhaps, occasional visits from the clergy. In this way the first moral restraints would be imposed on the savage, who would learn the value of order and subordination without alarm to his prejudices. It is the method which reason dictates, and experience enforces; but it is the one which, above all others, will excite the spirit of opposition, and we well know what arguments will be used, and the changes that will be rung upon them. Matt. xxviii. 19, 20.

In fact, the writer has vainly urged the consideration of this plan, both on Protestant and Catholic clergymen, who all condemned it from the text cited above. "We must," said they, "preach the Gospel to every creature." But how then does it come to pass, we might ask, as we have asked them in conversation, that you clergymen do not obey this positive command, and preach the Gospel to every creature? You have been located on the spot in question for the last thirty years; why not have preached the Gospel during all that time to "every creature?" You have not, so far as the heathen is concerned, preached to a tenth, a hundredth part of those around you! You have established missions on your own plans, as we have already noticed, and what has been the result? At this hour, the Indians are running as wild as ever in their native woods and prairies, nay, even in the settlement, and around your dwellings, and dying on every point, without the least regard to their lost state. Our assembling, locating, and training them, as proposed, cannot entail more guilt on the dying, or deprive them in any greater degree of the means of grace than your present system. If your arguments are worth anything, how are you justified in waiting till we locate the Indians, according to the plans you wish to dictate? Why not, in obedience to the divine command, go to their camps, their dwellings, and "preach the Gospel to every creature" now? Why wait till *anything* is done, if it is not lawful to wait till the right thing is done? So far from this, we may here state the fact, that from 1823, when Mr. West left the colony, up to 1842, when Mr. Cowley went to Partridge Crop, a period of twenty years, no Protestant missionary ever stepped out of Red River to preach once to the heathen, or preach to one of them, far less to "every creature;" indeed, with the exception of the Swampy Crees, in the village already noticed, no one has even preached to those within the settlement. Some plan, then, for benefiting the poor Indian is plainly necessary, and we know there is much difficulty in proposing one, especially as the very statement of these facts is calculated to raise a strong feeling against ourselves in the minds of those it would be our interest, as well as our sincere desire, to keep on our side—the very men, too, whose opinion on the subject is best entitled to respect. Nevertheless, our plan, under any circumstances, must eventually stand or fall by its own merits.

How short, after all, is the time we propose for ascertaining the result of our scheme, considering the great end in view; for what are the lapse of a few years, or even a few generations, when compared to eternity? We shall, indeed, have passed away before much can be done; but we shall pass away with the firm conviction, that those who come after us "will pluck the fruit of the tree we have planted." Nor have we anything really to fear from opposition, which can only lead to a more thorough investigation of the plan, and the more it is investigated, the more likely it becomes that it will, in the end, be adopted. "To everything there is a season, and a time to every purpose under the heaven," as the wise man says in Eccl. iii. 1. All we ask or expect, is an impartial consideration of the subject, by men who have had much experience in Indian life, studied their language, their habits and feelings, in their native wilds—where alone the savage is seen in his true character and not when under restraint among civilized men. It is but an essay, in the absence of anything better, that we propose. The apostle says, "To the weak became I as weak, that I might gain the weak: I am made all things to all men, that I might by all means save some."* Now if we can, as the apostle says, save some, our labour will not be lost.

After accomplishing the preparatory step, on the

* 1 Cor. ix. 22.

principle we have laid down, that the Indian must first be civilized before he is evangelized, the door would be opened for commencing spiritual instruction. " When a door is said to be opened, the meaning here is, that every obstruction or barrier is removed in the providence of God for going forward in the way of the moral and religious improvement of the heathen;" or in other words, after they are civilized, for that must be the first step. This course would be agreeable to the laws of our nature, the laws of civil and religious liberty: for they ought to know something of the one, before they can enter upon the other. For the success of our plan, however, three things must be kept in view.

First. The Indians must be located some distance from the whites—fifty miles or more; not, however, in villages, as has hitherto been the case, but in country lots by themselves, in some fertile place where wood and water might be conveniently got. Our reasons for this are, 1. Their being settled among the whites would expose them to too many baneful temptations, which would operate against temperance, industry, and independence. 2. Their being huddled together in villages would partake too much of their original camp habits, and foster a continuance of savage life which would be injurious to the progress of civilization. 3. The Indians in this quarter are too far removed by everything that can disqualify them from amalgamation with the whites by intermarriages, that they could never rise to an equality and independence among them; but, on the contrary, live in a state of slavery and degradation, as they now do. In a separate community, however, they might still retain something of their native spirit and independence — that gift by which God in his wise providence might mitigate the extreme penalty of barbarism.

Secondly. The establishment should be as nearly as possible in the centre of one tribe, and exclusively among the same people. 1. Because if it is on the frontier, or as it were between two nations, it will be subject to annoyance from both, without the support or protection of either. 2. There are many petty tribes in this quarter; but they are all more or less hostile to each other, except against a common enemy. Rivalry and jealousy between them would ever be at work, and the object of the mission ought to be unity and peace. This is an important point, and ought not to be lost sight of; for the collisions that would be unavoidable between the opposite tribes would alone be sufficient to frustrate the best devised plan for improving the heathen.

Thirdly. The place selected for their location should be as destitute of all wild animals as possible; the more ruined, the more easily will the natives be induced to relinquish the chase, and cling to habits of industry for subsistence. But a good fishery would be an additional recommendation to any place—in fact, absolutely necessary, as a failure in the crops, without some other stand-by, might ruin all; and besides, a fishery is a stationary thing, and would rather encourage than discourage settled habits. To become Christians, the natives would have to forego their roving propensities and the chase, but not the fisheries; nor do we mean that the habit of hunting should all at once be abruptly cut off—that would be attempting an impossibility. Till the earth yielded her abundant increase, the bow and arrow would have to supply the table, and supply the Indian with his blanket also. It will be for the Government to grant lands for missionary purposes; and if so, Government ought to protect the first creed against all unholy interference of a second, as religious opposition demoralizes the heathen. Of all other obstacles, all other evils, that of opposite creeds warring against each other, in the Indian camp, is the worst—the most fatal to the Indian, and to pure religion.

We might observe as we proceed, that this country is perhaps an exception to most other parts of the earth, and the course pursued by missionaries must be, in some measure, exceptional also. Our savages have almost thrown aside the gregarious nature of man, and show as much aversion from inclination, as other barbarous races have from necessity, to a stationary mode of life. Without industry and without subordination, they neither are willing, nor can they be compelled, to undergo steady toil. Reared with a taste for slaughter, they look with more of a butcher's than a herdsman's eye on any cattle they may have—a propensity, by the by, not disproved by the possession of a few animals, for an ox or two to draw fuel cannot be dispensed with, if a fixed house is to be rendered equal in point of convenience to a movable tent. Lastly, having long been in communication with traders, they have come to connect knowledge of all kinds with a good bargain. Education they regard in no higher light than as a means of living by their wits; and they can hardly divert themselves of the suspicion, that the very missionaries, more particularly when pitted under hostile banners against each other, have some mysterious interest of their own in the red man's conversion.

With these introductory remarks before us, we shall proceed to a short digest of our plan, which may be most conveniently considered under two general heads, or a first and a second stage of procedure, each divided into periods of five years.

The preparatory or first stage would occupy a period of ten years or more, for assembling, locating, and training the Indians under secular management. To accomplish these important ends, we require, at the very opening of the mission, the following staff of labourers, and other essentials, which may be considered sufficient for the first five years; our estimate is founded on the prices of Red River taken as a standard.

2 farmers, at 30*l*. each per annum for five years	£300
1 labourer, at 15*l*.	75
2 lads, at 10*l*. each	100
1 interpreter, at 20*l*.	100
6 oxen, at 6*l*. each	36
2 ploughs, at 6*l*. each	12
Outfit for general purposes	100
Expenses of first five years	£723

The first thing necessary is to set the ploughs at work, in order to benefit the Indians materially, by supplying them with food as early as possible. This is the mainspring of the whole machinery, the grand point of attraction, not only in order to keep the

Indians together, which would be an important step gained in advance, but for introducing with effect the habits of order and industry among them.

Supposing the mission thus far successful, we may presume the Indians would increase in number, which would be attended with increased expense. Accordingly, our estimate for the next period of five years would be as follows:—

The above items continued	£723
1 conductor, at 50*l*. per annum for five years	250
1 additional farmer, at 30*l*.	150
6 additional oxen, at 6*l*. each	36
1 blacksmith, at 30*l*.	150
1 carpenter, at 25*l*.	125
1 catechist, at 20*l*.	100
	£1,534

This sum of 1,534*l*. for the second period of five years, added to 723*l*. for the first five, gives a total of 2,257*l*. for the first stage of our process, occupying ten years in its accomplishment.

With reference to the Indians changing their habits of life and settling on lands, and the mode of locating them, Sir James Kempt, formerly Governor of Canada, observes:—" The locating of the Indians in country lots, would be found much more advantageous in producing habits of temperance and industry, than by assembling them in villages;" and then he goes on to say:—" Without the assistance of the Government, indeed, it is impossible to produce any extensive or effectual results on the Indian character and modes of life." This is exactly the view that we take of the subject; and though we are aware that no extensive plan for ameliorating the condition of the Indians can be entered upon without the aid of Government, we proceed to point out what can be done, in a small way, with the view of improving the system hitherto pursued: it is to this our task seems limited, for if we wait for Government aid, we may wait a day too long.

During the first stage, no great result should be expected; but this ought not to discourage us. The change would be gradual, but it would be sure. Soon would some families be inclined to throw off their roving propensities, follow the example of the whites, and fall into civilized habits. Food and care would have their due effect, and after these others would follow. The difficulties would gradually diminish with time. There would be more obstacles to overcome, and prejudices to smooth down, with the first family or two, than with a dozen after. Once the tide commencing to flow, it would flow rapidly, and as soon as one indicated a desire and willingness to settle, it would be for us to help him on, encourage and assist him. We should locate him on fifty acres of land, not wood but prairie, with a frontage of four chains; plough for him the lands he had first cleared, to the extent of an acre or more; and then give the means of ploughing himself, two oxen, an axe, a hoe, a spade, and a small dwelling-house. Give him also a deed for his lands; not merely for certain conditions having been fulfilled, but for so long as he remained on them, or transferred them to some other Indian, and no longer. The right of the property thus granted or given him, he should not be able to sell, alienate, or dispose of, before the end of ten years' occupation, when it must virtually become his own. During all this time the mechanics and labourers would be fitting up houses for the reception of the Indians, and in other respects contributing to their comfort.

This would be carrying out our plan fully: it would be the portion allowed to each converted family on settling permanently—a boon granted for encouraging civilization; and being the result of a regular system, would be the means of riveting the Indians to the soil. To those who might settle prior to the end of the first period, this would be the allowance; but those settling subsequently would, in lieu of the two oxen, only get one ox, and a cow, in order that they might have the means of rearing up stock for themselves.

Seeing now one or more regular settlers established as a land-mark in the wilderness, we might, indeed, take courage, and record a fair beginning. As others followed the example, they would, as a matter of course, be furnished with houses and lands in a similar manner, one alongside the other, so that there might be a uniformity of proceeding. Unity gives strength. How encouraging it would be to see the germ of civilization, rooted and grounded in hope, thus arise as it were by magic, and raising new feelings in the native mind, to humanize the barren desert. Nor would it at all be over-stepping the bounds of probability to expect, that within the short period of ten years, under civilized guidance, we might see two hundred families, averaging five each, or a thousand persons, comfortably established together, as the nucleus of a great and permanent good, round which thousands might in time be drawn to swell the stream of civilization, and worship the only living and true God, in spirit and in truth.

But we come now to our second stage of procedure, which would probably occupy a period as long as the first, and require a vigilant and active superintendence. This is the time for imposing moral restraints, bringing the Indians under social order, and for the introduction of elementary schools, to fit and prepare them for the next and most important step. During the first five years of this stage we would require, according to the anticipated increase of Indians—

In addition to the sum already computed of	£2,257
1 more farmer, at 30*l*. per annum, for five years	150
1 blacksmith, at 30*l*.	150
1 carpenter, at 25*l*.	125
12 draught oxen, at 6*l*. each	72
4 ploughs, at 6*l*. each	24
1 schoolmaster, at 25*l*.	125
1 catechist, at 20*l*.	100
	£3,003

This sum, with the 2,257*l*. of the first ten years, gives, for the total amount of expenses at the end of fifteen years, 5,260*l*. In the next five years, to complete the second stage, the farmers, with the exception of one, would be all withdrawn, as the Indians by this time ought to be farmers themselves. The mission then, prior to being left to its own resources, would only require, as a winding up, the following staff of labourers:—

1 intelligent superintendent, at 80*l*. per annum, for five years	£400
1 farmer, at 30*l*.	150
1 blacksmith, at 30*l*.	150
1 carpenter, at 25*l*.	125
1 schoolmaster, at 50*l*.	250
1 ditto at 25*l*.	125
1 catechist, at 20*l*.	100
2 school-houses, at 20*l*. each	40
	£1,340

The former total of 5,260*l*., added to this 1,340*l*., gives a grand total of 6,600*l*. This, of course, is exclusive of the property given to the Indians, namely, the lands, houses, axes, hoes, spades, and cattle; being, in short, neither more nor less than our estimate for an establishment for feeding the Indians.

Even this scale of expenses would not be perpetuated in case of neighbouring missions being entered upon. Once the desire of settling stimulated, a tithe of the present expenses would suffice to carry on the work. Make the Indian thoroughly sensible, as our establishment is calculated to do, that his food and comforts are more certain from the soil than the chase, and he will gradually fall into civilized habits of his own accord. With the aid of civilization to conduct him, the system only requires to be fully set going; it will then progress and prosper of itself.

Now, at first sight, this appears to be a very large sum, and perhaps very little good done for it, for the results of all new and limited experiments are doubtful;

but that very doubt ought to stimulate us to try, and try again, to arrive at greater perfection. If it be asked, Where is this sum to come from? we might answer the question by putting another: Where did the thousands and tens of thousands spent in the missions already described, come from? Or we might place the subject in another point of view. According to the working of the existing system, a missionary enters a new field, depending on his books and zeal; but neither books nor zeal will feed the Indian. Year after year rolls on; but still the missionary and the Indian are as far from each other as ever. Indeed, the labourer who remains ignorant of the Indian's language can never labour profitably. The best interpreter is but a false medium for conveying Gospel truth.

The missionary with an allowance of 200*l.* per annum, and 150*l.* more for his establishment, makes out to live indeed; but the poor destitute natives, if they would be converted, must at once give up their wandering habits of life, their hunting-grounds, their wives, their scalps, their gods, everything that is dear to them, and assemble round the missionary to starve; for in this arrangement no provision is made for them: they come and go, and go and come; but still no change in their condition. They are still the wild savages they were before; and during this coming and going, the missionary is left resting for lack of hearers, according to the variety of instances we have pointed out in the working of the Red River missions.

Suppose, then, the missionary remains at the station the time we have allowed for giving our experiment a fair trial—say twenty years—his expenses alone, according to our statement, would amount, not only to 6,600*l.*, but to 7,000*l.* Now we might ask any intelligent being this simple question: Which of the two systems is most likely to benefit the natives, and forward the great work of conversion? The answer is self evident. It is equally evident, that if we draw the Indians from their field of chase to a missionary station, and then neglect to provide food for them, we ruin them spiritually as well as temporally; for we assume it as proved that the mission is sure to fail, if the helpless natives are not supported materially.

This brings us to the closing period—that of their spiritual warfare; for the ultimate aim of all missions is to change the condition of the natural man. It has always been matter of remark here, that Indian converts have been too easily, if not hurriedly, admitted to church privileges. We should be careful not to force spiritual things upon them, nor allow them to receive them unworthily; for, of themselves, they must have but a withering conviction of what they stand in need of. This is the stage they are expected to know something of civil liberty. They can plough, sow, and read, and have a knowledge of temporal things. Knowing this, they are next brought to know something of liberty of conscience, or religious liberty, and their duty as Christians. It is at this point that the missionary steps in as their spiritual guide; the last boon in time, the first in end. As we have said before, the exact time of this change, or their getting a church and minister, would entirely depend on circumstances; if in a sufficiently advanced state to warrant it, they might get their minister and church at the end of the first, instead of waiting till the end of the second stage, or at any intermediate period. Up to this time, however, the mission should be visited, as we have noticed, at least once a year, by a regularly ordained clergyman.

As to the missionary himself, we would remark, that no man, however learned, pious, and zealous he might be, ought to be placed as spiritual pastor over a colony of new converts, without a knowledge of their language— and we may add, a knowledge of Indian life, acquired by at least some five or six years' residence among different tribes, to learn something of the Indian character. Nothing would be more absurd than to send a man direct from home to superintend such a mission, with only his learning to recommend him, as is too often the case, and has been the case here too. It takes even the man of business a year or two after his arrival to be conducted and instructed, step by step, before he is fit to be a common Indian trader; how much more, then, the missionary, the spiritual guide? We repeat the fact: any man with simply a knowledge of books, and utterly destitute of experience in Indian life, is, of all men, the most unfit to be entrusted with the civilizing and evangelizing of Indians; but more especially to be placed at the head of an Indian mission. We have seen enough of this to convince us that such appointments will result in failure, and do more harm than good in such a cause.

In the stage we have now reached, nothing ought to be forced or hurried on, if we would go honestly to work; for nothing is more deceptive than the character and demeanour of a savage in the presence of his spiritual instructor. Indifference is mistaken for modesty, cunning for diffidence, and the savage habit of hanging down his head and looking at the ground when spoken to on religious matters, is taken for reverence. In all these appearances, however, there is nothing real. An Indian never appears more pliable and devout than when he is meditating your destruction. We are imposed upon by comparing the habits of the savage with our own. Two things are often wanting to discriminate aright on these occasions—experience on our part, and the want of time on theirs: no wonder then, that men ignorant of the Indian character should be deceived and led into error, by adopting hasty conclusions. The missionary must keep a watchful eye on all changes, aspects, and appearances; he must confine his converts to a purely religious education, till the truths of the Gospel have fairly taken root, and a desire for instruction has been widely diffused.

The mission should be conducted, as all enterprises of the kind ought to be, on the most economical plan, and the means afloat for carrying on one mission might, with but little additional expense, carry on two, if within two or three hundred miles of each other; but this double advantage would depend on a variety of circumstances, unity of action, and a zeal only known to the traders; for no people in this country seem to get on so well among Indians as the trader; no other class of men have to depend so much upon them as the trader: his life, his fortune, his all, depends on the good or ill will he creates among them; consequently, no one takes so much pains to please, flatter, and conciliate them, as he does. In making these remarks, our object is simply to draw attention to the fact that there is, indeed, a way of pleasing and gaining over our heathen brethren to our views, if taken in the proper way, and that secular guidance at the beginning is more likely to be effectual than purely clerical superintendence. Everyone in his own time, and in his own sphere.

To give an instance or two in point. While travelling in the United States, the writer came to an Indian mission of the description here proposed, only on a somewhat smaller scale, conducted by a simple farmer, on an allowance of only 200 dollars a year. In answer to some queries I put, he answered, "I am the only farmer, schoolmaster, and catechist, about the place; myself and my family attend to the mission, but we are visited by a clergyman generally twice a year." And yet I was delighted to see everything working like clock-work, as things do when conducted aright. I said to myself, the Americans are a wonderful people, a people going fast ahead.

Another example may be drawn from a place nearer home—that wide and interesting field for missionary labours, known as the Saskatchewan. Here, for a number of years, no other labourer was sent by the Missionary Society but a native catechist, as farmer and superintendent; yet he managed matters so well, as to have prepared some 300 for baptism, and about 50 of the number for the sacrament of the Lord's Supper. This mission was likewise visited by a clergyman once a year. Just what we have proposed for our mission. These are encouraging instances. This last mission, however, might owe much of its success to peculiar advantages. The Indians live chiefly on fish, and are stationary; and besides, they are the relations of the Swampy Cree village in Red River, but entirely detached from the settlement. Their progress is far ahead of their brethren living among the whites. Mr. Budd, the zealous catechist alluded to, has been rewarded by being admitted to holy orders.

The Saskatchewan, or Cumberland mission, as it is called, had been long neglected; but is now in rather a thriving way. A few years ago, an excellent and indefatigable man, the Rev. Mr. Hunter, was appointed to that station, who, by his unwearied application, zeal, and talent, has made himself master of the Indian language, in order to preach in the native tongue—the only instance of the kind we have known among our Protestant missionaries in this quarter. This, indeed, is doing the work of a missionary in right good earnest.

Yet with all this pleasing prospect before us, we cannot shut our eyes to the fact, that like many other places, the Saskatchewan is a disputed field; so that little real good can be done. The Indians are distracted by opposite creeds. The Upper Saskatchewan was for some time under the Wesleyans—a very enterprising body of men; but they having left that quarter, it is now wholly under the Roman Catholics. In the neighbourhood of the Lower Saskatchewan also, near Cumberland, in a very extensive district called Isle a la Crosse, the Papists hold sovereign sway.

Had there been a zeal commensurate to the means, and that zeal exercised for the benefit of the Indians, the Red River missions would have appeared in a very different light from what they do. Mr. Cockran and his Swampies form the only instance of labour and zeal ever manifested in this quarter. Since his time, the missionaries have been doubled, trebled in number, and yet the more labourers the less work; verifying the old proverb, that " too many cooks spoil the broth."

But it is in a different aspect that the numerical force of the Protestant clergy is peculiarly hurtful. Being sufficient in number to form a party among themselves, they are now as independent of their flocks on social grounds as they have always been on most other grounds whatever. They are thus placed altogether beyond the influence of public opinion. Nor does this isolation affect merely the lighter matters of social intercourse, for the incidental alienation of mind thus produced, must be fatal, in a greater or a less degree, to the weightier relations between pastor and people. In the absence of any other Protestant creed (a blessing which may thus be too dearly purchased), these weightier relations are not strengthened by any pressure from without; while the same numerical force of the orthodox which occasions the evil, tends also to perpetuate it, by the ever ready shield of mutual example. It is an axiom, which no intelligent settler can doubt, that one-third of our Protestant clergy would do more good than the whole phalanx combined.

But, to draw this chapter to a conclusion, there yet remain one or two important observations to make, which we shall endeavour to comprise in a few brief sentences. The zealous missionary often raises a hue and cry against idols the moment he arrives among the heathen. This is not only premature, but absurd, and one great cause why the work of conversion progresses so slowly as it does. We should never busy ourselves over anxiously at first about the Indian's gods. If the desire to cast them away does not spring up among the Indians themselves, when they see us read, and pray, and worship God as Christians, there is no regeneration begun in the heart; and till then, the more pains we take to induce them to abandon their idolatrous customs, the less success we shall meet with in the attempt. This is a work of time, and time must be allowed; otherwise we deceive ourselves, and deceive them also.

Another evil in the existing system, more than once complained of already, has been to give spiritual things too rapidly, before they are prepared for them; a thing easily got is thought but little of. There is a time to give, and a time to withhold from giving. Progress is to be secured little by little, and especially by giving at the right time those particular things that can be received with thankfulness. Taking all this into consideration, no intelligent person, experienced in Indian life, will say that we have asked for too much time to do the work as it ought to be done, nor proposed a change of system without due reflection.

Before closing our remarks on the present subject, we might notice, and that with much pleasure, that the missionary cause in this quarter is likely to undergo a thorough change for the better, by the appointment and arrival of a bishop in Rupert's Land. This high functionary is a man of great diligence, energy, and zeal. Pious and exemplary, he is most anxious to promote the cause of the heathen, and to that end, is acting upon views which we cannot for the present fully appreciate. Being, however, a man of talent and means, there can be no doubt but, under an improved system, his pious efforts will be able to accomplish much good.

This much on spiritual things; and as to temporal matters, we may here quote, in support of our views, a passage from Sir George Murray's observations on the converting of Indians, penned by him when Secretary for the Colonies. "The white people," says Sir George, "by their habits of cultivation, are spreading everywhere over the country, like a flood of water; and unless the Indians will conform themselves to those habits of life, and will bring up their children to occupy farms, and cultivate the ground in the same manner with the white people, they will be gradually swept away by this flood, and will be altogether lost; but by occupying grants of land, and cultivating farms, they will gradually increase their numbers and their wealth, and retain their situation in a country in which they are so well entitled to have a share."

To conclude. Nothing but the postponement of spiritual instruction till the heathen are in a great measure independent of temporal aid, can ever enable merely human eyes to form a correct view of the religious state of aboriginal converts. When a savage is offered at once food and truth,—both or neither,—he is at least as ready as civilized men, whether laity or clergy, have often been, to take the one for the sake of the other; in fact, he is strongly tempted to consider what he calls " praying" as something that makes the pot boil. Nor is the Christianity in such a case less prejudicial to the civilization than the civilization is to the Christianity. Among those who know the Indian by experience, there can be no question, that he would be more likely to appreciate and embrace the sweets of a stationary life, if he were sure of not being attacked, before his own time, about his drum and his medicine, his gods and his wives. Let me not be misunderstood. Though undoubtedly Christianity be the end, yet civilization is nevertheless the best means,—not only the best means of introducing that end, but still more dearly the sole means of enabling it, when once introduced, to perpetuate itself.

CHAPTER XXI.

CONTENTS.—Sioux and Saulteaux—Treaties—Indian correspondence—Indian feelings—Two Indians shot—Result—Indian hung—Effect—The favourable change—Fulling-mill—The farce—Yankee fur-traders—The two foxes—Friendly intercourse.

IN a previous chapter we noticed the visits of the Sioux Indians, and likewise settled some difficulties between them and the Saulteaux, our neighbours; we have now to record their subsequent visits and difficulties with our plain-hunters; for it is hardly necessary to state that two such formidable bodies can seldom come in collision with each other, without difficulties, and even serious quarrels, sometimes ensuing. Every year, in fact, treaties of peace are made between the half-breeds and Indians, and every year they are as regularly broken.

The usages of peace and war among savages are often erroneously judged by the parallel customs of civilized life, while the fact is, that hostile tribes, like wild beasts of prey, are in the continual endeavour to destroy each other. The writer has never yet known an instance in which a treaty between savages held good a day, or an hour, after an advantage was to be gained by breaking it. For the last four years up to 1844, the half-breeds have suffered considerably: at last, however, they were roused to retaliate, and that retaliation gave rise to the following correspondence:—

No. 1.—SIOUX TO THE HALF-BREEDS.

White Bear's Lodge, 14th November, 1844.

FRIENDS,—We hang down our heads; our wives mourn, and our children cry.

Friends,—The pipe of peace has not been in our council for the last six days.

Friends,—We are now strangers. The whites are our enemies.

Friends,—The whites have often been in our power; but we always conveyed them on their journey with glad hearts, and something to eat.

Friends,—Our young men have been killed. They were good warriors: their friends cry.

Friends,—Our hearts are no longer glad. Our faces are not painted.

Friends,—You owe the Sisitous four loaded carts, they were our relations; the half-breeds are white men: the whites always pay well.

Friends,—The four Yanktons did not belong to us: but they are dead also.

Friends,—Tell us if we are to be friends or enemies? Is it to be peace or war? Till now our hands have always been white, and our hearts good.

Friends,—We are not frightened; we are yet many and strong. Our bows are good; but we love peace: we are fond of our families.

Friends,—Our hearts were not glad when we left you last; our shot pouches were light, our pipes cold; but yet we love peace. Let your answer make our wives happy, and our children smile.

Friends,—Send Langé with your message, his ears are open; he is wise.

Friends,—We smoke the pipe of peace, and send our hearts to you.

Friends,—Tell Langé to run, he will eat and rest here. He will be safe, and we will not send him off hungry, or bare-footed.

Signed by the chiefs.

WA NEN DE NE KO TON MONEY	×	La Terre qui Brule.
IN YAG MONEY	×	The Thunder that Rings.
ETAI WAKE YON	×	The Black Bull.
PIN E HON TANE	×	The Sun.

No. 2.—HALF-BREEDS TO THE SIOUX.

Grantown, 8th December, 1844.

FRIENDS,—The messenger which you sent to us, found us all sad as yourselves, and from a similar cause : a cause which may give a momentary interruption to the pipe of peace; but should not, we hope, wholly extinguish it.

Friends,—You know that for half a century or more, you and we have smoked the pipe of peace together; that during all that time, no individual in your nation could say, that the half-breeds of Red River lifted up their hands in anger against him, until the late fatal occurrence compelled them in self-defence to do so; although you well know, that year after year, your young men have killed, and, what we regard worse than death, scalped many belonging to us. Not that we were afraid to retaliate ; but because we are Christians, and never indulge in revenge. And this declaration, which may not be denied, brings us more immediately to notice and to answer the several points in your message to us.

Friends,—You say your people have been killed : we believe what you say, and sincerely regret it; but at the same time, you forget to express your regret that our people were killed also : the one fact is as well known to you as the other; and they were killed first. You forget to notice, that whilst La Terre qui Brule and party were in the midst of our friendly camp, smoking the calumet of peace in all confidence and security, your people at that moment were treacherously murdering our friends within sight of that very camp! You forget to mention that our dead were brought into the camp, the bodies yet warm, and laid before your eyes! Till then, never did it enter into the head or the heart of a Red River half-breed to seek in revenge the blood of a Sioux.

Friends,—You state that our people have often been in your power: we acknowledge what you say; but you must likewise acknowledge, that your people have often been in our power, and we sent them off with glad hearts also. Even on the late fatal occurrence, when our dead were before your eyes, and when a hundred guns pointed with deadly aim threatened La Terre qui Brule and party with instant death, yet more were for you than against you; so you were safe; La Terre qui Brule and party were safe in the camp of the half-breeds. The brave are always generous.

Friends,—You state that when you last left us, "your shot pouches were light and your pipes cold." There is a time for everything; was it a time to show you special kindness when murdering our relations? You demand from us four loaded carts for the four Sisitous: we never refuse paying a just debt, never consent to pay an unjust one. Let us see how far we are liable. In the first place, then, you know your people were the first aggressors. You, La Terre qui Brule, saw with your own eyes our dead, and you knew that none of your people were then killed, and we gave up all thoughts of retaliation, still clinging with fond hopes to that peace and friendship which had so long cheered our intercourse together; but the very next day after you left our camp, a party of your people were discovered rushing upon one of our hunters who happened to be a little on one side and alone; the alarm was given, when the first at hand scampered off at full speed to the rescue of their brother, and in the onset your people were killed. Four, you say, were Yanktons. The demand you make we cannot comply with, either for Sisitous or Yanktons, be the consequences what they may; because we consider it unjust. We may give a pipe of tobacco, or a load of ammunition voluntarily; but we will submit to no unjust demand.

Friends,—You put the question, "Shall we be friends or

enemies, or shall there be peace or war?" We leave yourselves to answer the question. They who would have friends must show themselves friendly. We have violated no faith, we have broken no peace. We will break none. We will not go to find you to do you harm. We will always respect the laws of humanity. But we will never forget the first law of nature: we will defend ourselves, should you be numerous as the stars, and powerful as the sun. You say you are not frightened: we know you are a brave and generous people; but there are bad people among you.

Friends,—We are fond of you, because you have often showed yourselves generous and kind to the whites: we are fond of you from a long and friendly intercourse, and from habits of intimacy. To sum up all in few words, we are for peace, peace is our motto; but on the contrary, if you are for war, and you raise the tomahawk in anger, we warn you not to approach our camp either by day or night, or you will be answerable for the consequences.

Friends,—You have now our answer; we hope you will take the same view of things, and come to the same conclusion we have done. Langé will lay this before the great chiefs; may your answer be the sacred pipe of peace. Put your decision on white man's paper. And may that peace and friendship, which has so long knit our hearts together heretofore, still continue to do so hereafter.

      (Signed)   CUTHBERT GRANT,
   Chief of the half-breeds, and Warden of the Plains.

To WA NEN DE NE KO TON MONEY.
 IN YAG MONEY.
 ETAI WAKE YON.
 PIN E HON TANE.

No. 3.—SIOUX TO THE HALF-BREEDS.

To CUTHBERT GRANT, *Chief of all the half-breeds, and Warden of the Plains.*

White Bear's Lodge, 12th Feb. 1845.

FRIENDS,—Langé is here, and your message is now spread before us in council. Ne-tai-opé called for the pipe; but Wa-nen-de-ne-ko-ton-money said no : all the men were then silent; but the women set up a noisy howl out-doors. Nothing was done till they got quiet. The council then broke up. Next day it was the same. The third day the council received your message as one of peace. We now send you our answer. Langé promises to run.

Friends,—I, the afflicted father of one of the young men killed by you, wish that he who killed my son should be my son in his stead. He had two feathers in his head.

NE TAI OPE.

Friends,—Among the young men killed by you, I had a nephew. He who killed him I wish to be my nephew. He was the smallest of all the unfortunates.

Friends,—You killed my son, he was brave, San-be-ge-ai-too-tan. He who pointed the gun at him, I wish to be my son. He had a feathered wand in his hand. I send it by Langé to my adopted son.

TAH WAH CHAN CAN.

Friends,—I wish the brave who killed my brother, should be my brother. He had a gun and many feathers in his head. He was young.

HAI TO KE YAN.

Friends,—I am old and bowed down with sorrow. You killed my brother-in-law. He was braver than the bear. Had three wounds, and a scar on the face. Whoever killed him, I wish him to be my brother-in-law for ever. He was bareheaded. Hair painted red. Many bells and beads on his leggings. He was tall and strong.

TAH TAN YON WAH MA DE YON.

Friends,—My cousin never returned. He is dead. Whoever deprived me of his friendship, I wish him to be my friend and cousin. He had been wounded before, and had a crooked hand. His feathers were red. He had garnished shoes.

WAH MA DE OKE YON.

Friends,—You killed my father last summer. I wish him who made me fatherless, should be my father. He was a chief, a Sisitou warrior, had a gun and a bow, had been scalped young.

His feathers reached the ground. Whoever will wear those proud feathers, I will give him a horse. I will be proud of him.

Friends,—You killed my uncle, Thon-gan-en-de-na-ge. I am sad. The man who was so brave, I wish to be my uncle. He was a Yankton. My face is always painted black. He had on cloth and leather leggings, and one feather.

KAN TAN KEE.

Signed by the chiefs.

WA NEN DE NE KO TON MONEY	×	La Terre qui Brule.
IN YAG MONEY	×	The Thunder that Rings.
ETAI WAKE YON	×	The Black Bull.
PIN E HON TANE	×	The Sun.

Considering now that peace and friendship were restored, our hunters returned to the plains as usual; smoked, hunted, and passed the summer among the Sioux, as if nothing unpleasant had ever happened: and all with one accord enjoyed the present, as they had done the past. On the strength of this friendly intercourse, and renewal of peace between all parties, for the Saulteaux were a party to the late convention, a party of the Sioux arrived at Red River on a friendly visit to the whites, and after a short stay returned again to their country in safety. A second party that reached Fort Garry on the 31st of August were less fortunate.

After a welcome reception, and a few hours passed at the fort, their curiosity was excited by the Roman Catholic cathedral on the opposite side of the river, and they crossed over to visit it. During this brief interval, a considerable number of Saulteaux gathered round the fort, as is usual on the arrival of strangers; but nothing occurred to raise the least suspicion of any hostile intention, so that the whites and Saulteaux were mingled promiscuously together, awaiting the Sioux' return. They had, however, no sooner landed—whites, Saulteaux, and Sioux, in a group—than a shot was fired, and instantly two Indians fell dead. The ball, after passing through the Sioux, killed a Saulteaux, and grazed a white man, who narrowly escaped with his life.

In the bustle and confusion that ensued, nothing could be learned for some time. The Saulteaux fled; and as soon as the Sioux were lodged safe in the fort, and the two bodies taken in, an inquiry was instituted, when the murderer was discovered to be a Saulteaux. Had the criminal sought his safety in flight, he might have been beyond our reach, before we were aware of it; but no: he was at last discovered by his own people, pointed out, and identified, standing with his back to a fence, not two gun-shots from the fort. He was pensive and mute, as if at a loss what to do or say for himself, and stood still till he was laid hold of; nor did he attempt to deny his guilt. On being questioned, he coolly answered, "The Sioux killed my brother, and wounded myself last year; from that moment I vowed revenge, that revenge I have now taken, and am satisfied; do with me," said he to the whites, " what you like." As a matter of course, he was committed forthwith to prison.

However justifiable the conduct of the Indian might be, according to his idea of things and the laws of his country, few acts more daring in its nature, or more insulting to the whites, had ever been committed in this quarter, and the universal voice called aloud for justice.

The fourth day after the murder was committed, he was tried in the regular way by a jury, found guilty, and condemned to be hung—the first instance of the kind in Rupert's Land. Being one of the Catholic converts, he was regularly attended in his last moments by the Reverend Mr. Belcourt, a Catholic priest. A gallows was erected over the prison gate, and there he was executed on the 6th September 1845.

At first, it was apprehended the Indians and their sympathisers might have made a stir; but the imposing appearance of 500 mounted cavalry, all armed, commanded respect; and everything went on with that awe and solemnity befitting the occasion. There were but few Indians present, to whom Mr. Belcourt made a short and appropriate speech, which seemed to have a good effect. During the novel spectacle, although more than a thousand spectators were on the spot, a voice was scarcely heard, and all parties left the ground in silence. Whatever the world may think or say of this act, any doubt or dissatisfaction that existed at the time arose from mere pity; the punishment, in the eyes of all present, was deemed just.

Long before this affair took place, the Indians had become insolent and overbearing; the peace and safety of the whites loudly called for some check on their growing audacity, and a fairer opportunity than now offered could never occur. Had we through a false sympathy overlooked this insult, our leniency would have been attributed to nothing but fear; and thus would have increased their assurance, and our danger. The propriety of the decisive course adopted has been proved by its salutary influence on the conduct of the Indians generally, demonstrating that they were amenable to the laws, and that crime, either by the whites or Indians, would not be tolerated within the colony.

A circumstance which took place in the previous year may here be noticed, by way of showing the tact, hardihood, and cunning, which distinguish the Indians. In the night of the 22nd of September, the Company's trading shop was robbed of its strong box, containing about 405*l.* sterling. The shutter had been forced, the window opened, and the box carried off; which done, the window was again closed, and the shutter properly replaced. This was done in the middle of the fort square—the fort being peopled on every side, surrounded by a high stone wall, and its gates shut; yet it was so well managed, that nothing appeared to excite the least suspicion, until the shop-door was opened in the morning, and the money missed.

Search being made, the strong box was presently found broken open, and concealed in some bushes behind the fort. A ladder also, with which the wall had been scaled, was discovered at the distance of a mile, although there were, at the time, several other ladders lying about the place which had not been touched. Suspicion fell on the whites and half-breeds, as everything indicated watchfulness, address, and caution; some few, and they were but few, thought it possible that it might have been the Indians; and this opinion gained strength when it was found that a young Saulteaux Indian had decamped in the direction of Pembina. The police were put on the scent, as far as Pembina; but the traces of the Indian went still farther. Beyond the lines, private individuals pursued the discovery for upwards of 250 miles, when they came up with the fugitive on the shores of Red Lake, and there, by the friendly assistance of the missionaries, they secured the fellow, and recovered the money, which he had still on his person, with the exception of some eight or ten shillings. The thief, being on American ground, was then allowed to go, and the poor fellow has been expatriated ever since, not daring to return to the colony.

The ladder alluded to was a heavy load for a man to carry, and yet the probability is, that the unaided villain went through the whole process himself, singlehanded. An act which for boldness and finesse could searcely be surpassed by the most expert burglars.

As this year witnessed the failure of the most signal efforts that had hitherto been made to open an export trade for the produce of Red River, we might here develope that subject at length, but it is necessary to proceed with caution, lest we encourage false hopes, and colour our subject too favourably. We have seen the plain-hunters as loud before in their demands for an export trade; but when put to the test, the whole settlement could not produce a boat's load for exportation. The plain business is as uncertain as the wind that blows. One year may prove abundant, and the next a complete failure. Indeed, since this demand has been a-foot, the plains have been known so far to fail, that not a pound of tallow could be found in the colony to make candles; and when got, not at $1\frac{1}{2}d.$ or $2d.$, but its cost was $4d.$

per pound. Such fluctuations must account for apparent contradictions occasionally in our own statements, as we cannot but follow, in the course of our history, the irregular and uncertain circumstances which compose it. System would, no doubt, do much towards creating a steady supply; and with all the ups and downs, doubts, and uncertainties we have described, it cannot be denied that a market is wanting for the farmer as well as the plain-hunter.

Our population, as we have before observed, is made up of two classes nearly equal in number; the European or agricultural party, and the native or aboriginal party, called hunters or half-breeds, differing as much in their habits of life and daily pursuits as in the colour of their skin. In the present state of things, their interests are exactly opposed to each other, inasmuch as a market for one party shuts up all prospect against the other. When the plains fail, the farmer's produce is in demand; and when the crops fail, the hunter finds a ready market; but when both are successful, there is not a tithe of a market for either within the colony. Such a state of things as now exists, we need hardly remark, cramps industry, and renders labour—the great source of wealth in other countries—utterly fruitless. Hence, an idle, vagrant, and grumbling population—a population with barns full, stores teeming with plenty, and yet their wives and children half naked, insomuch that the more industrious and wealthy can scarcely command a shilling to pay the doctor's bill, or their children's education. Singular assemblage of wealth and want, of abundance and wretchedness!

On the graver side of the subject, namely, the administration of the laws, a word still remains to be said. How long, it may be asked, will a people in this wretched state of things, without any profitable pursuit, or power to maintain order, yield obedience to the laws? The aboriginal inhabitants of the soil, without profitable employment, without means, without care, impatient of restraint, by nature wild as the country which gave them birth, free and independent as the air they breathe, where is the power to command subordination? or what boon is offered them for obedience? Their advantage, on the contrary, is to be found in breaking the laws rather than obeying them. Even at this moment, it requires not only a vigilant eye, but the exercise of patience and forbearance, to administer justice. It is almost dangerous to own property, and that danger is increasing hourly. "Take our produce," is the universal cry—the universal threatening voice. Nor is it the voice of the native class alone: all classes unite in calling aloud for a market; and will the united efforts of a whole people be disregarded by the few whose duty it is to remedy such evils? If so, it may be convenient for them to bear in mind, that sooner or later, a storm may burst forth, and the first burst of that storm may fall on their own heads, if it does not prove fatal to the colony.

Not to recount a hundred other arguments which occurred to me at this time (for I can here most conveniently speak as a narrator), I had resolved to bring the question of an export trade before our council, at its first meeting; and such were the assurances of support I had received, that, in imagination, I had the ball at my foot. At length, the long-wished-for day arrived, and thrusting my papers into my pocket, I repaired to the council-room full of hope that the day of better things for Red River was at last come. Alas! a strong under-current had been at work, and my warmest supporters had grown cold. The measure was offensive in a certain high quarter, and the council considered it the wisest policy to look upon it in the same light. It was apparent, in a moment, from the side glances, grave looks, and long faces about me, that the export trade was about to expire in the struggle for birth. After two or three ineffectual attempts to be heard, without any other reason given, it was observed to me, "Your motion is premature;" on which the president remarked, "It is not a subject for this Council; but for the Governor and Council of Rupert's Land." This was a most convenient foreclosure of the subject; but right or wrong, the decision admitted of no alternative. From that day the halfbreeds turned their thoughts towards the Americans and the American Government: the farmers meanwhile looked at each other in silence, and kept dragging on as usual.

But the failure of our export trade project did not prevent us from entering into another, and the last we shall have occasion to notice in the catalogue of experiments. Notwithstanding the limited number of sheep in the colony, and consequently the scarcity of wool, nothing would do but we must have a fulling-mill. So the project of a fulling-mill was set on foot—and a very useful article it is in a place where it is wanted, or where wool and cloth, to any extent, occupy the attention of the people; but for a community like ours, with never as much wool as would keep us in mittens and socks, a more foolish and useless speculation could scarcely be imagined; especially as its tendency must be to diminish, not encourage manual labour, and by so doing, swell the list of idlers, already too great. When this whim took us, an American on the spot offered to bring us a small fulling-mill from the States, and erect it, and set it going, at a cost of 50*l.* sterling. Nevertheless, from a deeply-rooted prejudice against everything American, we preferred obtaining one from England, at an expense, including cost and charges, landed in Red River, of 300*l.*

Our mill being erected, we waited three months or more for a bit of cloth, and then discovered that it would not go. It was altered in some respect, and now we hoped all was right; but after waiting a month or two longer, a farmer brought 25 yards of cloth to be fulled, which proved too small a quantity: the mill required 100 yards to give her a fair trial. A second month elapsed, and we got 30 yards more; but the mill refused to go without its full allowance, and before more cloth could arrive, the man that brought the first, took it away as it was; by and by, the second did the same; and from that day till this—a period of five years—the fulling-mill has been silent and motionless. All we have for our money is the edifying spectacle of this specimen of our liberality fast mouldering to decay.

We have mentioned that the people of Red River have strong prejudices against our republican neighbours of the south; but to prevent misunderstanding, this remark is meant to apply only to the fur-hunters on the frontier, whose grasping propensities have proved so offensive. It sometimes happens that we have to rebuke them for an infringement of rights—a fox or a lynx carried off, perhaps—in which case they bluster and bully, and throw the fault on us for showing the example, forgetting, that if we take a few wild buffaloes from them, they take many valuable furs from us. They also keep tampering and meddling with our people, not forgetting to tell them how much better their Government is than ours, and how liberal their traders; as if we could forget the Missouri tariff!

One of their plain-rangers happening to meet some of our hunters, one of whom had two black foxes for sale, he inquired where they were conveying them, and what price they were to get. The reply was "Fort Garry;" and the price "twenty-five shillings a-piece for them." "Tut, man!" said the American, "they cheat you; come with me, and I will give you thirty shillings for each." A bargain was struck for one; the man could not part with the other. Taking the fellow to his shop, he gave him a blanket and a knife for his thirty shillings. The man refusing the price offered, demanded his fox-skin. "No," said the trader: "you cannot take furs across the line; it is now on American ground; you must either take the price offered, or forfeit the skin." So the fellow had to content himself with what he got, or go without! For the other, he got his twenty-five shillings in cash at Fort Garry; which brought him two blankets and two knives. Such is a frontier trader's liberality!

In other respects, the Americans are on the most friendly terms with us. Notwithstanding the high rate they charge for their goods, our hunters are devotedly attached to them, and their interests of late have partaken of much in common. With them, everything American is praised, everything British dispraised; and yet all agree that American goods are very inferior to English. There is a well-grounded reason for this preference. Since the road to Saint Peter's has become practicable, thither all the moneyless and poor go every summer, to find a ready market for their robes, leather, provisions, and garnished work—articles which they could not sell in the colony; and in return for which they get all their wants supplied—stoves, iron, tea, tobacco, and a thousand other articles of great value to them—a resource which puts the poor of this settlement on a footing with the rich. Saint Peter's, to them, is what London is to the moneyed man. Under such circumstances, it cannot be wondered, that the attachment grows stronger and stronger every day.

CHAPTER XXII.

CONTENTS.—Cause of the Presbyterians resumed—Governor Finlayson—The petition—The clergy at work—Criticisms—Correspondence with Leadenhall-street—Affidavits—Doubts removed—The church site question—Company's ultimatum—Appeal to the Free Church of Scotland—Time lost—Friendly aid of Sir George Simpson—The four propositions—The minister in view—Correspondence sent to England—More delay—Bishop of Rupert's Land—The secession—The Presbyterians at home—The churchyard—Frog Plain—The church and the manse—End of the forty years' agitation.

CONTINUING the thread of our history, we find the cause of the Presbyterians again brought under our notice, and now, indeed, for the last time. The innovations daily being introduced into the English churches, developing more and more strongly their Popish tendencies, so disgusted the Presbyterians that they determined on making another strong effort to get their own minister; and the arrival of a new Governor at this time opened the door of hope once more to them.

We have, from time to time, had Governors of all classes—some good, some bad, English and Scotch, Catholic and Protestant; but it was Mr. Finlayson's lot, from the impartial and straightforward course he pursued, to unite and to please all. A man of business habits, liberal principles, and strictly just, he knew nothing of party and its objects, but at once took his position in the interest of all, and especially as the friend of the poor. With Mr. Finlayson's arrival, everything underwent a change. The settler was invited to bring in his produce without reserve; and the farmer, for the first time, saw himself placed on the same footing with the hunter. There was now an end of favouritism; and Mr. Finlayson showed such a determination to promote the general interests of the colony, that we resolved at once on laying our case before him. At a meeting, therefore, of the Presbyterian community on church matters, a petition was prepared for the new Governor.

With the petition a deputation waited on Mr. Governor Finlayson, who received it courteously, and stated his opinion frankly and favourably. He told the deputation that he regarded the treatment of the Scotch emigrants, in respect to their long and grievous want of a minister of their own persuasion, as a blot in the history of the colony; it was a question, however, that rested chiefly with the Committee of the Hudson's Bay Company; and he strongly urged upon the aggrieved party the propriety of petitioning that body on the subject. Acting on his suggestions, we addressed the following petition to the Governor and Committee, and put it into the hands of the Governor-in-Chief of Rupert's Land, Sir George Simpson, in June, 1844, to be by him presented at home:—

ITS RISE, PROGRESS, AND PRESENT STATE. 343

To the Governor, Deputy Governor, and Committee of the
Hon. Hudson's Bay Company, London.

The Petition of the Presbyterian Inhabitants of Red River Colony,

Humbly showeth,—

That about thirty years since, say in 1815, the greater part of your petitioners were brought from the north of Scotland to this country, either by the late Earl of Selkirk for this colony, or by your Honourable Company, as artisans and labourers for your service. That emigration from Scotland and the service, and other causes, have since continued to increase their number to about 2,600 persons, who may be considered to have been during that period without a pastor, at least of their own persuasion, to administer to their spiritual wants.

That your petitioners, before leaving Scotland, had a solemn promise from the late Earl of Selkirk that a clergyman of their own Church would either accompany them to this country, or join them the following year in it. That when his Lordship visited the colony in the year 1817, this promise was then renewed; but the troubles, or rather the law-suits, in which his Lordship was engaged in Canada, detained him long there; and the state of his health, after going home, rendered it necessary for him to travel on the continent of Europe, when he unfortunately died, put an end to the hope which they, up to that period, had cherished, and which has not since been realized.

That the attention of your petitioners has long been turned with painful solicitude to their spiritual wants in this settlement; that widely as they are scattered among other sections of the Christian family, and among many who cannot be considered as belonging to it at all, they are in danger of forgetting that they have brought with them into this land, where they have sought a home, nothing so valuable as the faith of Christ, and the primitive simplicity of their own form of worship; and that their children are in danger of losing sight of those Christian bonds of union and fellowship which characterize the sincere followers of Christ.

That your petitioners do not deny but they have enjoyed some Gospel privileges in this place, nor to insinuate that the promises of Christianity belong exclusively to their Church; but rather to state that they are strongly attached to their own form of worship, and wish to enjoy the freedom of serving God according to the dictates of their consciences, and the rules prescribed by their own Church, within whose bosom your petitioners have been nurtured; and they believe and are persuaded, that it speaks more forcibly and powerfully to their hearts than any other, and that within its pale, and within it alone, they wish to live and die.

That your petitioners, forming, as they do, one of the more orderly, industrious, and intelligent part of this community, and feeling, as already stated, conscientiously devoted to their Church, can no longer abstain from appealing to the generosity and liberality of your honourable board, in the fond hope that the prayer of their petition will not pass unregarded, and that you will not withhold from them the boon which you have afforded to other denominations of Christians in this country—that is to say, the means of spreading God's word, and fulfilling his purposes of love towards mankind, and of making Him more fully known in this land to his fallen creatures, for their adoration.

That your petitioners are mortified to see year after year Roman Catholic priests brought into the settlement—at present no less than six over a population of some 3,000—and Church of England missionaries, no fewer than four over a few; while your petitioners are left to grope in the dark, without even one. And yet your petitioners were the first, the only regular emigrants in the colony; and on the faith of having a clergyman of their own Church they left their native country.

Therefore your petitioners would most humbly and respectfully implore your honourable board to send to this colony a Presbyterian clergyman of the Kirk of Scotland, for their edification and instruction; and as their means will furnish him with but a small stipend, you would be pleased, according to your usual liberality, to contribute something towards his support, in like manner as you have done to all the missionaries sent to your territories.

And your petitioners, as in duty bound, will ever pray.

ALEXANDER ROSS.
ROBERT LOGAN.
JAMES SINCLAIR.
And forty other heads of families.

This step of the Presbyterian party alarmed the missionaries, who did their utmost, both in word and deed, to defeat our object. Every head and pen were at work. Our petition was roughly handled, and pronounced unintelligible. It was analyzed, scrutinized, and criticised; whole sheets were written exposing the errors in our petition, and doled out as wholesome advice to the people in this emergency. A holy crusade was raised against our lawless proceedings, as had always been the case whenever an attempt was made, either in word or deed, to revive the obnoxious subject of a Presbyterian minister; for we are told the Jews and Samaritans have no dealings together. Our "expressions were intolerable;" our principles were taunted, and our conscientious scruples pronounced "absurd." The phrase, "Presbyterian form of worship," said one more knowing than the rest, "can give no definite notion either of our religious tenets or of the Church to which we belong;" adding, "the Presbyterians may seek, but shall not find: persevere, but shall not prevail." "Your language," said another, "offends both grammar and Scripture." "The Church of Scotland," said a third, "is rent asunder; it is no longer a Church," and the use of the term "Presbyterian," obsolete. In short, all our "moods and tenses" were out of place; an assertion which they were very welcome to make, as our lives had not been spent in adjusting "moods and tenses." This, however, was not the worst; for the next Sabbath-day we were told from the pulpit that "No Presbyterian would ever enter the kingdom of heaven!" At length, in June, 1845, the following letter was received from London in answer to our petition:—

Hudson's Bay House, London, March 31st, 1845.

GENTLEMEN,—I am directed by the Governor and Committee of the Hudson's Bay Company, to acknowledge the receipt of your petition, dated 10th of June, praying that they would send out to Red River settlement a clergyman of the Church of Scotland, for the edification of the Presbyterian inhabitants, and also that they would contribute towards his support.

The reasons urged in support of the petition are the granting of similar indulgences to missionaries of other denominations, and a promise made by the late Earl of Selkirk to the original settlers of Red River; with respect to which, the Governor and Committee have to observe, in the first place, that the indulgences granted to missionaries can form no precedent for maintaining the minister of a Presbyterian congregation at Red River settlement, as these indulgences are allowed in consideration of the services rendered by the missionaries in instructing and converting the aboriginal inhabitants, who are unable to provide religious instruction for themselves; and, secondly, that they know of no such promise as that stated to have been given by the late Earl of Selkirk.

During the time that the settlement was under the direction of the late Earl of Selkirk, no steps appear to have been taken with a view to the appointment of a Presbyterian clergyman; nor, when it was transferred by his Lordship to the Hudson's Bay Company, was any stipulation to that effect made with them. Nevertheless, if you and those you represent are prevented by conscientious scruples from availing yourselves of the religious services of a clergyman of the Church of England, the Governor and Committee will order a passage to be provided in one of their ships for any minister, to be supported by yourselves, whom you may think fit to engage.

I am, Gentlemen, your most obedient servant,

A. BARCLAY, *Secretary.*

To Messrs. A. Ross, Robert Logan, James Sinclair.

On receipt of this letter, in order to remove all doubt as to the promises that had been made to us by Lord Selkirk, both before and after coming to this country, we made the subjoined statements on oath, and forwarded them to the Honourable Committee, together with the following letter :—

To the Governor, Deputy Governor, and Committee of the Hudson's Bay Company.

Red River Settlement, 18*th July,* 1845.

HONOURED SIRS,—We have the honour to acknowledge the receipt of your letter in answer to our petition, dated 31st March last, wherein you state, first, " that you know of no such promise as that stated" by us " to have been given by the late Earl of Selkirk." Secondly, that " during the time that the settlement was under the direction of the Earl of Selkirk, no steps appear to have been taken with a view to the appointment of a Presbyterian minister; nor, when it was transferred by his Lordship to the Hudson's Bay Company, was any stipulation to that effect made with them." With reference to the first of these points, we beg most respectfully to refer your honours to the accompanying affidavits, which, we trust, will leave no doubt on your minds but that a clergyman of our own persuasion was promised us by the late Earl of Selkirk, both before and after leaving our own country ; and permit us also to say, that we know nothing of the transfer you mention, further than hearing it now and then rumoured that such was the case ; but as to the fact, we knew nothing of it until we saw it stated in your honour's letter ; therefore could not, at the time, have made any " stipulation to that effect." This we know, however, that in 1833, when the building of the stone church, noticed in affidavit second, was contemplated, we were distinctly told by the Governor-in-Chief, that a Mr. Noble, a Presbyterian minister, was engaged, and would be out for us the year following, or surely we had never allowed a place of worship for any other sect to be built on our church lot; but we never heard anything more about Mr. Noble or any other up till this hour.

"Further, we, the party now applying to your honours for a clergyman of our own persuasion, only ask for our rights—rights solemnly promised to us—being the conditions on which we left our own country: and further, we beg to state, and that without fear of contradiction, that we have, one and all, to the utmost of our power, faithfully and zealously fulfilled all the promises, obligations, debts and dues, we owed, both to his Lordship and to the Hudson's Bay Company, from the day we left our native country up to this day. And this fact encourages us to hope and expect, that your honours will be pleased to re-consider our case, recognise our claim, and grant the prayer of our petition.

We are, honoured sirs,
Your obedient humble servants,
ALEXANDER ROSS.
ROBERT LOGAN.
JAMES SINCLAIR.

For and in behalf of the Presbyterian inhabitants of Red River.

AFFIDAVIT FIRST.

We, the undersigned settlers in Selkirk's Colony, Hudson's Bay, make oath on the holy evangelist, that in the spring of 1815, at Helmsdale, Sutherlandshire, when we and the other emigrants agreed with the late Earl of Selkirk to come out to Red River as colonists, one of the conditions stipulated, and solemnly promised by his Lordship, was, that a minister of our own persuasion should accompany us. That the Rev. Donald Sage, now minister in the parish of Rosolis, was the gentleman agreed to, and he was to have 50*l*. a year from his Lordship. Our minister along with us, was the strongest inducement held out to the emigrants for coming to Red River, and without which we had not left our native country. And the reason why Mr. Sage did not accompany us, as agreed upon, was this—his father, Alexander Sage, then minister in the parish of Kildonnan, requested the Earl of Selkirk to leave his son for another year in order to perfect himself more fully in the Gaelic language, which request his Lordship submitted for the consideration of the emigrants, who yielded their consent on condition that his Lordship would answer for his being sent out the year following.. This was agreed to, and Mr. Sage remained; his Lordship, in the mean time, appointing one James Sutherland, an elder of our church, and one of the emigrants, to marry and baptize during that year till Mr. Sage should arrive. But Mr. Sage never came out, and Mr. Sutherland was, during the troubles in the country, forcibly carried off to Canada by the North-West people, and from that day to this, we have been without a settled dispensation of the means of grace; not being able to obtain a minister.

Over and over again have we applied to every Governor in the colony, since its commencement; to Mr. Halkett, also his Lordship's kinsman, and to the Governor-in-Chief of Rupert's Land; and time after time petitioned the men in power among us; but all to no effect. What other step, then, could we have taken? This is the truth, and nothing but the truth, so help us God!

ANGUS MATHESON.
ALEXANDER MATHESON.

Sworn and subscribed before me at Red River settlement, this 18th of July, 1845—GEORGE MARCUS CARY, J. P.

AFFIDAVIT SECOND.

We, the undersigned settlers in Selkirk's Colony, Hudson's Bay, make oath on the holy evangelist, that in the summer of 1817, when the late Earl of Selkirk visited the colony, he assembled all the Scotch settlers together, and held a meeting on the west bank of the river, some two miles below Fort Garry, on the identical spot on which now stands the upper stone church, being lot No. 4,

original survey; and on which was settled at the time John Mc
Beath, one of the deponents; and on lot No. 3, the next to it on
the south side, was settled his father, Alexander Mc Beath, another
of the emigrants. "These two lots," addressing the two Mc
Beaths, said his Lordship, " I intend granting the former for your
church, as you have already formed a church-yard on it, and the
latter for your school; if you will give them up for that use, in
lieu of other two lots which I shall give you, in any place you may
select. To this proposition they willingly agreed; and all the
people were highly pleased at his Lordship's arrangement. His
Lordship then, in presence of us and the meeting, said to Mr.
Alexander McDonell, then Governor of the colony, and on the
spot at the time, " You will give Alexander and John McBeath,
in lieu of the lots they now occupy, and which are to be hence-
forth reserved for their church and school, a lot to each, in any
place within the colony which they may think fit:" and they did
select other two lots, and removed to them accordingly. His
Lordship then observed to the emigrants, "These lots are to be
reserved for your minister, to be ready for him by the time he
comes." On mentioning their minister, the Scotch people got a
little warm on the subject. " Our minister " said they, "ought to
have been here before now." On their making this remark, his
Lordship was touched, and drawing his hand across his neck,
exclaimed, " You might as well cut my throat as doubt my word;
you shall have your minister; nothing but the troubles in the
country prevented Mr. Sage from being here before now; but you
shall have your minister; Selkirk never forfeited his word."
And so anxious was his Lordship to see his promise fulfilled, that
immediately on reaching Canada, seeing he would be detained
there longer than he wished, he ordered his agent, a Mr. Pritchard
of Red River, and now alive, to engage and forward a Presbyterian minister without delay, as Mr. Sage had not come out; but
his return to England, and the bad state of his health, rendered
it necessary for him to travel on the continent, where he died;
and unfortunately for the Scotch settlers, Mr. Pritchard belonging
to the Episcopal Church himself, took no further interest in our

affairs; so that up to this day the Scotch emigrants have not got their minister. All this is the truth, and nothing but the truth, so help us God!

> JOHN MCBEATH.
> ALEXANDER MATHESON.
> JOHN MATHESON.
> ANGUS MATHESON.
> ALEXANDER SUTHERLAND.

Sworn and subscribed before me, at Red River settlement, this 18th of July, 1845—GEORGE MARCUS CARY, J. P.

It will be noticed that the Committee state, "that they know of no such promise as that stated to have been given by the late Earl of Selkirk;" as much as to say, if we interpret right, that had a promise been made, it would have been attended to, and acted on. Now, we think we have made it pretty clear, that not only a promise, but promises were made; and yet, what is the effect? Not one word about our affidavits! as shall appear in the following letter, which we received in reply:—

Hudson's Bay House, London, 6th June, 1846.

GENTLEMEN,—I am directed by the Governor, Deputy Governor, and Committee of the Hudson's Bay Company, to acknowledge the receipt of your letter of the 18th July last, with accompanying documents, and to acquaint you that they can neither recognise the claim therein advanced, nor do anything more towards the object you have in view than they have already stated their willingness to do.

> I have the honour to be, Gentlemen,
> Your obedient servant,
> A. BARCLAY, *Secretary.*

Messrs. A. Ross, Robert Logan, James Sinclair.

Such was the Company's ultimatum; and as our hopes were now at an end in that quarter, the writer lost no time in opening a communication with the Free Church of Scotland. To relate the result in this place we shall be compelled to anticipate our history by a year or two; but we shall prefer this course to that of resuming the subject in a future chapter. A duplicate of our correspondence with the Company, and other documents, were transmitted to the Rev. Dr. Brown, of Aberdeen, then Moderator of the General Assembly of the Free Church, which he, on his part, lost no time in transmitting to the Rev. John Bonar, of Renfield Free Church, Glasgow, Convener of the General Assembly's Colonial Committee. Three years elapsed before we received a reply, owing in part to the great distance between Red River and the old country; but in a still greater degree to the difficulty experienced in transmitting our letters, and their frequent miscarriage. Its terms were as follows :—

Glasgow, May 16*th*, 1849.

MY DEAR SIR,—I am grieved to say that we have not yet succeeded in finding a suitable minister to be sent to the Red River Settlement. I have opened communications with two or three on the subject; but none of them have seen it their duty to accept. I will not, however, relax my efforts, and hope, by this time next year, to be able to send some one, as the Colonial Committee has set itself, with all earnestness, to find one; and in the meantime, I am, my dear sir, with great regard,

Yours truly,

JOHN BONAR,

Convener of the Colonial Committee of the Free Church of Scotland.

Alexander Ross, Esq., Red River Settlement.

Thus encouraged, we addressed two letters to Sir George Simpson, on the subject of our church and school lots, which had so long been occupied by the English missionaries, that they regarded church and lands as their own. It will be remembered, however, that the lot was in our possession, and that the burying-ground on it had been used by our people exclusively, for eight years before the first English missionary for Red River crossed the Atlantic. To these letters the following reply was sent:—

Fort Alexander, 7th July, 1849.

My dear Sir,—I have only time, in passing this place, to acknowledge your two letters of June, which I found here. With reference to the transfer of the Upper Church to the Presbyterians, and the other arrangements connected with the minister expected out this season, I must defer giving any opinion on the subject; it being one of so much importance, that I must communicate thereon with the Governor and Committee.—Believe me, my dear sir, Yours very faithfully,

(Signed)   George Simpson.

Alexander Ross, Esq., Red River Settlement.

Seeing that Sir George's arrangement would throw the matter back for at least one year more, the writer next opened a communication with Mr. Chief Factor Ballenden, the Company's chief officer at Fort Garry, through whose agency a full statement of all the points to be settled were laid before Sir George Simpson. His Excellency returned the following reply:—

Upper Fort Garry, 2nd July, 1850.

Dear Sir,— I have just received from Mr. Chief Factor Ballenden, three papers addressed to him by yourself and others, respectively purporting to be "Presbyterian Question," "Church Question," and "Claims respecting Church Lands." On a careful perusal of these documents, I find that you and your friends refer to various points, which not only require, but also appear to deserve, a more extensive and patient investigation than my very short stay will permit me to bring to a satisfactory conclusion.

In a few weeks at most, however, Mr. Governor Colvile will reach the colony. He, I feel confident, will be ready to adjust your claims in the premises on equitable and liberal principles, and meanwhile, you will have the goodness to hand to Mr. Ballenden the whole of your evidence in detail, for Mr. Colvile's consideration. Accept for your friends and yourself my assurances, that I shall rejoice in the amicable settlement of a question that has been so long agitated, and believe me to be, dear sir,

Yours truly,
(Signed)   GEORGE SIMPSON.

Alexander Ross, Esq., Red River Settlement.

During this time, Dr. Bonar took a lively interest in our cause; yet all great bodies move slowly, and much time was necessarily spent in discussion before any decision was arrived at. At length it was determined to transfer the matter to the Presbyterian Church of Canada. This gave a new impulse to the business, and rendered the correspondence more certain, by bringing it a step nearer to our door; besides which, Dr. Burns, at the head of the Church in Canada, entered into the matter, heart and hand. From this time, the cause of the Presbyterians in Red River became more and more known; and the more it became known, the more lively was the interest manifested in its favour. On this occasion, a correspondence of some length took place between the late Reverend Mr.

Rintoul of Montreal, and Sir George Simpson: the former was warmly devoted to our cause, and, at the eleventh hour, the latter gave it his best support; even the Committee at home now began to view the cause of the Presbyterians in a favourable light, and this was the main-spring of the whole machinery. Meantime, Mr. Eden Colvile had succeeded Sir George Simpson as Governor of Rupert's Land, and to him, as a matter of course, our appeal had now to be transferred. The subjoined letter will show how it was received:—

Lower Fort Garry, 30*th Oct*. 1850.

DEAR SIR,—I have to acknowledge the receipt of your letter of 28th ult., written in behalf of the Presbyterian community of Red River Settlement, and am much pleased with the moderate tone it bears, which seems to hold out a fair prospect of finally settling the question. I now beg to hand you, for the information of the said community, the following reply. The propositions I have to make are as under:—

1. That the present church should be valued by arbitration or otherwise, and a proportionate amount be paid to each seceder from the congregation.

2. That the right to burial in the existing churchyard be reserved. With these two propositions the Bishop of Rupert's Land has expressed to me his entire concurrence.

3. That a grant of the Frog Plain shall be made to the trustees of the Presbyterian community, to be held by them in trust for the congregation, for the purposes of sites for church, churchyard, school-house, and glebe. I should be willing to make this grant as soon as the church shall be erected, and a Presbyterian minister in occupation thereof.

4. That at the next meeting of the Council of the Northern Department, I shall recommend a grant of 150*l*. sterling towards the erection of the church, such sum, if voted, to be paid into the

hands of the trustees of the congregation, so soon as preparations are made for commencing the work.

You may consider this arrangement, as far as I am concerned, as definitely settled; but I deem it right to inform you, that I have no instructions on the subject from the Governor and Committee, and that it is possible, although I think not probable, that they may take a different view of the matter.—I remain, dear sir,

Very truly yours,
(Signed)   E. COLVILE.

Alexander Ross, Esq., Colony Gardens.

Here, then, were the "liberal and equitable" conditions offered to us as an equivalent for our church and school lots; and yet, had they been free of all doubt and uncertainty, rather than see the missionaries disturbed, we would have accepted them. The second proposition in the original stipulation made by us was thus worded :—" That the right of burial in the existing churchyard be secured to the members of the Presbyterian community in all time to come, according to the rules of the Presbyterian church of Scotland." Yet, abridged as it was, we did not object. The third and fourth propositions, however, were so vague, that the correspondence with reference to them was sent home for the consideration and decision of the Committee; and we heard nothing further on the subject till the writer was favoured with the following communication:—

Lower Fort Garry, 16th April, 1851.

MY DEAR SIR,—I beg once more to address you on the subject of the claims of the Presbyterian community, and with reference thereto, have to direct your attention to the annexed extract from a letter from Mr. Secretary Barclay to myself, under date, "Hudson's Bay House, London, 6th Dec., 1850," which I received per winter packet. "As the settlement of the vexed question of the Presbyterian claim, in the manner proposed—namely, a grant of the Frog Plain, with the sum of 150*l.*, in full of all claims and demand, and free of all conditions—meets the entire approbation of the Governor and Committee, they confirm it."

In conclusion, I beg to express a hope that you and your friends will do me the justice of believing that I am actuated with a sincere desire of settling this long vexed question, and that you and the other members of the Presbyterian community will meet me in a like spirit. Trusting that I shall have a favourable reply to this letter, I remain, my dear sir,

Very truly yours,

(Signed)   E. COLVILE.

Alexander Ross, Esq., Colony Gardens.

It is but justice to observe, that we have had every reason to allow Governor Colvile full credit for sincerity, which, indeed, was sufficiently proved by the ready kindness with which he endeavoured to adjust whatever differences prevented a settlement. The same spirit, as the above letter must demonstrate, now animated the Hudson's Bay Company; who, by one stroke of the pen, has set this "vexed question," as it has been called, at rest for ever. Soon after receiving the Company's decision, putting us in possession of the Frog Plain, a public meeting was convened, a committee of management appointed, and a manse erected for our minister. Within a week or two of the same date we also received the first certain tidings of our minister coming from Canada, as shown by the official letter subjoined:—

Toronto, C. W., 8th May, 1851.

DEAR SIR,—As serious difficulties have come in the way of an immediate mission to the Red River, I beg in name of our committee to state that we have every reason to rely on a missionary of approved character being prepared to go forward by the caravans from St. Anthony's Falls about the beginning of July; and in the confident hope of this, we have to request of you to make the arrangements to which you referred in your conversation with the Reverend Mr. Rintoul at Montreal.

In name of the members of our Presbytery and Synod, who have been consulted with on the present occasion, I feel myself authorized to give this pledge; and farther to return you our hearty thanks for the deep interest you have taken in this important matter, and to express our regret that it has not been in our power to take advantage of the kind offer you made, to carry up with yourself an approved labourer for this interesting field.—I have the honour to be, dear sir,

Faithfully yours,
ROBERT BURNS, D.D.,
Chairman of the Committee on
Mission to Red River.

J. *Ballenden, Esq.*

A party sent to the falls of St. Anthony at the period fixed upon, returned on the first of August without meeting the promised minister. On the 19th of September, however, our long-cherished hopes were at length realized by the arrival of the Reverend Mr. John Black from Montreal, the first Presbyterian minister to this neglected colony, and for whose conveyance across the long and dreary plain, we are under many and deep obligations to Governor Ramsey of Minnesota. As the manse, which it was intended should for the present serve as a place of worship, was not quite ready for Mr. Black's reception, application was made to the

Bishop of Rupert's Land, the present occupier of our property, for leave to preach an afternoon's sermon in the church built on our lands. Although his Lordship's church had enjoyed the free use of our lands for more than thirty years, this request was denied us. It made little difference. Mr. Black's arrival was the signal for every flock to follow its own shepherd, and no less than 300 Presbyterians left the English church in one day.

We have said that the " vexed question" was settled, and set at rest for ever; but this was not exactly the case, as the Bishop, after some little time, started a new difficulty, by refusing to acknowledge the second proposition. This after-thought of his Lordship's was in direct opposition to our arrangement with Governor Colvile, notwithstanding his Lordship, as we learn from a glance at the proposition itself, had expressed his " entire concurrence" in it. In short, this part of the settlement was the basis of the whole arrangement; for we had really acted from beginning to end on the faith of the " churchyard" being secured to us by the compromise. The result, as might be expected, involved the head of the Government and the head of the Church in a sharp and vexatious controversy; which, after both had exhausted their reasoning powers to no purpose, had, like the third and fourth propositions, to be sent to England for final decision. Nothing further was heard on the subject till the 12th of June, 1852, when we received the Committee's final decree in our favour, that neither church nor churchyard should be consecrated, but left open to all.

Our history of the Presbyterian question may now draw to a close. A stone church, erected for the Scotch congregation on Frog Plain, was finished in 1853; and, though small, it is considered the neatest and most complete church in the colony. It is seated for 510 persons, and is always well filled. Its cost was 1,050*l.* sterling. The manse is also completed; and it is pleasing to add that, when finished, there was not a shilling due on either church or manse. Our indefatigable and gifted minister, the Rev. Mr. Black, in addition to his usual clerical duties at both stations, has had to teach a French and Latin class ever since Bishop Anderson prohibited Presbyterian pupils from attending his schools. Mr. Black's stipend is 150*l.* a year; of which 100*l.* is paid by the congregation, and 50*l.* by the Hudson's Bay Company. The day-school at Frog Plain numbers about 80 scholars, and the Sunday-school, for a year preceding the date at which we are writing, has averaged 110. They are both increasing.

It is to be hoped the noble example thus set by the smallest community in the colony will not be without its effect, and that other congregations will have the ambition to become self-sustaining congregations, build their own churches, and pay their own clergymen, which they are all well able to do. Thus may be obliterated the disgrace of having for the last thirty years been supported by charity, at the expense of the Church Missionary and other Societies; and the means thrown away upon congregations comfortable in their circumstances, be extended to the conversion of the poor and degraded Indians, who are living and dying without the means of instruction. The people of Red River possess singular advantages and incitements to self-support. Their salt, their soap, their sugar, their leather, is supplied by the colony. Their lands, if not free, are almost so; for they have no land-tax, no landlord, no rent-days, nor dues of any kind, either to Church or State. Every shilling they earn is their own. With the exception of iron, all their essentials are within their grasp every day in the year, and as for luxuries, they are easily procured by labour at their very door. No farmers in the world, on a small scale, no settlement or colony of agriculturists, can be pronounced so happy, independent, and comfortable as those in Red River. Their tea, their coffee, beef, pork, and mutton, and their wheaten loaf, may be seen on the table all the year round. These things being incontestably true, is it either just or necessary that men in such circumstances—importers, merchants, freighters, artizans, and the husbandman, enjoying plenty—should be upheld by the hand of charity?

CHAPTER XXIII.

CONTENTS.—The decades—Epidemic of 1846—State of public feeling—Deaths—The 6th Royals—The effect—The pensioners—The Company's policy—A military Governor—Government inquiry and result—Character of Major Caldwell—Isbister's controversy—Earl of Elgin's views—Real grievance of the half-breeds—The fur-trade question—Mob meeting—Celebrated trial of Sayer—The Court in jeopardy—Reasons and opinions—Hints for consideration—Judge Thom and the laws—Sacredness of the oath.

RETURNING back the few years that we anticipated, in order to complete the history of the Free Church, we have now arrived at a period which reminds us that our calamities are numbered in decades. We have already described, as they occurred, the massacre of 1816, the flood of 1826, and the failure of the crop and loss of supplies in 1836; our fourth decade, now to be treated of, is the epidemic of this year, 1846. During this pest, for we can give it no milder name, the colony was overwhelmed with terror. The winter had been uncommonly mild. In January the influenza raged, and in May the measles broke out; but neither of these visitations proved very fatal. At length, in June, the bloody flux began its ravages among the Indians of the White Horse plains, and soon spread with fearful rapidity and fatal effect among the whites. In " Rama was there a voice heard, lamentation, and weeping, and great mourning." In Red River that voice was heard this year: like the great cry in Egypt, " for there was not a house where there was not one dead!"

In no country, either of Europe or America, in modern times—not under the severest visitation of cholera—has there been so great a mortality as in Red River on the present occasion. Not a smiling face in a summer's day. Hardly anything to be seen but the dead on their way to their last home; nothing to be heard but the tolling of bells, and nothing talked of but the sick, the dying, and the dead. In other more populous places such things might be more common and less horrifying, but in a country hitherto so healthy, and a population so scant, it was a new and awful sight. From the 18th of June to the 2nd of August, the deaths averaged seven a day, or 321 in all; being one out of every sixteen of our population. Of these one-sixth were Indians, two-thirds half-breeds, and the remainder whites. On one occasion thirteen burials were proceeding at once. Many houses were closed altogether; not one of the family, old or young, being left in them.

In September this year, before the settlement had recovered from this sad affliction, the boon of royal protection was granted us from England, as if to solace and cheer us up in the day of our troubles. This was the arrival of several companies of the 6th Royal

Regiment of Foot, for the protection and defence of the colony, amounting to 500 strong, including artillery and sappers, under the command of Lieut.-Colonel Crofton, who was appointed Governor of the colony. For this addition to our population, our thanks were due, perhaps, to the unmeaning fuss and gasconade of the Americans about the Oregon question; for we are not aware of any inducement but the protection of the frontiers that could have moved our Government to send out troops to this isolated quarter. Whatever their real object, the soldiers proved of great benefit to us. From the moment they arrived, the high tone of lawless defiance and internal disaffection raised by our own people against the laws and the authorities of the place, were reduced to silence. All those disaffected to the existing order of things, and to the principles of subordination, immediately sneaked across the boundary line to the land of freedom, and became *pro tempore* subjects of the United States. We have heard say that a bad Catholic seldom makes a good Protestant; and if we may paraphrase this bit of proverbial wisdom, we think it unlikely that a bad subject north of the line will become a good subject south. However, to let that pass, the good we enjoyed from the presence of the military was but of short duration, for in 1848 they were recalled, and their recall was the signal for the recommencement of our troubles.

The officers of the 6th were, to a man, highly respectable and exemplary in their conduct. They improved our society, gave a new impulse to everything in Red River, and threw a market open for our produce.

During their short stay, the circulation of money was increased by no less a sum than 15,000*l.* sterling; no wonder then that they left the colony deeply regretted. We may here remark, that an available force, say of one hundred men, backed by the local police, would amply suffice to maintain peace and order in Red River for many years yet to come. Indeed, the general opinion here is, that if the people had confidence in the authorities, we should require no military at all; but this can never be the case so long as the courts and council are the haunts of favourites and sinecurists, to the exclusion of others, in whose administration of the laws, and conduct of public business, the public could have full confidence. At present, either a protective force, or a thorough change in the administration of justice, are imperiously demanded; and the Hudson's Bay Company would be well advised to look to it.

On the departure of the 6th, in the same autumn, arrived a motley squad of some seventy pensioners, and the year following as many more, to take the place of the Royals. The troops were commanded by a Major Caldwell, who was also dignified with the title of Governor of Red River. If the people on the arrival of the 6th were ready to chant a *Te Deum,* they were no less ready, on seeing the conduct of the pensioners, to "hang their harps on the willows" and sing a *Requiem.* The soldiers and their Governor, indeed, were well matched, and about equally fitted for the duties they had to perform—performed, by the way, at an annual expense of some 3,000*l.* sterling. In the pensioners we recognised a second edition of the de Meurons; and the good old Major was so destitute of business habits, and of the art to govern, that after a few sittings the council and magistrates refused to act with him; he was therefore, superseded, merely that the wheels of Government might keep moving. As for the pensioners, all the authorities, civil and military, in the colony, could not keep them within the bounds of order. The half-breeds were meekness and loyalty itself, in comparison with them. Governor Colvile, in his charge to the jury on one occasion, observed, " We have more trouble with the pensioners than all the rest of the settlement put together."

We must not omit, however, that Major Caldwell was appointed by the Queen's Government in terms which should have left him in no doubt about his duties. The following is a despatch from B. Hawes, Esq., addressed to this gentleman when appointed Governor of Assiniboine:—

Downing Street, 10*th July*, 1848.

SIR,—I am directed by Earl Grey to acquaint you, that so soon as circumstances will admit, after your arrival at Assiniboine, Her Majesty's Government will expect to receive from you a full and complete account of the condition of affairs at the Red River Settlement, and particularly of the mixed and Indian population living there: charges of maladministration and harsh conduct towards the natives having been preferred against the Hudson's Bay Company, which it is of the utmost importance should be either established or disproved. Her Majesty's Government expect from you, as an officer holding the Queen's commission, a candid and detailed report of the state in which you find the settlement you have been selected to preside over.

I would particularly direct your attention to the allegations which have been made, of an insufficient and partial administration of justice; of the embarrassments occasioned by the want of a circulating medium, except promissory notes payable in London; the insufficient supply of goods for ordinary consumption by the Company; and the hardships said to follow from an interference which is reported to be exercised in preventing half-breed inhabitants from dealing in furs with each other, on the ground that the privileges of the native Indians of the country do not extend to them. These, however, are only mentioned as instances, and your own judgment is relied on for inquiry into other points.

I have, &c.,

(Signed)   B. HAWES.

Now let us see what steps Major Caldwell, as Governor of Assiniboine and armed with the Queen's commission, took to inform the Government at home of the condition of affairs in this quarter. Five months after his arrival in the colony, he sent round to a few select individuals, all of whom, in general terms, were favourable to the Company, a few simple, not to say childish queries, which they were desired to answer categorically; there were two questions for the Indians, and two for the whites; and the writer can speak positively to the fact, that no statement which deviated in any degree from the tenor of a simple answer to these queries was admitted, although in strict accordance with Her Majesty's commission. Moreover, if any person below what the major considered a gentleman—especially if unfavourable to the Company—presumed to mention a grievance to him, it mattered not of what sort, his reply was ready; " Sir, I ask you no questions." Such was the Major's mode of conducting the " full and complete" investigation required by Her Majesty's Government!

Turning to the reality of things, however, all happened well; because the allegations of "harsh conduct and maladministration" preferred against the Hudson's Bay Company by Mr. Isbister and his party, were in general totally unfounded and "disproved," and therefore, neither Major Caldwell's inquiries, or the inspiration of his genius, were required. So far, good; but the case might have been otherwise; and if it had, what information could the Government have got, or what redress could the people have expected, from a man of Major Caldwell's judgment and capacity? Yet in all fairness, although the Major had never studied the art of governing a people, we are willing to give him full credit for his good intentions; believing, as we do, that there was no intention on his part wilfully to betray the confidence reposed in him by the Government: on the contrary, the questionable course he pursued may be attributed to an error in judgment; for, in other respects, the Major is an exemplary and pious man.

With reference therefore to the complaints set forth by Mr. Isbister as the organ of a disaffected party, it is scarcely possible to entertain a clearer and correcter view of the subject than is expressed by the Governor-General of Canada in his despatch to Earl Grey, stated in Mr. Isbister's correspondence (page 9.) As his Lordship's opinion fairly and clearly embodies all the facts of the case, we shall here take the liberty of transcribing the passage. "It is, indeed," says the Earl of Elgin, "possible that the progress of Indians towards civilization, may not correspond with the expectations of some of those who are interested in their welfare. But disappointments of this nature are experienced, I fear, in other quarters, as well as in the territories of the Hudson's Bay Company; and persons to whom the trading privileges of the Company are obnoxious, may be tempted to ascribe to their rule the existence of evils which it is altogether beyond their power to remedy. There is too much reason to fear, that if the trade were thrown open, and the Indians left to the mercy of the adventurers who might chance to engage in it, their condition would be greatly deteriorated."

This, then, is precisely the state of things in Red River, in Rupert's Land: throw the trade open to all, and not only would the Indians be ruined, but the country also: the introduction of free trade would be the introduction of opposition, strife, and bloodshed. We have seen enough of this in by-gone days; and with a revival of such scenes, neither coloured nor white men of character could live in the country.*

While thus disposing of the popular claims, we must not forget that the half-breeds have grievances of which they may have cause to complain. We shall, in fact, devote some pages to illustrate this point; especially the Company's prohibition against bartering, buying, or

* We cannot dismiss this part of our subject without acknowledging our feeble tribute of praise, due to Mr. Isbister for the able and zealous efforts he has made in behalf of the natives of this quarter; at the same time that we regret he should have been betrayed into so great a sacrifice of time and talent, by the unfounded representations of his countrymen. They are justly rewarded for their folly by vexation and disappointments, while he, by his praiseworthy efforts in the cause of humanity, has gained for himself a name that will live in days yet to come.

trafficking in furs with the pure Indian, both being natives of the soil. We know something of the fur trade, and must confess we cannot see the policy of this interdict, or how the prohibited traffic can be supposed to operate against the Company; on the contrary, we think it would prove rather favourable to them. On the other hand, it may easily be seen, that such a prohibition is a grievous restraint on the half-breed. Living, as he does, constantly among the Indians, and furs being the only circulating medium they have, their use in traffic and exchange must necessarily be beneficial to both.

To illustrate this by an example on either side. First, it is a well-established fact, that the Company's rate for furs is fixed and regulated every year; they have but one price. Suppose, then, that an Indian and a half-breed agree to hunt together; when the hunt is over, the Indian is naked, ill-provided, and unable to go to the fort with his furs; in that case, he offers them for sale to his associate, and if he cannot buy them, he must cut the skins up on the spot to clothe himself and family. But the half-breed buys them, carries them to the fort, and sells them to the Company, who are clearly so much gainers by the transaction; for if the half-breed had not bought the furs, they might have been cut up and destroyed. What difference, we might ask, could it make to the Company, whether the half-breed, or the Indian, or a Turk brought the furs, providing they got them, and got them at the fixed price? The Indian could not be imposed upon, for he knew the Company's price as well as the half-breed, nor was the half-breed likely to give more for them than he was sure to get from the Company. The transaction is therefore a fair and equitable one; and this is all the half-breed knows or cares about the question of the fur trade: give him this privilege, and he is satisfied.

The other side of the question may be illustrated thus:—A half-breed, in his rambles through the wilderness, stumbles on an Indian in great distress, either for want of food, or the inclemency of the weather; he applies to the half-breed for relief, offers him some furs, the only thing he possesses. The half-breed cannot afford to give for nothing what he has got; and if he accepts of what the Indian offers him, he breaks the law, although by the act he saves the Indian's life! Or we might look at it in this light: suppose the half-breed falls in with a sick or frost-bitten Indian, far from his camp (which is not an uncommon case), he offers the half-breed some furs, to convey him to his family, or he dies. The half-breed, as already stated, cannot well abandon his own business to attend upon the Indian for nothing; and if he takes any furs, he is prosecuted for an infringement of the Company's regulations! We might multiply instances without number, all tending to establish the fact, that the existing law not only places the half-breeds in an awkward position, but operates strongly against humanity, in so far as the Indian is concerned. Any benefit the Company can derive from this law is purely imaginary, and yet, to support it, we had well nigh completed the circle of folly by upsetting Red River Colony, as shall presently appear.

In the spring of 1849, William Sayer, a French half-breed, who had been implicated and imprisoned, but afterwards liberated on bail, and McGillis, Laronde, and Goullé, three others of the same class, held to bail, but not imprisoned, were to stand their trial at the first criminal court, for illicitly trafficking in furs with the natives. This was the charge against them, namely, their accepting of furs from the Indians in exchange for goods, which was construed to be contrary to the rules and regulations of the Company's charter, wherein it is stated, "That the Hudson's Bay Company shall have the sole and exclusive trade and commerce of all the territories within Rupert's Land."

Notwithstanding the hue and cry that had been raised against the Company's misrule of late years, no half-breed or other, we may here observe, had been deprived of his liberty, or molested for meddling in the fur trade, with the exception, as already stated, of one solitary instance, during the whole quarter of a century in which the Company's officer presided over the affairs of the colony. It was reserved for Major Caldwell, a Government man, to exhibit this new feature of severity. Had his Excellency, however, issued an official notice, giving the people timely warning beforehand that they were to be so dealt with, the Major, as well as Recorder Thom, might have escaped that odium cast upon them in the present instance, nor would they have been taught this severe lesson of humility, nor the public peace have been disturbed as it was.

The 17th of May was the day appointed for the

Criminal Court to sit and decide this celebrated case, "Hudson's Bay Company *versus* Sayer." For some days previous it was rumoured about, that a hostile party would be prepared to watch the motions of the authorities during the trial. About 9 o'clock in the morning of that day, the French Canadians, as well as half-breeds, began to move from all quarters, so that the banks of the river, above and below the fort, were literally crowded with armed men, moving to and fro in wild agitation, having all the marks of a seditious meeting, or rather a revolutionary movement. As the hostile demonstration proceeded, boats and canoes were laid hold of wherever found, for the purpose of conveying over the crowd, who no sooner reached the west bank of the river, than they drew together about Fort Garry and the court-house. This movement took place about half-past 10 o'clock; and the whole affair was watched by the writer from his own door, At this moment a deputation of the ringleaders called on me (for I must here speak in the first person, as I am sometimes compelled to do) to announce the fact, that they intended resisting the proceedings of the court. "My friends," observed I to them, "you are acting under false impressions. Beware of disturbing the peace! The 6th are gone, but the 7th may come," alluding to the military; "and those who may now sow the wind, may live to reap the whirlwind for their pains." With this deputation, however, I walked up to the fort, as the hour of the court approached. The object of the mob was to resist the infliction of any punishment, whether of fine or imprisonment, on the offenders; and their anger was provoked by a report that the Major was to have his pensioners under arms on the day of the trial to repel force by force. The pensioners themselves had imprudently boasted what they could do, and what they would do, if the half-breeds dared to show themselves.

At 11 o'clock, the authorities, not intimidated by the storm which threatened them, entered the court, and proceeded to business; but what business could be done under the menace of an armed rabble? At this time 377 guns were counted; besides, here and there, groups armed with other missiles of every description. Imminent as the danger appeared to us—for an accidental shot, or a fist raised in anger, might have set these inflammable elements in a blaze—many incidents occurred to cause a reluctant smile. Some running one way, some another; one party taking up a position here, another there; whilst many present knew not for what they had come, kept running amongst the crowd, yelling and whooping like savages, calling out, "What is it, what is it? Who are you going to shoot? who are you going to shoot?" This was the aspect of things when the court was opened, and the Major, Judge Thom, and magistrates, took their seats on the bench; on this occasion, however, the Major dispensed with his usual guard of honour, and walked to the court-house like another private gentleman.

As soon as the court was opened, Sayer, the first on the court calendar, was summoned to appear; but he, with the other offenders, was held in close custody by an armed force of their countrymen out-doors, and we were not so imprudent as to direct the application of force, or even to insist on his bail bringing him forward. Other business of minor importance was taken up to pass away the time, which occupied the court till 1 o'clock, when Sayer was again called for, but in vain: at the same time, a Mr. Mc Laughlan, an Irishman, who was not a settler, being on a visit to a relative, and who considered he possessed some influence over the halfbreeds, attempted to interfere, but was suddenly repulsed; and, in fine, peremptorily ordered off. The court then held a consultation, and sent word to the half-breeds, that they might appoint a leader, and send in a deputation to assist Sayer during his trial, and state in open court what they had to urge in his defence. This suggestion was ultimately adopted. A gentleman named Sinclair, well known among the half-breeds, and eleven others of his class, took up a position in the court-room, with Sayer under their protection.

At the moment Sayer entered, about twenty of the half-breeds, all armed, took up their station at the court-house door, as sentinels, and held in their possession the arms of the deputation. At the outer gate of the court-yard, about fifty others were placed as a guard, and couriers kept in constant motion going the rounds, and conveying intelligence of the proceedings in court to the main party outside, so that at a moment's warning, had anything gone wrong, a rush was to have been made to rescue Sayer and the deputation from the fangs of the law. While all this manœuvring occupied their attention out-doors, the proceedings within the court were not less interesting; nine out of the twelve jurymen were challenged by Mr. Sinclair, but it was a needless interruption to the trial. Sayer confessed the fact that he did trade furs from an Indian. A verdict of guilty was recorded against him, upon which Sayer proved that a gentleman named Harriott, connected with the fur trade, had given him permission to traffic, and on this pretext he was discharged. The cases of Goullé, McGillis, and Laronde, were not proceeded with, and they all left the court together, greeted with loud huzzas.

As the offenders troubled themselves very little with the subtleties of the law, it was their own belief, and that of their people, that they were honourably acquitted, and that trading in furs was no longer a crime. Not a word was said whether the half-breeds were, or were not to trade furs in future, and so obscure were their perceptions of the real value of the decision, that one of the jurymen, on reaching the court door, gave three hearty cheers, and in a stentorian voice bawled out, " Le commerce est libre ! Le commerce est libre ! Vive la liberté !" a *crié de joie* which was soon repeated by another. These men, we ought to observe, were Canadians, but the half-breeds soon followed their example; and in the midst of yelling, whooping, and firing, kept shouting over and over again, " Le commerce est libre ! Le commerce est libre !" all the way from the court-house to the water's edge, and that in the midst of the court officials, Governor, Judge, and Magistrates. As soon as they were boated across, they gave three cheers, followed by three volleys in testimony of their victory, and from that day, these deluded people have been incited and worked upon by disaffected demagogues to entertain the idea that the trade is free. When this is really the case, we much fear, with such elements of disaffection, it will be the signal for every honest and peace-loving man to leave Red River; and the more so, as the Americans are on the eve of planting their starry banner at our door.

The trial we have just described suggests for our consideration several leading questions of importance; and first—Why this perpetual hostility against the authorities on the part of the French inhabitants?

In answering this query, we must repeat what we have already stated more than once, namely, that the French Canadians and half-breeds form the majority of the population; and, to a man, speak nothing but a jargon of French and Indian. In all fairness they ought to have been represented in the Legislative Council, and have had the laws expounded to them in their own language in the courts of justice. The facts, however, are as follows:—

1. There are twelve legislative councillors, exclusive of the Governor, who is president; of these, nine are Protestants, and three Catholics; that is, three to one in favour of the former.

2. Mixed juries have never had the benefit of a competent French interpreter, nor have the laws bearing on the cases been otherwise explained to them.

3. The laws have always been administered in the English language, as indeed ought to be the case in an English colony; but they have never been professionally interpreted in the French language, which is a real grievance.

4. The laws have all been framed for the benefit of the commercial and agricultural classes; but not one for the half-breeds or hunters.

5. Their being legally disqualified by Mr. Thom's interpretation of the charter, from trafficking in furs with the Indians, is the greatest of all their grievances; as furs are the only circulating medium the country affords, beyond the limits of the colony.

Secondly. We may here inquire for what reason Judge Thom became so obnoxious to all our subjects of French extraction? To answer this candidly, we believe that Judge Thom's unpopularity has grown up, not from any dereliction of duty, or defect in his official character as judge, but simply because he was the professional organ of the court. As the interpreter of the laws, and the Company's legal adviser, he was looked upon by an uninstructed people as the cause of all their grievances; and this unfavourable opinion was grounded on the impression they had formed of him on his first arrival in the settlement, which was stated in a previous chapter. In short, any other judge without a knowledge of the French language must prove as objectionable here as Mr. Thom has been. To remedy these evils, either reduce the councillors to an equal number on both sides, or grant the people of Red River a constitution similar to that of Vancouver's Island. Take care also that the judge of the colony be equally independent in his official capacity of the populace and the Company. Above all, a knowledge of the French tongue is indispensable.

Thirdly. Did the court pursue the wisest policy in

proceeding to business in Sayer's case? We think not. So long as the court authorities were menaced by the hostile rabble, their wisest proceeding had been to shut up the court and retire without proceeding to business at all.

Fourthly. It may be worth inquiring, Of what use are the pensioners, as a protective force, in Red River? As they are, squatted down as settlers, and scattered about, they neither are, nor ever will be, of any manner of use. Any efficient force, either here or elsewhere, must be under strict military discipline. With these suggestive remarks before us, relative to Sayer's case and Judge Thom, we may be permitted to pass a comment on the laws generally.

Under the letters patent of Charles the Second, the Governor and Council of Rupert's Land, in addition, of course, to executive functions and legislative authority, exercise also judicial power. But as the union of these incompatible duties must have been sanctioned through necessity rather than enjoined from choice by the framers of the charter, other tribunals have long been established in the respective districts of the settlement, with the view of more speedily and conveniently adjusting civil causes of inferior importance.

According to the terms of the same document, the laws of England are to be the rule of decision. But in the absence of professional aid, every tribunal becomes, in a greater or less degree, a court of conscience or equity; and the more numerous the bench (particularly if the equal units have been educated in different countries, and under different systems) the more extensively must this be the case. In such a state of things, there remains no room for a jury; and as those who are thus arbiters both of law and of fact cannot be forced to unanimity, the results are little likely to give satisfaction. At the same time, it must not be omitted that the decisions have been satisfactory where the grounds upon which they were formed have been clearly expressed. To these inherent evils must be added the difficulties incident to the primitive condition of our little community: that everybody knows everybody; that people of all classes are closely connected by blood or marriage; and that any story, good or evil, with all its additions and deductions, reaches every ear.

It was for these and other like reasons, therefore, that the Hudson's Bay Company introduced into the settlement in 1839, as already noticed, Mr. Thom as Recorder of Rupert's Land, who, as senior member of the Governor's Council, was virtually to preside in the general court. In order to secure the great object in view, namely, the separate consideration of law and fact, a municipal regulation was immediately passed to the effect that every criminal issue, and every such civil issue as could come before the general court, should be tried by a jury.

The reader must not suppose, however, that we were now enabled to reduce into actual practice the laws of England. For instance, in civil cases, thanks to the " plentiful lack" of practising attorneys, we have no written pleadings, while execution may be stayed by the Company's notes, which, though practically better than Her Majesty's stamped gold, yet neither are, nor can be declared to be, a legal tender. In criminal cases, again, with the exception of a few floggings, and the terror of one execution already mentioned, we have no resource but imprisonment,—no tread-mills, no hulks, no pillory, no penitentiary, no white sheets, no Botany Bay. Fortunately, our only available punishment is generally speaking quite sufficient. The mere confinement is far more severely felt in a state of nature than in civilized life, and as the daily ration of a pound of pemmican, and water at discretion, is adhered to in all cases, it is rendered more irksome. We are neither rich enough nor philanthropic enough to feed our gaol-birds with dainty fare, and the mere support of life must afford to a denison of the wilderness but poor compensation for such misfortunes as loss of liberty, privation of gossip, and prohibition of beer and tobacco.

Nor are our juries more punctiliously modeled after the pattern of the old country than our laws. Without regard to any rules of selection, we desire nothing more than the presence of twelve householders, as little interested as possible in the victory or defeat of either of the parties. So powerful is the obligation of an oath over the unhackneyed consciences of the mass of the population—for, on all administrative points, we are contented with an unsworn declaration—that wilful perverseness, in a jury of Red River, is hardly to be imagined for a moment. On the trial of Sayer, notwithstanding the alarm excited by the popular feeling against the Company and the court, the jury unhesitatingly returned a verdict in conformity with the laws. A still more remarkable fact may be mentioned, as showing that scrupulous regard of our common people for an oath which forms the grand justification of our apparently loose mode of selecting jurymen. In addition to the proof of the defendant's own voluntary confession—a confession not sufficiently circumstantial to have convicted him by itself—the only evidence was that of the defendant's son, who, under the stern injunction of one parent, told the whole truth, without any attempt at delay or equivocation, against the other.

In what court of England or Scotland could the moral beauty of this scene have been surpassed? However, to give an instance of more decisive character and wider application. Our local enactments against the selling of beer to Indians, besides imposing a public fine on the seller, condemn him to make restitution for every article of barter thus received, at first price. Under all the temptations of these enactments, the original buyer of the article is admitted as a witness; this being the only means of preventing an entire failure of justice. Perjury, in such cases, the writer has never known, and if the Indian has hesitated, the reluctance obviously arose from the feeling, that speak the truth he must, if he speak at all. What an example does our untutored savage thus show to those who call themselves civilized, in most parts of the world!

The intelligent reader can hardly require to be told, that the position of our Recorder was, from the beginning, rather an invidious one. As the only professional man in a country where printing was unknown, he was exempted from nearly all the checks which might be expected elsewhere to influence a lawyer on the bench. So far as any knowledge of law at all existed in the settlement, it was derived from the systems of Scotland or of Canada, which differed essentially from our chartered rule of right; and even if some few of us could be said to have made a study of the system we were bound to administer, it proved of little advantage to us when the Recorder announced his principle, (doubtless a correct one) that our "Laws of England" were not those of the present day, but those of the date of the Letters Patent, namely, the "Laws of England" of the 2nd May, 1670. Nor was our legal associate much less independent of control with regard to our local enactments, whether such enactments professed to provide for the indigenous peculiarities of this secluded colony, or to modify and modernize our imported code. It was the Recorder that penned them; it was the Recorder that argued them through the council in a masterly manner; it was the Recorder that interpreted them, so as to make their inevitable generalities fit particular cases. In these respects, he may be said to have always had his own way—less would not satisfy him; and this often raised up difficulties between himself and his colleagues. People said he possessed the gift of twisting and untwisting his interpretations, so as always to fit his own cause.

Accordingly, with his command of language, and his fertility in argument, Mr. Thom was supposed by the many to be able to mould the law to his own wish. To meet a difficulty, which he appeared to foresee from the very beginning of his residence among us, he resolved, (at the hazard, as he seemed to be aware, of being tiresome) to expound the law of each case so fully as to forestal himself, as he expressed it, against any other exposition of the same on his part. He strove, in short, to make the public a present of the *argumentum ad hominem* against himself. But the more diligently he showed that he could split hairs, the more readily did the many believe that he would split them, whether they needed splitting or not. On another point, also, Mr. Thom has been less circumspect and less successful than most of his colleagues in uniting public sentiment in his favour. He has had far less to do with the people, generally speaking, than any of the other officials; nor has he ever wished to interfere with our more purely ministerial duties; and yet it was generally thought he had too much in his power. It was in vain he guarded—by publicly stating the extent of his intervention, in open court—when circumstances had connected him, perhaps, with the preliminaries of any measure. So it was on the bench. As might have been expected, his charge was almost uniformly echoed by the verdict: and yet this uniformity of success, which would elsewhere be reckoned a proof of the truth and reasonableness of a judge's views, tended here to inspire the multitude with a notion, that Mr. Thom could turn black into white, and white into black.

Again, the Recorder's influence in our little legislature was sure to be regarded as disproportionably great. Any measure that he proposed was pretty sure to be carried—not that he ever attempted beforehand to make a party, for everyone opposed him in turn; but that, by dint of talking, he always brought over some majority or other to his side. Nor was Mr. Thom so careful as he ought to have been under such circumstances, to blend the *suaviter in modo* with the *fortiter in re,* though his demeanour, to do him justice, savoured rather of a confidence in his own views, than of any disregard of the feelings of others. Some of his measures, too, were by no means acceptable to a certain section of the people. We allude more particularly to those enactments which subjected our traffic with the United States to the differential duties of such Imperial statutes as regulated the foreign commerce of colonies. Although that law affected the settlers of French origin far more extensively than their English brethren, Mr. Thom introduced a measure to impose a duty of ten per cent. on all American articles, with some trifling exceptions; while the English importer paid only four! The measure, however, fell to the ground; but the odium it created lives to this day; though, in point of fact, the exemptions in favour of the actual adventurers were so large and liberal as to render the trade free as the wind to all but the wealthiest individuals that were engaged in the business. The import duty from England and the United States are now both the same; namely, four per cent.

In this state of public feeling, the single prosecution of an interloper in the fur trade caused, as we have already related, a considerable degree of popular excitement, on the part of the French settlers. From words they flew to arms, chiefly, as they alleged, in consequence of believing, whether right or wrong, that Major Caldwell had threatened to call out his pensioners against them. In this struggle, legality, in a certain degree, carried the day; but in such a way, that public opinion was left as dissatisfied on the point as before, and the law as vague as before. Hence, it has happened, through a dread of the renewal of such a conflict between reason and force, that we have, since then, been deprived of the advantages of Mr. Thom's ability, public spirit, and independence. Such a result, clearly traceable to this gentleman's perverse use of his talents, by constantly exercising them to support his own opinions in opposition to all others, is deeply to be regretted.

CHAPTER XXIV.

CONTENTS.—Climate and productions—Woodlands and pasturage—Rearing of cattle—Horses—Brick-makers and other artisans—Prices—Domestic servants—Barter and long credit—The truck system—Imports—Exports—How the money comes—Police—Magistrates—Minnesota and the half-breeds—Fortune's own child—Pembina and the Americans—St. Peter's again—Minnesota government—Vancouver's Island and the constitution of Red River—Danger of neglect—Appendix.

As our task is now drawing to a close, we shall throw together in this chapter such observations or facts as could not conveniently be inserted elsewhere. The physical characteristics of the country have been briefly described, and as to the natural productions, there is but little either to amuse or interest the general reader. Red River is more of a plain than a wooded country, bleak and almost shelterless. The burning sun of summer is oppressive; the winter no less severe in the opposite degree. The heat reaches 98° in the shade, and the cold descends 45° below zero. Summer and winter are of equal duration: no jealousy between the heat and cold, for each claims six months. Yet, though subject to these extremes, the climate is healthy, crops abundant, and everything in nature attains its full growth.

The only timber worth mentioning, either in Red River or the surrounding country, is the oak, pine, and white wood, used in the building of houses: oak for the frame, pine for the floors, and the white wood, in the States called bass wood, for the furniture. Poplar is generally used for fencing; and when peeled, keeps straight, is free of cracks, and lasts long. Clumps of this wood, like islands in the ocean, stud the plains; maple and elms adorn the banks of the rivers, stunted birch the higher ground, and swamp ash may be seen here and there sparsely scattered over the country. In the low ground, there is a sprinkling of cedar, which, although not large, makes excellent shingles; but being somewhat far off, the few who do indulge in the luxury of shingled houses, generally use the oak. As the great summer heats, however, warp the oak shingle, and make it curl up like spoons, the best roofs made of this material seldom last more than twelve or fifteen years. The generality of the people use straw thatch roofs, which are light, water tight, and durable.

Wild fruits grow to perfection; but the variety is small. Cherries, strawberries, gooseberries, bearberries, hawthorn-berries, poires or pearberry, and wild plums, are among the most abundant. These, and the like, form the Indian's food during summer.

The natural grasses abound everywhere, and are very nutritious; but again the variety is not great. Red and white clover have been tried repeatedly, but without success; and the failure is attributed to the long and severe winters. Grasses generally appear the first spring after sowing, and then,—we allude especially to the red,—disappear ever after. A question then arises, will red clover resist a winter of six months long, and a cold of 45° below zero? Timothy thrives well, although but little of it is used; as the natural grass is esteemed fully as good, and is produced without labour. Red River is peculiarly adapted for the rearing of flocks and herds; and although cows do not generally give so much milk as we have seen at home, and in Canada, or the United States, yet the milk is rich. A good cow well fed in the open plains, will yield her pound of butter daily. The writer himself having tried the experiment, obtained from one of his best cows $24\frac{1}{2}$ pounds in twenty-five days.

Nothing has yet been done here in the way of stall-feeding for fattening cattle for the slaughter. In this year, say 1850, an "Agricultural Association" has been formed by a number of intelligent individuals, one of whose objects is to encourage stall-feeding, and other branches in which the farmer is deeply interested; so far, however, cattle have roamed about at large in the open plains till late in the fall, and are then killed; and yet, many of them would be considered fat in any country. A cow seven years old, belonging to the writer, was killed some time ago, and yielded 105 pounds of clean rendered tallow. This, however, was above the average.

It is generally believed that the best mode of raising cattle, in order to have a fine stock, is to allow the calves to suck, and this appears but natural; yet the practice is condemned—so far, at least, as our own experience is of any value. To be sure they are sleek and very fine for the first year; but the calves that suck generally breed sooner than those that are hand-fed, and the sooner heifers calf, the more stinted will be their growth ever after: for they will lose more the second and third years by having their first calves when two years old than they would gain the first by sucking. It is the better plan to raise calves, not altogether on skim-milk, but half warm and half skim mixed together; and although they may be somewhat stinted at times in the quantity, no harm is done. It will no doubt retard their growth a shade the first year; but as this very circumstance secures a longer period before they have their first calf, the more likely they are to become large cows. This is found to be the case in Red River. Ragged and pinched boys often become stout and robust men.

For want of care, our cattle are deteriorating fast in size, although costly bulls, and of the finest breed, both from England and the United States, have been imported into the colony. The local government has taken no steps to restrain a multitude of dwarfy bulls from running at large in all seasons, to the great injury of the breed; and as one evil generally begets another, the large oxen keep at bay the small bulls, and not only destroy the cows, but injure themselves into the bargain. The best farmer and dealer in cattle in the colony, excepting one, has no more than forty-two head; yet pasturage costs nothing, and every man that is a farmer has four times the quantity of land he requires for every useful purpose. Formerly, our best oxen weighed 1,000 pounds; but the largest killed during the last five years only weighed 852 pounds; the general run of the best weighs 700 pounds. The best oxen in the colony can be purchased for 6*l.* sterling a head, and the finest cows for 4*l.* Pork is not raised to any extent, there being no demand for the article; the heaviest pig hitherto killed in the colony weighed 604 pounds. Sheep are declining fast in number from the ravages of the dogs and wolves; neither do they thrive well even under the best circumstances. During the last year, hogs have diminished one-third in number; and the sheep were fewer by 1,000 than in the year before.

Pork and mutton sell at $2\frac{1}{2}d.$ per pound; beef, 2*d.*; butter, 7*d.*; cheese, 5*d.*; and eggs, 6*d.* per dozen. Average weight of the best wheat, 66 lbs.; though instances have occurred as high as 70 lbs. per bushel. The price of wheat is 3*s.* 6*d.*, and barley, 2*s.* per bushel. Peas generally sell for the same price as wheat; oats, 1*s.* 6*d.*; and potatoes, although generally a sure crop, fluctuate more than any other article, being sometimes as high as 2*s.*, and at other times as low as 4*d.* per bushel.

No article of produce is exported, consequently no provisions are salted but what people require for their own use. Each farmer raises grain and cattle enough for his own establishment, and no more; but the generality of them, with the exception of the Scotch, fall more frequently below, than rise above this standard. As a proof of this, provisions of every description are generally 50 per cent. dearer in the spring than the fall of the year.

Horses, the only staple article in the colony, always meet with a ready market and good price. While buffalo-hunting continues, they must always be in request. For improving the breed, old Fire-away, noticed already, was invaluable. Indeed, the only good breed of horses we have ever had in the colony, were the cross breed of that noble animal. They were excellent draught horses, good for the saddle, and highly prized for docility and enduring fatigue. Full-grown animals of this class sell for 25*l.* sterling; country nags half the price. The value of first-rate buffalo-hunters is, of course, regulated by caprice. As to bottom, shape, and power, no horse, either before or after, has stood so high in public estimation as Fire-away. Another full-blooded stallion, however, came out from England, a year or two ago, at a cost of 300*l.*, superior in size and bone to his predecessor, but inferior in model and action. From the scarcity of money among the people, two guineas for the chance of a foal was regarded high; yet, all things considered, it was certainly moderate. In New South Wales, horses of their class cost four times the amount. We have had some fine horses from the States also, but they were inferior to those we had from England; nor did they stand the climate so well. The great expense attending the importation and keep of such animals is a strong proof of the Company's anxiety to improve the breed, and advance the colony.

Nearly all the horses here, with the exceptions we

have noticed, are obtained from the Indians of the plains: their appearance, generally speaking, is not prepossessing; but they are better than they look. They are hardy, easily kept up, and sure-footed. Few horses could be better adapted for the cart and the saddle, and none so good for the climate. To improve the breed, the colonial law imposes a fine of 20s. on all stallions rising two years and upwards found at large: had the same restraint been imposed on bulls, the settlement would have derived far greater benefit from it.

One of the most profitable speculations a man of means could turn his attention to in the colony, and that with the smallest risk of capital, would be the breeding of horses. In a country like this, where pasture is got without cost, a few parks enclosed is all that would be required in the way of keep, and that would be a mere trifle; and yet, notwithstanding the great and increasing demand for horses, no person as yet has turned his attention to it.

Brick-making has hitherto been entirely neglected here: a few attempts at different times have been made, sufficient only to test the quality of the clay, which in many places has been found good; but with the exception of a few brick chimneys, we have nothing as yet constructed of that useful article. The samples hitherto produced, though not of the best quality, cost 2l. per thousand; while in New South Wales, where labour in general is much higher than in Red River, they are purchased for 12s. a thousand. This difference arises from the want of competition, and the small demand; as all partial trials must be costly and imperfect. Sir George Simpson, some years ago, brought a professed brickmaker from Russia, but he had soon to leave for want of employment. Ere long, brick must necessarily be adopted as a substitute for wood.

The bulk of the agricultural labour is performed by the members of each family thus occupied, which is the only way to succeed; but when hire becomes absolutely necessary, the custom is to engage servants by the day, the month, or the year. Men generally get 20*l.* per annum, and women 10*s.* per month, nominal value, for they are seldom paid more than a part of their wages in money; the rest is given them in articles as they require, at the long credit rate (as they are generally taken up in advance), which exceeds the money price by a third. Job-work is not much in practice: the people are not up to such undertakings. A daily labourer, during hay and harvest season, gets 2*s.* 6*d.*, and in the dead season, 1*s.* 6*d.* per day; the employer always furnishing food, and a blanket to sleep in. Tradesmen are paid from 3*s.* to 5*s.* per day. There are, however, but few regular workmen among us. Under this head, we might name four blacksmiths, three house-carpenters, two millwrights, and one mason. The half-breed natives of the place, and their value as servants, need no farther observation, having been amply treated of before.

Formerly, the petty traders were looked upon as a public good; but the system has become highly detrimental to the colony in its late development. Scarcely a shilling is to be seen afloat; and if it meets the eye, it no sooner reaches a shop door—and almost every door is now a shop door—but it disappears, and is kept locked up to swell the amount devoted to a new importation. The servant may go without, or take truck: " Take goods, take goods," is the universal cry. Nor is it the agricultural servants alone that complain. Since the Company made a present of its patronage by transferring the freight business into the hands of the petty traders, the voyageurs and trip-men, in place of being paid in money as formerly, must now submit to the truck system, or go without employment. This state of things presses hard on the servant: his wants are many, the temptations are great. Where goods and good things are to be got on credit, he runs deeply in debt, and can never be his own master. Indeed, he cannot call the little property he possesses his own: it may be seized the next hour to pay his debts. The system chains him down to perpetual servitude and dependence. This evil is so widely spread that it is no longer a private but a public wrong, and demands a public remedy.

In order to show the excess to which the barter and petty trading system have been carried on, we may state, that in 1847, there were no less than 102 English importers in the colony, and nearly as many more from the United States, on a smaller scale, whose united invoices amounted to 11,000*l.* sterling, exclusive of the Company's outfit, amounting to as much more. Nay, we might select ten individuals out of the petty traders, whose united book debts at this time amount to 3,750*l.*, divided, of course, among hundreds of penniless subjects, who have but little to support their families with, and still less to pay their debts. With such work for the courts of justice, with such misery as these facts imply, will any one say, that the system has not become monstrous and intolerable?

Having stated the amount of our imports, is it necessary to remind the reader, that our exports are of incomparably small amount? the result of the struggle for an export trade having already been explained. Apart from the fur trade, there is no commerce carried on in the colony with the mother country, the United States, or any other place in the wide world; unless the few articles of garnished work and other trifles that make their way to St. Peter's can be dignified with the name of commerce. As to manufactures, the only articles produced in the colony, as already noticed, are a few coarse woollens for home use; and yet, in our present infant state, we enjoy a good share of the essentials, and many of the luxuries of life.

But, it may be asked, if we export nothing, where does this 11,000*l*. that we send to England and the States for our goods, our fineries, and our luxuries, come from? It has already been stated, that there is but 5,000*l*. in circulation in the colony, and also that there are but few men of means among us; our answer may be anticipated, therefore, that the money comes from the Company, who afford a market to the settlers, one way or other, to that amount. The Church of England throws about 2,000*l*. annually into the settlement, and the Red River Academy or Hudson's Bay Company's School, patronized by Sir George Simpson, and many gentlemen connected with the fur trade, nearly another 1,000*l*.; from these establishments, the colony derives considerable benefit, even in a pecuniary point of view. The Company's transactions, as regards its connection with the settlers, are carried out on the most equitable and liberal principles.

Our police force—for we cannot take the pensioners, as at present organized, into the account at all—are by far too few, and so managed that it is impossible they can answer any good purpose. They are paid too much for all that they really do, and by far too little to induce them to devote their time and energies to such duties as are required of policemen. The only effective force that has ever been embodied in the colony was the volunteer corps established in 1835, and which continued till 1845, a period of ten years. So peaceable and orderly was the settlement during that period, that a hue and cry was raised against keeping up and paying a force that had nothing to do; but their having nothing to do was the best sign of their efficiency. The council, however, in an evil hour, gave way, and they were disbanded, not without disturbing the peace of the colony. The subsequent arrival of the 6th Royals from England, and how they were succeeded by Major Caldwell's pensioners, has been recorded in its place.

The only class of public men who have laboured assiduously—we might say, successfully—and from whose local knowledge of men and things the colony has derived any absolute benefit, are the district magistrates. In short, all that has been done in the way of maintaining peace and good order is due to them; for they, in their magisterial capacity, have possessed the confidence of the people. Some of these, however, have been subject to much annoyance and loss of time; and fortune not having placed them in such independent circumstances as to be beyond the necessity of attending to other duties, they are dropping fast off the list to attend to their own affairs: a result, we regret to add, which has been accelerated by the reinstatement of Major Caldwell, in whose administrative abilities very few could feel any confidence. Other men, less influential, and still less fortunate in circumstances and in talent, are now filling the places of these old servants of the public, who retire with the proud consciousness that they have done their duty, and left behind them an example worthy of imitation.

The greatest hurt to the peace of the colony is occasioned by the frequent visits of our citizens to St. Peter's of late years. They fancy that the magic-like progress of the Minnesota territory, rising with mushroom rapidity at their door, compared to Red River, must be altogether owing to the constitution of its government; it never strikes them, that the Americans are at work while they are idling. Nevertheless, with all their hue and cry about the marvellous difference between the two places, when any of them go thither to reside, they can never eat, drink, or sleep comfortably, till they get back again to their Red River homes.

Having now travelled through all the tortuous windings of the task we had laid down for ourselves, and brought our sketch of Red River history almost to a close, we have a word or two more to say, not of the colony, but of an individual belonging to it: one whose fertile genius and manifold dexterity have enabled him to overstep all competition, and to take his stand at the head of our colonists as a man of enterprise and general usefulness. The gentleman we allude to is at once a merchant, a farmer, a horse jockey, and a dealer in cattle. In barter, traffic, and bargain-making, he stands unrivalled. He has tried everything, and everything he has tried fortune has turned to his advantage. Of him we may say, that he was never above stooping down and picking up a pin, observing as he put it in his sleeve, that great things were made up of small, as pence make shillings, and shillings pounds; and although he sometimes sold his commodities at exorbitantly high prices, and occasionally prided himself in over-reaching his neighbour, yet he was liberal and charitable withal—the poor man's friend, and the rich man's companion. Governors have consulted him, and many have benefited by his good offices. He is the man above all others who has raised himself by his own merit, until, from nothing, he has become the wealthiest person in the state.

Who, then, the reader will naturally ask, is this extraordinary man? Ireland is his country—the land of noble spirits and warm hearts. But with his lineage or pedigree, beyond the twelfth century, when Dermud the Bold carried off Queen Orork of Meath, we shall not trouble ourselves or our readers. The names of his ancestors have been handed down to us in a long list of Irish nobles, called Dermud, Diarmuid, Diarmot, Dermot, and lastly Mac Dermot.

Andrew McDermot was born in 1791, and came out to Hudson's Bay as a clerk in the fur-trade in 1812. Young, active, and ambitious, it was his pleasure, amongst other things, to learn the Indian language; and paradoxical as it may appear, he could speak it better than the savages themselves. In this necessary qualification for an Indian trader, he soon outstripped all his colleagues; he was, at the same time, an excellent walker, ran like a deer, and could endure cold with any Esquimaux dog. With these qualifications he became a good trader; and being esteemed by his associates, high and low, he was before long particularly noticed by the magnates of the fur trade. With Mr. Halkett, one of the committee, and Mr. Governor McKenzie, he was a great favourite; and more recently, he was regarded by Sir George Simpson as a man of superior abilities. Notwithstanding these advantages, he disliked the slow and tardy steps that led to preferment in the fur trade. His genius, like that of many of his countrymen, became impatient under restraint; he longed to become his own master, although the prospect before him on going free, was to ordinary minds dark and ominous. His release from the service forms the beginning of his career in Red River, where, we may say, he arrived almost friendless and penniless—a sum of 75*l.* being all he had to begin the world upon.

The whole of this little capital Mac did not hesitate to spend in an outfit of horses, carts, and servants, to try his fortune in the plains. Accompanying the hunters, he made his first essay in 1824. Kind, open, and obliging, and as full of wild adventure as themselves, he soon became a favourite among the Nimrods of the plains. Taking advantage of the field thus opening before him, he kept a keen and watchful eye to his own interest: never was known to "sell his hen on a rainy day." While the freemen were frolicking away their time in a losing business, he was doubling his money every trip; and, by a system of barter and traffic carried on in the plains, he next monopolized the chief part of their hunts, which threw the provision market into his own hands, and the money of course into his own pocket. Thus, the plain business suiting his genius and turn of mind, he followed it for a period of ten years, till his run of success and good fortune placed him at its head, and in the possession of ample means to extend his future operations.

Two years after he had commenced these plain speculations, the writer entered into co-partnership with him; but a joint-stock concern did not long suit Mac; he got as impatient in that as in the service. In all his arithmetical calculations, he never admired the rule of division. It was a common saying of his, "Where one man can do the work there is no need for two;" the field must be his own.

Having secured his interest among the hunters, he left the rude and savage life of the plains and settled in the colony. Here, being favoured by the ruling authorities, he became an extensive importer from England and the States. By his address and accommodating qualities, aided a little by no lack of Irish wit, he soon drew public attention to his business. He was everybody's man, and formed the centre of attraction; for he could lend a horse, change an ox, or barter a dog, as circumstances required. If a stranger, of whatever rank, chanced to visit the place, although he kept neither inn nor hotel, yet accommodations for both man and beast were always ready. A house to let, a room to hire, and every want supplied. If a contract was contemplated, or an enterprise proposed, or if money was wanted, who but Mc Dermot was the man to do the good turn? Such being his character and services, ten years had not elapsed before he overstepped all his competitors in the settlement, as he had done in the plains. Uniting the resources of the plains with his affairs in the settlement, he stands at the head of both, in point of popularity and enterprise. It is a common saying here, " that the bush he passes by must be bare and barren indeed, if he does not pluck a leaf off it." His discriminating knowledge of men is proverbial: nor is it confined to men alone; as a judge of horses, he stands unrivalled.

As Mc Dermot's means increased, his aspiring genius expanded. He became a general dealer, engrossed the freighting business, acted as the Company's right-hand man in all contracts and public undertakings, speculated in houses and lands, built mills, encouraged manufactures, and lately commenced forming a little colony, of which he himself is the head.

On the arrival of the 6th Royals, the officers and men complained that their pay was of no use to them in a country where they could get nothing to buy. " Go to Mc Dermot," said Colonel Crofton, "and then you will get everything you want." The soldiers did so, and soon found out that what they had been told was true; for their pay was no sooner in their hands than it was transferred to Mc Dermot's pocket. With the exception of second-handed coffins, there was nothing they could ask for but they got. In a few months he had received in gold 1,400*l.*; treble the amount gained by all the rest of the colony during the same period.

We have remarked in a previous chapter that on the failure of the export trade agitation, the half-breeds turned their thoughts towards the Americans and the American Government. That circumstance, at least, was the pretext at the time; but we shall here state what we believe to have been the real cause.

The Pembina squatters are chiefly half-breeds from Red River; many of them without house, home, or allegiance to any Government—wanderers at large, citizens of the wilderness. They have crossed the British line, as the gold-hunters of California cross the mountains, in search of gain. Ever since the road to St. Peter's has been opened, it has been rung in their ears what large sums of money the Americans pay for Indian lands; and that half-breeds, being the offspring of Indians, come in for a good share of the loaves and fishes on all such occasions. Their cupidity being thus excited, is the real cause of the half-breeds having settled down on the American side; their movements being accelerated of late by the report that the Pembina lands were to be purchased forthwith by the American Government, and that all British subjects were in future to be debarred from hunting south of the line. As to any definite grievance under the government of the Hudson's Bay Company, or their calling for American protection, it is all pure fiction; let the Americans but withhold from them the anticipated boon they have in view—that is, a share in the sale of the Pembina lands—and they will soon return again to their cherished haunts in the north. Even should they attain their end, if there is any truth in their creed, they will still return; for it is not in the nature of either Indians or half-breeds to change their country, even if for a better, still less for a worse. We have ample proof of this feeling in those who have gone to reside at St. Peter's; for scarcely one has remained who could get back. No earthly advantage will induce them to farm; they care nothing for lands, save for the chase.

This whim of the half-breeds, again, was turned by interested individuals to their own selfish purposes. A torrent of abuse was poured out against the Hudson's Bay Company, for "injustice and oppression," by a perfect stranger, and echoed far and wide by that scum along the frontiers who, like the cat in the fable, make the best of both neighbours, and pay them back with ingratitude. The latter is not much to be wondered at; but that a gentleman holding a commission under his Government, and possessing its confidence, should have made his report the vehicle of circulating false and unfounded statements is, at least, surprising, and certainly cannot tend to increase the good understanding which exists between the two countries: we allude to the report of Captain Pope, of the Topographical Engineers, published in the United States, in 1850.

The Captain states (page 28 of the report), " that the population of Pembina within the territory of the United States amounts to 1,000 French half-breeds." And in speaking of Pembina (page 29), " that the United States will consent, by the merest neglect, to have withdrawn from their authority and influence a population of 7,000 hardy and industrious people, who are only awaiting the slightest encouragement to settle, is no less deplorable than true, and is only to be accounted for by the belief that this melancholy state of affairs has never been properly represented." Truly, the American Government is deeply indebted to Captain Pope for the important information; and we should be as much indebted to his penetration and judgment, did he condescend to inform us where the 7,000, or even one half of the 1,000 French half-breeds, came from, and where they are " awaiting the slightest encouragement to settle !" Does Captain Pope expect all the colony of Red River to fly across the line like a flock of geese ? Even then, 2,000 would still be wanting to make up his number. Where are they " awaiting " the call ? We can assure this sanguine Captain, and that with the best feelings, that if Pembina is to be peopled, it must be from the south, not the north. Instead of 1,000 French half-breeds " settled within the American territory at Pembina," we never yet could discover 500, nor is the number likely to be increased from this quarter.

Again, at page 32, it is remarked, that " the settlers of Pembina are not permitted to trade or hunt upon the English possessions, and that the troops of the English forts will, for such offences, or any other, invade the territory of the United States, and carry off American citizens to Fort Garry for trial and punishment!" Where, we may ask, did Captain Pope get this information? Can he refer to one instance of such a thing as he alleges? We might point out a thousand such absurdities. In short, the report, as far as regards Red River and Pembina, is totally at variance with facts, and calculated to mislead those most interested in obtaining correct information.

But Captain Pope is not the only one the world is indebted to for information on Pembina: our neighbours 500 miles off seem to know more of the mysteries of that place than we, who live on the spot. At the very time Captain Pope was penning his graphic report, we were reading in the *Minnesota Register* of 11th August, 1849, that the " Town of Pembina contained 636 inhabitants, and that the women manufactured most of the woollen and linen fabrics necessary to clothe their families." Now, what amount of truth is there in these statements again? In all Pembina, town and country, there were not 250 squatters—for really we cannot dignify them with the name of "inhabitants;" nor was there, to our knowledge, a single head of sheep, nor a single pound of either wool or flax, nay, nor a spinning-wheel, rock, or distaff, in the whole community.

Again, we read, that the " Town of Pembina " sent 500 carts to St. Peter's annually. How different is this from the fact: with the exception of Mr. Kittson, the American fur-trader, and Mr. Belcourt, the French priest, we are not aware of their ever having sent half-a-dozen carts of their own to St. Peter's; although the good people of the States are made to believe that the few carts from Red River—and they are not a fourth of the number stated—are all from the Pembina squatters. The half-breeds, however, are not answerable for these misstatements; they are mere hunters, and pretend to nothing else. It is only the Americans who are gifted with the double sight, that will have them a commercial and agricultural people.

The Pembina half-breeds have now been hovering about the boundary line for the last seven years, and to this day have not raised as much grain in one year, *en masse*, as would feed a single family; nor have they manufactured, up to the hour we are writing, 1 cwt. of flour. When the American officials reach the "Town of Pembina," if their Minnesota stores run short, they must send down to us for new supplies, both for man and beast, or go to bed supperless. The agricultural resources of Pembina have not yet been developed: the soil is good, but low for farming purposes, and the country subject to inundation. Its hunting resources are drawing fast to a close; for the wild animals are fast retiring from it, and will soon be out of reach.

The territorial Government of Vancouver's Island, and also that of Minnesota, are by some envied for their advantages, but on considering these systems, with all their happy appliances of civilization, and the systematical operation of their laws, we are strongly impressed with the opinion, that the plain and simple Government under which we live, were it but revised, is the most desirable for Red River colony. By its revision, we mean, were the local Governor invested with fuller powers to act, that we might not be compelled to refer every question, however trifling, to England, and were the Legislative Council placed on a more healthy footing. It is true that in both the Governments alluded to, the members of the Legislative Assembly are elective; and in both, also, the people, along with the local Governor, have secured to them the power of forming such a constitution as may be best suited to their political views: these privileges, indeed, Red River has not; but then the political views of one people may not be the political views of another. Our population are as different in their pursuits and passions from the subjects of the Governments alluded to, as our laws and institutions; and each may be best, under its respective circumstances. Nevertheless, we are compelled in honesty to declare our settled conviction, that if the framework of the constitution is not altered, and based on more equitable and liberal principles, it will soon cease to inspire confidence. Should this be the case, and the people once feel that they are compelled to think and to act for themselves, a representative government will be the result.

APPENDIX A.

CENSUS 1849.

MEN.		WOMEN.		SONS.		DAUGHTERS.		TOTAL.	
Married and Widowers.	Unmarried.	Married and Widows.	Unmarried.	Above 16.	Below 16.	Above 15.	Below 15.		7 Churches, 12 Schools, 2 Water and 18 Windmills.
873	145	877	135	382	1314	373	1292	5391	

LIVE STOCK.

Horses.	Mares.	Oxen.	Bulls.	Cows.	Calves.	Pigs.	Sheep.
1095	990	2007	155	2147	1615	1565	3096

DWELLINGS.

Houses.	Stables.	Barns.
745	1066	335

IMPLEMENTS.

Ploughs.	Harrows	Carts.	Canoes.	Boats.	Acres Cultivated Land.
492	576	1918	428	40	6392½

A.D. 1855.—There is no later census than the above, but the population of the colony this year is supposed to be about 6500 souls.

B.

A LIST OF THE GOVERNORS OF RED RIVER COLONY FROM THE YEAR 1812 TO THE YEAR 1855.

Capt. Miles McDonell was Governor from August, 1812, to June, 1815—2 years and 10 months.

Mr. Alexander McDonell was Governor from August, 1815, to June, 1822—6 years and 10 months; but the colony was broken up in June, 1815, and the settlers did not return till the summer of 1817.

Capt. A. Bulger was Governor from June, 1822, to June, 1823—1 year.

Mr. Robert Pelly was Governor from June, 1823, to June, 1825—2 years.

Mr. Donald McKenzie was Governor from June, 1825, to June, 1833—8 years.

Mr. Alexander Christie was Governor from June, 1833, to June, 1839—6 years.

Mr. Duncan Finlayson was Governor from June, 1839, to June, 1844—5 years.

Mr. Alexander Christie was Governor from June, 1844, to June, 1846—2 years.

Colonel Crofton, 6th Regiment, was Governor from June, 1846, to June, 1847—1 year.

Major Griffiths, 6th Regiment, was Governor from June, 1847, to June, 1848—1 year.

Major Caldwell was Governor from June, 1848, to June, 1855—7 years.

C.

PEMBINA TREATY.

The Honourable Governor Ramsey, of Minnesota, and suite, arrived at Pembina in September, 1851, and concluded a treaty with the Indians, the provisions of which are as follow:—

"Article 1. A tract of land, in the valley of the Red River of the north, is hereby purchased, containing from 4,000,000 to 5,000,000 acres: being 30 miles on each side of the river, and extending up to Buffalo River on the east side, and the south branch of the Goose River on the west side. The international line is the northern boundary of the purchase.

"Article 2. For this, the United States agrees to pay the Indians 30,000 dollars in hand, 'to enable them to make provision for their half-breed children, and to arrange their affairs.'

"Article 3. Provides for their being paid annually, for twenty years, the sum of 10,000 dollars in cash, except 2,000 dollars of it, which may be reserved by the President, and applied, under his direction, to farming, educational, and other beneficial purposes.

"Article 4. Provides for their union with the other bands of Chippewas, and holding all lands and annuities in common, whenever the United States shall secure from these bands a reciprocal arrangement.

"Article 5. Provides that rules and regulations to protect the rights of persons and property among these Indians, may be prescribed and enforced among them by the United States Government."—*Extract from the Min. Pio., of* 30*th Oct.,* 1851.

The terms of this treaty have proved a sad disappointment to the poor half-breeds, after their long struggle to obtain a settlement, in the belief that they themselves would have been recognized by the American Government as the rightful owners of the disputed lands of Pembina; on what grounds, however, we have always been at a loss to discover. Seeing, at length, that nothing is secured to them but what the Indians choose to give, they are dropping back, as we anticipated, to their old haunts.

If we may judge from the mode of concluding the present compact, the Americans are not very particular in forming their treaties with the Indians. Pembina was disputed ground. The Assiniboines, Crees of the plains, and the Saulteaux of the woods, all laid claim to it as their land; but the title of the last has always been the most disputed: yet, being found on the spot, they were, without hesitation or inquiry, recognised as the lords paramount of the soil, and with them the treaty was concluded; nor were the principal Chippewa chiefs themselves present—they were distrustful and lukewarm—not willing to sell their lands, and therefore declined to attend. Regardless of this want of formality, however, the business went on, and the treaty was finally ratified by those of secondary rank who did attend.

D.

HIGH WATER IN RED RIVER, 1852.

To our chapter of accidents we have to add a renewal of the scenes of 1826, a flood of water having recently deluged the colony again.

On the 7th of May the water had risen eight feet above the high water mark of ordinary years, overflowed the banks of the river, and began to spread devastation and ruin in the settlement: boats and canoes in great request for the saving of lives and property. All hurry, bustle, and confusion. Some had to take shelter in the garrets, some on stages, some here, some there in little groups, on spots higher than the rest, anxiously waiting a boat, a canoe, or some friendly hand to save them from a watery grave. From 150 yards wide, the usual breadth of the river, it had spread to three miles on each side, and rose for several days at the rate of nearly an inch per hour.

On the 12th, half the colony was under water, and had made a clean sweep of all fencing and loose property on both sides of the river, for a distance of 22 miles in length. In all this extent, so low and flat is the country throughout, that not a single house was excepted—all was submerged—not an inhabitant but had fled. The crying of children, lowing of cattle, squeaking of pigs, and howling of dogs, completed the strange and melancholy scene.

On the 22nd, the water was at its height, and the coincidence is remarkable, inasmuch as on the same day of the month the water was at its height during the former flood twenty-six years ago; but it was then 18 inches higher than it has been this year; still, the people being fewer, the damage at that time was less. During eight days before the change, dwelling-houses and barns were floating in all directions, like sloops under sail, with dogs, cats, and poultry in them. Outhouses, carts, carioles, boxes, cupboards, tables, chairs, feather beds, and every variety of household furniture drifting along, added to the universal wreck.

In the former flood one man was drowned, and it was so in this, one man only lost his life. Some few horses, horned cattle, and pigs, in the hurry and bustle, were likewise drowned. The destruction in other respects was general: the very mice, the snakes, and the squirrels, could no longer find a hiding place either above or below ground—all their efforts to save life were vain—the destructive element forced them to surrender—they struggled and died. Even the frogs were overcome in their favourite element, and might have been seen sitting and seeking refuge on every log, plank, and stick that floated along; the very birds and insects deserted the place, so complete was the desolation. Nothing was to be heard but the howling of dogs in the distance, nor seen, as far as the eye could reach—but water, water, water! No cock crowing in the mornings; not a plough at work; not a bushel of seed in the ground; men, half bewildered, pensive, and mute, looked at each other and mourned their loss. The Sabbath almost undistinguished from the week days; the church-going bell mute; the churches empty; the sound of the millstones no longer heard. Where cattle used to feed, boats sailed and fish swam. Twenty-six years' labour of man and beast hastened to be engulfed in Lake Winnipeg. Many, many houses gone; many deprived of their all. The loss to the sufferers, who can estimate? but especially that which must be felt by the Canadians and half-breeds? The people, like a retreating army, lost much in the course of flight. Little firewood, less shelter, few tents, the weather cold, and ice on the water, deprived them of all comfort.

On the breaking up of the river, the channel got choked up with ice, which caused the water to rise seven feet in an hour or two. This occurred at night, after the people had gone to bed; and it came on them so suddenly, that before they were aware of it, themselves and their beds were afloat, cattle and sheep were drowned, and two men, who had gone to rest on a small rick of hay, found themselves in the morning drifting with the current, some three miles from where they had lain down the night before. Others, again, in the absence of canoes or other assistance, had to resort to the house-tops; some took to the water, and hung to the branches of the trees and bushes, till daylight brought them relief; and what may seem somewhat remarkable, in the midst of this scene of distress, some pigs were swept away, one of which was known to swim for two days and two nights together without relief, and yet was caught alive. The cold, as well as the water, pressed so hard, that one man was reduced to the necessity of cutting up his plough into firewood, to save his children from freezing. Articles of furniture shared a like fate.

No sooner had the water overspread its usual bounds, but Governor Colvile, with his usual affability and kindness, manned his light canoe, and kept going from place to place, cheering the drooping spirits of the people, and encouraging them to bear with Christian fortitude the difficulties and trials Providence had doomed them to suffer.

At its height, the water had spread out on each side of the river six miles, for a distance of fourteen miles in length. Not a house was excepted. Loaded boats might have been seen sailing over the plains far beyond the habitations of the people. The spectacle was as novel as it was melancholy. Three thousand five hundred souls abandoned their all, and took to the open plains : the loss of property, besides that of the crop this year, and the risk of but a small one next, is already estimated at 25,000*l*. sterling. The people were huddled together in gipsy groups on every height or hillock that presented itself. Canadians and half-breeds on the Assiniboine, pensioners and squatters at the little mountain, and the Scotch with their cattle at the strong hill, twelve miles from the settlement. The Right Rev. the Bishop of Rupert's Land was frequent in his visits of consolation. The Rev. John Black accompanied his flock all the time.

The falling of the water allowed many of the people to approach their cheerless homes about the 12th of June; and even at that late period a favourable season may give them barley and potatoes. For the cause of this and similar high waters in Red River, we refer our readers to the reasons annexed to the flood of 1826, noticed in chapter ninth.